Mothers and Daughters a
Origins of Female Subjec

Mothers and Daughters and the Origins of Female Subjectivity challenges the theory of the Oedipus complex, which permeates psychoanalytic theory, psychology, semiotics and cultural studies. The book focuses on the re-examination of women's development through the theories of primitive mental states.

Women's subjectivity has been profoundly limited by continuing anxieties about the mother's body. Jane Van Buren describes how women are gradually escaping the curse of inferiority and finding a voice, enabling the mother to provide their daughters with a legacy of rightful agency over their bodies and minds. Drawing on the theories of Klein, Bion and Winnicott, and incorporating recent developments in psychobiology, this book provides a novel approach to subjects including the dreams, myths and phantasies of individuals, the nature of mother and daughter relationships, sexuality, pregnancy, menstruation and the idea of the mother's body as problematic and dangerous.

This interdisciplinary investigation into curtailed female subjectivity and its many ramifications in society, culture and individual mental growth will be of great interest to all practising psychoanalysts, and those studying psychoanalytic theory and gender studies.

Jane Van Buren is a psychoanalyst in full time private practice in Los Angeles, California. She has written widely on the themes of women and children, culture and psychoanalysis.

Mothers and Daughters and the Origins of Female Subjectivity

Jane Van Buren

Routledge
Taylor & Francis Group

LONDON AND NEW YORK

First published 2007 by Routledge
2 Park Square, Milton Park, Abingdon, Oxon OX14 4RN

Simultaneously published in the USA and Canada
by Taylor & Francis Inc
52 Vanderbilt Avenue, New York, NY 10017

*Routledge is an imprint of the Taylor & Francis Group,
an informa business*

Typeset in Times by Garfield Morgan, Swansea, West Glamorgan

Paperback cover design by Lisa Dynan

British Library Cataloguing in Publication Data
A catalogue record for this book is available from the British Library

Library of Congress Cataloging in Publication Data
Van Buren, Jane.
   Mothers and daughters and the origins of female subjectivity / Jane Van
Buren.
      p. cm.
   Includes bibliographical references and index.
   ISBN-13: 978-0-415-38673-9 (hbk)
   ISBN-10: 0-415-38673-X (hbk)
   ISBN-13: 978-0-415-38674-6 (pbk)
   ISBN-10: 0-415-38674-8 (pbk)
   1. Mothers and daughters. 2. Mothers and daughters–Psychology. 3.
Daughters–Psychology. 4. Identity (Psychology) I. Title.
   HQ755.85.V34 2007
   155.3'33–dc22

                                                             2006024343

ISBN 13: 978-0-415-38674-6 (pbk)
ISBN 13: 978-0-415-38673-9 (hbk)

To my grandsons, Quentin and Marcus

Contents

Plates

Foreword by James S. Grotstein

When Nietzsche exhorted, "God is dead!" in his *Ecce Homo*, his readers then and now never really fully comprehended the meaning and significance of his profound pronouncement. "God" has long constituted the reassuring Absolute Force that protectively hovers over us. This "God" has since time immemorial been addressed as "He." History and scripture have been written by men and largely about men. Today the Absolute is enshrined in godless, hyper-moral religion on one hand and in technological science on the other. The "excluded middle" is the domain of spirituality, the numinous, the emotional, the implicit, the sensual, i.e., the domain of the subjectively feminine, the domain to which Dr. Van Buren's work is dedicated and which she engagingly and persuasively explores. When we pray in churches, temples, synagogues, or mosques, we read or speak from texts that begin with references to "the Patriarchs." The conception of "the Matriarchs" is missing. We are gradually awakening to a realization that women in general and mothers in particular have been erased from history and from social significance. God is dead, perhaps, because "He" can no longer survive without "Her." We are gradually awakening to a realization that women in general and mothers in particular have long been erased from history and from the hegemony of significance.

Associated with the feminine-matriarchal principle is the domain of the numinous, to which I have already alluded. This is the non-moral, non-"religious" mystical realm of spirituality which Jung has so meaningfully explored but which has not until Bion's contributions found its way into psychoanalysis. It is the region of the infinite, the awesome, and the ineffable. Along with the numinous there exists another region, that of proto-emotions that are inchoately formed in the Register of the Infinite and which need to be transformed so as to be expressed and ultimately felt as feelings. Emotions are mediated by the right cerebral hemisphere, which some now call "the feminine hemisphere." As religion since historic memory has been masculine and left hemispheric (linear) oriented, so has science and psychoanalysis. It is only in recent times that positivistic, deterministic, linear science has had to make room for uncertainty, relativity, chaos, complexity, and non-linearity, a new "science" which Bion terms "mystical science."

This latter trend is in concert with the emergence of the female-matriarchal principle, which is associated with newfound importance of emotional and sensual mental life in psychoanalytic theory and practice – in place of the importance of the instinctual drives. The hegemony of Freud's masculine, patriarchal Oedipus complex in the phallic phase is now yielding to the hegemony of Klein's feminine, matriarchal Oedipus complex in the late oral phase. It is with Bowlby's concept of bonding and attachment, however, that we witness the full effects of this gender-oriented paradigm shift. The prime, organizing importance of the quality of attachment between the infant and its mother in all its conscious and unconscious permutations can only be underestimated in its predictive significance and importance – as the most salient element of child development. Dr. Van Buren explores the intricacies of this revolution in both broad and microscopic ways.

Put another way, it is almost as if human history can be viewed as an enduring "manic defense," a defensive protest of masculine potency against the realization of man's (including women) basic, fundamental, and inalienable experience of *dependency*, originally on mother. Why has this manic defense persisted so long unnoticed? Dr. Van Buren superbly delineates the reasons historically, socially, and utmost psychoanalytically. Her case illustrations are powerful, evocative, and poignant clarifications of this issue. Utmost, she reawakens our awareness of the catacombs into which feminine subjectivity (the woman – and mother – as subject, not object) has long been banished. This book says it all!

In emphasizing the idea of the mother's and the daughter's *body*, however, Dr. Van Buren significantly raises the level of inquiry to new heights. Freudian psychoanalysis referred to the body only as the origin of the instinctual drives. Klein, however, claimed that infant mental life begins as its conscious and unconscious phantasies (conjectures) about what is occurring in mother's body, including the infant's own desires to enter mother's body to "know her all up!" In returning to the inside of mother's body as the scene of the Oedipal "crime" Klein, and now Van Buren, are explicating the hidden order of the Oedipus complex, the murder of the mother as rival (envy) prior to the murder of father as rival (jealousy).

Here is *my* view, which I wish to append to Van Buren's own elegant view. First, some background: early in her career Klein postulated that when the infant becomes a toddler and enters the anal stage of development, (s)he experiences the beginnings of anal-sadistic impulses simultaneously with epistemophilic impulses, each of which enters into a coalition with the other for the purpose of the toddler's entering and exploring the insides of mother's body in unconscious phantasy, possessing her valuable insides and murdering her "internal babies" and father's penis, which is believed to have been confiscated by mother in intercourse in the primal scene. Of importance for our purposes is the notion that mother possesses father's penis, which renders her into the image first of an *omnipotent phallic woman* and then later of a *combined parent* in which the mother and father are united but in which situation the mother maintains hegemonic dominance and *omnipotence*. When father achieves dominance in the later phallic Oedipal phase, he does so with far less omnipotence than did mother earlier. This is my point: the unconscious image of the omnipotent combined parent mother becomes transformed into such chimeras as the medusa, the sphinx, the Sybil, and other horrendous omnipotent monsters which hover over us in our internal world and remind us of our uncompleted dependency-on-mother experiences. Thus, they devolve into frightening, horrendous reminders of unfinished business with a Cyclopean female monster, which is too dangerous to confront.

In reintroducing mother's body – and the daughter's body – into her discourse, Dr. Van Buren has added a badly needed dimension to our understanding of why feminine subjectivity has languished so long in the shadows. In Klein's terms, after we read this work, we feel compelled to offer reparations to female subjectivity. Let us hope that we may soon be able to say: "And the voice of the woman is heard in the land."

Acknowledgments

I wish to thank the following people for their support and good thoughts during the development of my book: Jim Grotstein, Shirley and Jim Gooch, Arnaldo Chuster, Maxine Anderson, John Stone, and Marianne Robinson. I also wish to express appreciation to my friends Johanna Wilheim in Brazil and Elizabeth and Marcello Bianchedi in Argentina.

I also want to thank my grandchildren Quentin and Marcus, who have provided me with ongoing infant and child observations throughout the writing of this book, as well as love and support. Lastly, I wish to give my deep gratitude to my analysands, who have provided me with so much knowledge of their experiences.

I want to express my deepest gratitude to Kate Hawes who has realized this project through conception, pregnancy, and delivery.

Introduction

The challenges to organized connections to spirituality have left us floundering in a secular universe with scarcely any impetus for believing in some system of defined purposefulness or morality. Secular society has depended on scientific proof for the scaffolding for some sense of rightness or truth; while another approach lies in attempts to maintain or revive religious notions of morality. Both have leaked into psychoanalytic theories blocking and stagnating contact with the unknown or unborn. Blame or fault finding need not come up here, that is the very trap we would want to avoid in seeking out the blockages to our potential sense of purposefulness.

We are now in a phase of culture and concepts of society that depend more and more on human thought, behavior and emotions as the foundation of survival though as we know many theories of ethics, concepts of human goodness and politics are constructed around fear of change and the challenges to traditional belief systems. Of late psychology and in particular psychoanalysis have discovered the richness and complexity of the infant's emotional life and the profound necessity of human bonding and attachment opportunities for the mind's normal growth. At the same time the mother–infant relationship is unfolding as a critical aspect of human survival,[1] not in its obvious physical dimensions exclusively but as an emotional experience which protects and makes possible a mind that functions with capacities for vitality, compassion and creativity, capable of happiness, self-respect and respect for others (Fonagy et al., 2004; Stern, 1985, 2004; Trevarthan, 1993). The psychoanalyst, Wilfred R. Bion, analyzed by Melanie Klein, and a great innovator of both Freud and Klein, provided the realization that the human mind, particularly the infantile mind, survives and grows through maternal reverie. Bions' original departure from instinct theory changes our concepts of the relationship between mother and child and the unconscious to the conscious in the way that Copernicus

---

1 Happily father's reverie and bonding capacities are given more respect and are appearing in contemporary child care practices across ethnic groups and classes.

changed our view of the relationship of the earth to the sun. Bion's conceptions about dreaming the as yet unknown helps us to make contact with emotional forces as difficult and painful but expanding the parameters of the contribution of the unconscious as messages from the infinite.

Bion addresses this contact with the ineffable and the unknown in *Taming Wild Thoughts* (1997). He explains that fear of the unknown plays a significant role over the eons in deeper feelings becoming translated, better yet, transformed. He adds that our efforts can be seen as a clumsy archeological dig; a camel brush is needed, not a shovel. He suggests that the wisdom that lies fast asleep, somewhere in the thickets, is somewhere buried not only literally under the mounds of the Ziggurat or the site of Ur of the Chaldees or Knossos, but perhaps with the Oracle at Delphi. And inquires is that voice in any way audible? Bion emphasizes that the full emotional impact of mental life is often profoundly aborted. Spirituality dressed in religious garb reveals profound hunger for meaning beyond the messages of the here and now presented in its limitations and horrors. Philosophy has extended a hand in the exploration of spirituality as we move through the challenges to superstition and the emergence of scientific knowledge. The grasp of the significance and functions of reverie have indeed been buried under mounds of fear and confusion. The infant's voice and maternal dreams have remained largely unacknowledged in the human record.

Freud's majestic discoveries of the unconscious, primary process messages and the paths and codes to the as yet unknown, or unborn, universal and infinite enter western scientific cultural inquiries into concepts of human nature, mental life and development slowly and painfully. In Freud's dream book he spins out the many complex threads of human emotion, some hidden deeply, in complex dream work, some distorted beyond recognition or feeling (the Rat Man (Freud, 1909) is a case in which all feeling is severely mutilated leading to compulsion and disassociation). But it is through the dream work, mainly displacement and condensation, metonymy and metaphor that Freud discovers the two logics and argues for their complementarities and their need of one another. Bion carries on Freud's ideas that dreams make up a large part of how we do or do not tolerate and respect human emotional complexity. His understanding of the function of the dream is that it is an outcome of alpha function, or mother's reverie.

Bion's theory of dreams and reverie are closely related; they emerge from his realization that the infant needs the mother's help in passing through painful emotional and physical experiences, standing by the infant through their anxious and fearful responses to unwelcome, overwhelming stimuli. Since these are often felt to be life threatening, the mothering one might shun the infant and its experience (the reaction of counter-projective identification or countertransference). Within this new view the idea that the repetition of the failure of the container–contained is toxic to mental growth and toleration of emotional life and that what had been identified as innate states of envy and greed and violent projective identification might instead be related to the parents' need of the infant as their container, which was thwarted in themselves. Bion's realization of the child as container as well as the source of urgent messages emerging in the infant's projective identification, is a monumental leap connecting the generations. As will be discussed, mothers and fathers in failing to accept their own emotional challenges, their own fears and anxieties pass the dilemmas onto the infant partners. Dreams are an extension of reverie and with the contact barrier,[2] create a bridge between different aspects of the mind, beta elements and preconceptions in such a way that dream function is possible and comes alive encouraging the presentation of meaning.

Voices from the deep

Two main ideas that have appeared consistently at the conscious level are the preparation of boys to separate from mother's realm (and her body) and the preparation of girls to care for infants and children, to become mother. Of course social arrangements have included matriarchal cultures however the power of maternity has most often been signified as questionable, weak, corrupt and immoral. The unconscious meaning of the terror associated with the non-verbal is found in the articulated antagonism between male and female culture in which women's marks disappeared underneath male-dominated culture (Campbell, 1959; Harrison, 1962; Van Buren, 1989, 2004, 2005).

Women denied self-expression and the authority to create significance in permanent public marks continued to communicate in other than verbal modes within the childrearing and domestic culture. Mothers responded to their children not only in words but also through the languages expressed from one unconscious to another. Thus, rituals, customs, and myths are laced with women's unconscious overtly silenced feelings and thoughts. As we pursue the roots of these bifurcations, we shall plunge into the depths of women's internal reality and attempt to make contact with lost, encrypted and sacrificed aspects entombed there. The daughter's subjectivity has remained an enigma as well; one surmises that it was disappeared or was minimized along with the burial of matriarchal powers. The argument about the power and the existence of matriarchy is transduced into the silent woman without her own words and often without her own thoughts.

We might be greatly helped by Melanie Klein's emendation of Freud's theories of the child's relation to their imaginary or mythic parents. She

---

2 Bion's contact barrier is differentiated from Freud's notion of the censor. The contact barrier as Bion explains is made up of alpha elements and is able to connect and blend emotional and meaningful elements of experience in dreams and phantasies; to access what has remained inaccessible.

proposes that the infant's first postnatal dramas take place in a phantasied re-entry into mother's body, now conjured as containing powerful rivals and predecessors, such as father's penis and the other babies. Depending on the intensity of the infant's postnatal anxiety, mother's insides feel to be filled with ordinary perturbations encountered in mental life. In that situation, fear of being left out is experienced as manageable with hope and faith that mental birth will be gradually accomplished, sponsored by parental support. In this version the infant is able to gradually give up the refuge of mother's insides and omniscient powers felt to be dominant there. In dire circumstances departure is largely prevented and the felt hostilities turn into battles with demonic internal figures (Grotstein, 2000a, 2000b, 2000c; Klein, 1945). The dreaded monsters and anxieties are then projectively identified as the enemy, often as the evil woman and consequently as a broken couple unable to realize their potential fertility. Following these ideas makes it possible to recognize and trace the tendency to cut women out of the creation of the symbolic order.

From the vertex of the myth of the re-possession of mother's body, mother's thoughts and words may be feared in a paranoid way due to the emotions associated with her body and presence in the infantile mind. Allow me to caution the reader to include the failure of attachment and reverie as critical here though often not recognized in psychoanalytic literature until the late twentieth century. Recall Freud's writings emphasized infantile sexuality and the libidinal phases as most formative in the development of personality and omitted maternal capacities as influential in the development of human infants and children. The formal discovery of holding, containing and empathy has greatly overcome these misconceptions.

However, Bion's notions of *Wild Thoughts or Thoughts without a Thinker* (Bion, 1977c) challenges us to expand our notion of the unconscious and the roots of meaning. As we move in a diachronic line we are also immersed in synchronic dimensions. We find ourselves in the realm of the dream work or of myth making. Though the narratives told in an oral tradition or interpreted from the figures and relics of the era insist on a historical reality and provide explanations based on those versions, the synchronic links lead us into other levels of contact. These are the messages erupting out of the dream work that are illuminating, disturbing and disorienting causing pain and anxiety. The extreme outcome of the dream work that fails or disguises rather than illuminates is associated with nameless dread (Bion's designation for a dream without a dreamer, the force and signified of which functions similarly to content without a container: Bion, 1967a; Grotstein, 1981, 2000a).

Some work on infants and neurobiology has confirmed Bion and Winnicott's discovery of the absolute necessity of containment and holding (Fonagy, 2001); a failed dream can be thought of as a nightmare (see Chapter 2) or a web of lies. Deception in this context is a rerouting of messages from the dreamer to dilute the pain of the latent meanings. We might think of this process as the killing off of the realizations that inform the mind of the dreamer from several layers of mind.

The notion of a vast well of potential meanings comes to us from myth and archaic artifacts. Freud's *The Interpretation of Dreams* (1900) elucidated a new theory of dreams, including the assumption that dreams might be de-constructed with the caution that there were deeper levels of the dream that would never be reached. Jung also brought to our attention the mythic and dreaming mind as communicating to us the messages and meanings from the universal unconscious. Bion and Matte Blanco pushed the concept of the unconscious to include the possibilities of vast dimensions of experience beyond the notions attached to the primary repressed and repression of the forbidden impulses of the instincts. Their explorations lead them to hypothesize further dimensions in mental life that they conceptualize as infinity, transcendence and the ineffable.

My realizations, assisted by other theorists who are seriously committed to tolerating the deepest infantile experiences and the vastness of the potential of mental life,[3] have led me to resonate with my own dreamer. I became aware of my own silenced feelings, emotions and thoughts, the ways I had lost or aborted parts of myself as a woman, an infant, and as a mindful person who could speak or write from my depths. I made the journey into mindedness at first from the vertex of my own lack of belief in my existence and my going on being. I was also dealing with surface manifestations of profound disconnection or dissociations. Through my studies in social and cultural history of ideas, and signification theories I began to appreciate the distortions and misconceptions by which I made some sense of the chaos and inauthenticity internally and externally.

In this context I have emphasized the notion of the *illness of the signifier* as the manifest or symptomatic outcome of the failure of realizations to fulfill their emotional destiny. I suggest that the compromise formations are most deadly at the point of stillbirth of transformations in "O," the utmost emotional truth arising from the infinite, unbound by time and space. Bion explains the "O" experience as bringing us to transcendence momentarily overcoming the limitations of fear and hatred of the unknown and mortality. A breaking down of the barriers to emotional truth and potential knowledge is made possible through the dream work that brings new and fresh realizations from deep structures and a porous alpha screen, a screen made up of the elements of dream, memory and myth. Preconceptions are

---

3 There are far too many pioneers to acknowledge here but I would like to express my gratitude to Melanie Klein, D.W. Winnicott, R.W. Fairbairn, Karl Abraham, Sandor Ferenczi, W.R. Bion, Frances Tustin, James Grotstein, Shirley Gooch, James Gooch and Julia Kristeva.

not only mated at the level of the accessible unconscious that which turns into phantasies, dreams and symptoms but also unfolding from the domain of the inaccessible (Bion, 1967a; Chuster, 2005). How then are we to make contact with that which is too far off from the accessible parts of the mind?

I think that the silencing of mother's voice or the undervaluing of her subjective contributions is passed on through projective identifications into the fetus and into the offspring. In this case the intergenerational messages are unconscious and manifest as inhibitions and doubt, about the significance of one's thoughts and feelings. The mother's relation to her powerful effect on the survival of the species is disavowed. Not only are her capacities to carry the fetus to full term and to provide needed sustenance often underestimated, but also they are ridiculed and given low priority in culture and society. We find ourselves caught in continuing arguments and intense debates over the care and protection of children and their mothers. Only recently have the ideas about mommy–baby early relationships become important enough to study thoughtfully and to include as part of the training of health professionals. Infant analysis and infant observation are also recent arrivals in our understanding of human development. My inquiry in this book focuses on the primitive roots of mother–daughter projective identifications and the reciprocal structuring of patterns of realizations, foreclosure or cultural and individual growth.

All of us are estranged from our infantile and ineffable selves to some degree. Many of the translations and transformation that are gestated in the psychoanalytic process are the birthing of thoughts without a thinker, likely those thoughts that are denied birth or become captivated by lies, distortions and misconceptions. I think we can link mind-blindness about infant and children's mental capacities to the terror of psychic pain without the solace and cushioning of reverie. Ironically mother's potency has often been signified as faulty, weak and troublesome. This pattern reaches deep into the infant's originary "O" experiences and involves overwhelming experiences and the knowledge of death. The evolution of "O" into signifiable elements rarely takes place unscathed, however the degree of distortion, mutilation and murder is of serious concern and/or also fosters hope.

In the chapters that follow, the unconscious messages to the next generation of women is explored from cultural and psychoanalytic perspectives including material from psychoanalytic work with women since the early 1990s. Some of these women were young, in their twenties, some of these women were in their forties, fifties and sixties. Some were childless, others became pregnant and gave birth to two children. A particular case brought to mind vividly the endangered infant. This baby could not swallow due to anomalies formed prenatally. She often stopped breathing and had to be brought back to life.

Almost all the infants are explored as internal figures, inside mother and inside daughter. I propose that the significance of death as it is accompanied by the possibility of a longer and longer life span continues to be disfigured and killed off. The origins of genocide, ethnic cleansing, and the vicious battles over abortion and stem cell research are buried in the folds of the pains of psychic birth. The efforts to make contact with the terrors of being human and the awareness of the need to protect and nurture brings fresh hope.

The chapters that follow are part of a template drawn out of my explorations into curtailed female subjectivity and its many ramifications in society, culture and individual mental growth. In my way of thinking the signifiers of mother's body appearing in dreams, phantasies and myths are the Rosetta Stones guiding us through the evolution of mindedness in our own human brains and minds.

Chapter 1

Silences from the deep

Women's subjectivity and the voice of the turtle

The concept of a woman subject is barely known to us yet another century has ended. This concept as a realization has been buried, encrypted, split, disguised, distorted and aborted through centuries of symbolic culture. Subjectivity is itself a newly emphasized concept that has grown alongside interest in the functioning of signification and its relationship to psychoanalysis (Freud, 1900; Lacan, 1977a). The former emphasizes the significance of language and symbols as colored and constructed through compromise formations between the ego and the drives; the latter proposes that the power of desire and the impact of loss or the awareness of "twoness" are powerful forces that create signification structures (Grotstein, 1990a; Kennedy, 1997; Lacan, 1977a; Tustin, 1981b). Jacques Lacan also emphasizes the gap in which to signify, the space in which substitution and combination take place. From these realizations the notion of the subject of speech, with the capacity to transform desire into symbols and signs is acknowledged. The subject, with capacities for signification and ultimately thought, include a reasonable receptivity to unconscious themes and desires, and a porous membrane between unconscious and conscious messages. Bion has designated the latter as made up of alpha elements stemming from dream work processes. The contact barrier, as he named it, allows a discourse between unconscious/conscious elements enabling the subject to dream and remember (Bion, 1965, 1992). As we shall see, the dream work not only is dedicated to taming wilder messages from the infinite but also helps the mind of the dreamer to take small doses of potential vastness. Bion understands the messages from the deep to carry intense disturbance but slips out the constraints of economic forces and rides with the belief in powerful meanings.

From Bion and Matte Blanco we are able to comprehend that dream work alpha transforms primal chaos into readable messages, but that it is also the instrument for harvesting elements from the infinite deep of our other side – the symmetrical unconscious, where all the meanings of all time reside waiting to potentate into little births. Freud came close to mapping these processes in his theory of the dream work in which the subject creates a dream narrative that grows out of elements of both symmetrical and asymmetrical logic (Matte Blanco, 1988). But Freud, as we know, thought from the perspective of drive theory. He believed that the ego, at first designated as secondary process, needed to check the fulminating drives, and transform their antisocial quest for gratification into sublimation, that brought acceptable compromise solutions between the pleasure and unpleasure principles.

Freud's dream work theory, however, also contained the blueprint of the path of burgeoning subjectivity. Freud's (1913) work on the Oedipus myth in *Totem and Taboo*, built upon archaic anxieties, and displayed their transformation through displacement and condensation. His understanding that myth and dream explained and illuminated important semiotic processes was crucial. However, the ways in which Freud justifies the death instinct are devoted to justifying his theory to the scientific community. Freud, like Klein and Lacan, responded to the mythification of the fear of death which Klein called "annihilation anxiety," and Lacan, "the awareness of lack and alienation." Freud builds his concepts of the death instinct around the nirvana principle. Each theorist had their own way of understanding phenomena that overwhelms the organism with stimuli and is felt to be a threat to life or are unbearably painful. Today we might think of these phenomena as the failure of alpha function. The version that is constructed is a heavily autochthonous reading by the subject as to what has occurred, or what is happening now, or will always be repeated. Grotstein has written on the importance of autochthony as the infant's or patient's self-created stream of myths and narratives functioning to ward off an awareness of helplessness, and to find agency in creating their world (Grotstein, 1998, 2000a). These proliferating signs are available to be presented and employed by language and conscious thought within the symbolic order.

We need to remember that human speech and literacy evolved only a few thousand years ago. In Shlain's book, *The Goddess Versus the Alphabet* (1998), he makes the case that until the left brain developed, offering dual hemispheric functioning, literacy and abstract symbolic functioning were only potential. One might say the pull to speak and write connected with a more settled agricultural culture stimulated the development of the left hemisphere. Thus, we cannot read the earliest messages from the history of marks left by human culture. We would need to be in the exchange itself, to feel the heat of the emotions as we do in the session when words fail, or are not able to carry the innermost affects. Shlain (1998) believed that the right brain contributions suffered a loss of prestige at the advent of left brain functioning. Today, in psychoanalysis, we are challenged to find a helpful balance between the two. In any event, signs and symbols developed slowly and were found at first in tools and objects for daily living. These concrete signs appear only as recently as 30,000 BC. A critical shift may be seen in the images placed on the walls of the French caves. These images left behind by the people of that era provide us with signs through which we can read about their civilization and daily life. The images of wild animals signify the literal and figurative aspects of their existence and the anxieties of survival. They also reveal some reflective capacity on the part of the painters about their situations and feelings. The images inside the caves suggest the beginnings of some signs of inner reflection and the projection of this mental activity outside the mind for communication purposes and further reflection.

Out of this change in brain functioning arose a profound psychological and social shift. Shlain explains that the dominance of patriarchal culture over matriarchal culture came about not because of the northern hunters invasion of the southern matriarchal cultures, but from a shift inside. The right brain sphere of mental functioning associated with mother–infant communication, and deep emotional experience, was sacrificed to the needs of left brain tasks; such as attention to the domain of symbols placed in orderly structures that themselves obeyed laws of time and space. Non-linear dreams and mythic structures were counterpoised to linear conscious apprehension. The different sides of mental life affect each other profoundly, and cannot be split away from each other without distortion of experience.

Similarly, the ability to reflect on one's mental experience and the concepts of inside are not clearly represented. The boundaries that delineate a sense of self, and not self, were not reflected in cultural artifacts largely until the Renaissance in Western Europe. You may recall the two dimensional renderings of human and religious figures of the medieval period. Similarly, landscapes were not yet presented as a subject of human interest. The human gaze focused heavenward until the outdoor scenes of nature appeared in the new space of perspective.

Also, we are accustomed to contemplating the emergence of individualism as an integral part of the awareness of internal mental life or subjectivity. This approach rests on the idea that the inner life of the individual is lost in the group or clan, or never develops out of enfoldment into the group mentality. In addition, hierarchical or authoritarian societies are known to mitigate against individual thought, as they are directed by the thoughts of the leader or elite group.

A fascinating possibility comes to mind! The new realizations made possible a sense of inside and outside that was mediated by perception and percepts. Perception is shaped by the inner eye and brings forward the artifacts of dream, myth, and phantasy. Percepts are the images formed through the physical eye. Intriguingly, we know that the two kinds of seeing, one more subjective and projective, and the other, more dominated by facts and external reality, mingle and blur the edges of subjective and objective. We must add that the very notion of reality has been severely challenged as has empiricism and scientism. Similarly, the notion of truths that can be found and used as guides for living the virtuous, worthwhile life, have been deconstructed unmercifully, particularly in the latter part of the twentieth century.

At the same time, the development of increasingly symbolic means of expression has seen a profound imbalance between the marks of men and those of women. In many instances, culture outwardly seems to be exclusively chiseled by men. Schlain's hypothesis is that as the alphabet and literacy developed, the left brain began to dominate.

An articulated antagonism between male and female culture is seen in the repeated death of matriarchal cultures, overthrown by male dominated hunting groups, in which women's marks disappeared underneath male dominated culture (Campbell, 1976). Women, denied self-expression and the authority to create significance in permanent public marks, enunciated in oral modes within the childrearing and domestic culture. Mothers in particular spoke to their children not only in words but also through the languages expressed from one unconscious to another. Thus, rituals, customs and myths are laced with women's unconscious overtly silenced feelings and thoughts. As we pursue the roots of these bifurcations, we shall plunge into the depths of women's internal reality and attempt to make contact with lost, encrypted and sacrificed aspects entombed there.

In keeping with these splits, men enunciated in discourses that assigned natural and biological causes to the concepts of sexual difference. The attempted burial of matriarchal culture, and the dominance of patriarchal culture, were justified by arguments about women's special capacities, defined by her childbearing, child-raising functions, and limited mental capacities. It was inevitable that both Freud and Lacan constructed and interpreted the nature of the symbolic order, along these lines. Despite their superb efforts at piercing the origins in which meaning and value are constructed by internal forces and social responses, they continued to split apart aspects of human experience. The signifiers that carried the utmost anxieties are designated (M) Other,[1] and influence the placement of women outside the symbolic order, as well as the failure to recognize female mental capacities as potent and equal.

Freud and Lacan were ensnared within the gender concepts of their time and place, not only because they themselves spoke their "mother tongue," but also by the same psychic forces that influenced the interpretation of male and female gender in binary oppositional terms; superior/inferior, known/strange, passive/active, culture/nature, sun/moon, which remained powerfully alive in language and culture.

---

1 Lacan's notions of the "Other" are useful here in exploring the inner dimensions of the man/ woman dichotomy. The Mother is also the "other," the lost object and the vessel for the forces of the unknown and uncontrollable.

Hélène Cixous describes the structure of binary opposition as a metaphor, which carries through all our discourse:

> Always the same metaphor: we follow it, it transports us, in all of its forms, wherever a discourse is organized. The same thread, or double tress leads us, whether we are reading or speaking through literature, philosophy, criticism, centuries of representation of reflection.
>
> (Cixous and Clément, 1975: 63)

She continues:

> Men and women are caught up in a network of millennial cultural determinations of a complexity that is practically unanalyzable. We can no more talk about "woman" than about "man" without getting caught up in an ideological theater, where the multiplications of representations, images, reflections, myths, and identifications, constantly transform, deform and alter each person's imaginary, and in advance, renders all conceptualizations, null and void.
>
> (Cixous and Clément, 1975: 83)

Freud and Lacan were ensnared in a discourse that arose out of a great paradox that itself contained a labyrinthine knot. Within their explanations of sexual difference, cultural belief, and practice, they proposed that women's capacities for thought and symbolization were less than those of men. Though Freud and Lacan differed in their concept of the symbolic order and sexual difference, both were seriously impacted in their views by the notion of castration. I propose that the emphasis on the phallus as present, and masking the fear of lack, also produces the ritual of circumcision; of enduring a tiny loss, the tip of the penis, implemented as a metonymy that both eases terror and anxiety, and disavows the implied realizations of loss and finitude (Lacan, 1977a).

Among these are fear of mortality, loss, lack of connection to the Godhead and impotence or helplessness, or the quest for omnipotence regained, the latter usually signified by patricide or domination of mother's powers.

The paradoxical knot that maintains the concept of sexual difference, as based on the inferior capacities of women to symbolize is a manic defense against the realization that neither man nor woman is insulated from the uncertainty of postnatal existence. The female person is linked with the failure to attain symbolism and to forever remain unborn or in pieces; psyche subordinated to soma.

In this scheme, the phallus substitutes for the umbilicus. Thus, males are offered a safe tether in place of fusion privileging them to create the symbolic order. Within the legend of phallic privilege, the male person is given confidence in his power to think, speak and create, while women are designated as creatures of the body and the instincts. The escape from what I have named "the shadow of the phallus" remains difficult, and the mandate of phallic privilege maintains the inferiority of female symbolism. Girls and women are defined as those who do not "master" thought or speech.

More recently, the mythologies of gender emphasize the notion of the subject or development of the sense of "I"-ness. Freud's notions of the latter were replete with the idea that men/women were unseated from their center as persons of agency, and will, by the forces of the "it." However, in the battles between the ego and the drives, men fared better in achieving capacities for speech and symbolism. In this reading of the Oedipus complex, the female person is at a disadvantage in the process of repressing Oedipal desires since she is already castrated. Her Superego remains flabby, her Oedipal desires not well resolved, she tends to mourn what is not there, and looks for the antidote to her sense of lack in father's phallus, husband's phallus and a baby.

Lacan's (1977b) essay on the "Significance of the phallus" deconstructs the concept of the phallus as a real biological entity, and reveals its semiotic function as a protection against engulfment by the mother. Lacan understands the phallus to be the signifier of signifiers that structures space in the subject's mind, allowing for the development of symbolic functioning. The newly acquired boundaries, named as "The Law of the Father," act as a barrier against the undertow of fusion. Lacan's Achilles heel is found in his use of language, particularly his designation of the onset of dual hemispheric functioning as brought about by the onset of Law of the Father; as if the infant and mother are always precariously perched on the edge of the well of fusion. Lacan is unclear here and leaves himself vulnerable to feminist criticism. Thus, Jane Gallop is able to say that the major fallacy in the phallocentric theory of psychic space is based on the physical presence, or absence of a piece of flesh, in place of attitudes and emotional states of mind (Gallop, 1982).

The best reading of Lacan's (1977b) essay and his theory about the implementation of the "Law of the Father" is justified through the theory of significance. Lacan understood the developing subject as discovering the yawning horror of lack or the void. The realization of separate existence from mother drives the infant subject or person to find substitutes for the other. The rationalization for phallocentrism takes the position that though woman/mother's body is the source of life and its provider, and the womb, the placenta, birth canal, vagina and breasts belong to mother's body, their power is overcome by the phallus. The potency of the female body and mind are greatly underestimated and represented by their opposites, lack of dependability, solidity and bounty. Thus, one can see the etiology of the many cultural rites in which women and girls are demeaned and denigrated, defined as inferior to men and destined for a subordinate life. The signifier of the phallus carries the truth of the struggle to bear realizations in which the veils of autochthony, phantasy and omnipotence are lifted (Bion, 1962a, 1962b; Grotstein, 2000a; Tustin, 1990; Winnicott, 1958).

Legends, myths and discourse over thousands of years of human culture reveal profound dread of female potency; in particular the insides of mother's body that are portrayed as both compelling and horrifying. As discussed the French prehistoric caves with their great drawings of animal life and hunting scenes suggest the profound association of survival with mother's insides, and the images of hunting and provision of animal food. As we know, children of both genders are stirred to both awe and hatred at the experience of the breast or extreme dependence, particularly if the experiences of helplessness are stimulated by premature awareness of psychic birth (Bion, 1962a, 1962b; Grotstein, 1998; Meltzer, 1988, 1992; Paul, 1997; Tustin, 1981b).

Several themes come to mind in the context of the cave art. The concepts of bonding and feeding stand out. The human infant phantasizes a privileged return to the blessed safety of the internal spaces of mother's body as a flight from anxiety and pain. In the robust infant's mind, the internal voyage is playful and temporary, but in the case of the disturbed or vulnerable infant, the journey to the inside of mother's body is felt as a fusion state and become more a prison than a refuge (Grotstein, 1990a; Joseph, 1975; Klein, 1957; Mason, 1981; Meltzer, 1992; Steiner, 1993a; Tustin, 1990).

The more intense and desperate are the feelings of disconnection in the infant, the more it is felt that the maternal insides are entrapping and malicious and/or the more the sense of survival is undermined. All channels of feeding and caves of safety are laced with persecutory images and later on with guilt (Klein, 1952). The cave paintings provide a semiotic framework for the negative and positive poles of the infant's transference to mother's postnatal presence. The cave paintings suggest the creation of a chain of signifiers that may tell the presence of bounty, and a balanced relationship with the cave mother, who provides for the helpless babe; or the cave paintings may suggest the tensions with the real predators as well as anguished rage at living through vulnerability, intensifying phantasies of possession, and plunder of maternal bounty and potency.

The concept of lack, and the threat of the ultimate void, in the sense of the experience of abjection and failure to find meaning, gives rise to language in the deepest emotional ways (Grotstein, 1990a, 1990b; Kristeva, 1982; Sullivan, 1991). Lacan interprets the significance of the cave paintings as placing a circle of meaning around the void. He is referring to anamorphous, a distortion in representation which expresses something beyond the literal meaning; in other words, not mimesis, but establishing meaning to fill the void of the unknown. In this case, more than physical subsistence, but the effort at using language for the demarcation and limitation of the void (Sullivan, 1991). The cave art may also sign the myth of the labyrinth, the caves themselves representing mother's body – the paintings the images of life, which are felt to dwell inside the caverns of mother's body. In psychoanalytic interpretations of the myth of the labyrinth, the infant wishes to explore or repossess mother's insides in order to regain security of attachment, to discover the origins of life, to possess the contents, and prevent the other babies or daddy's penis from stealing mother away, and to rehearse the odyssey of finding one's destiny by overcoming the obstacles to fear, and dread of psychic responsibility. In this way, the labyrinth may be seen as a metaphor for the map of the pathways that lead to the capacity to take on the responsibility of subjectivity (Grotstein, 2000a).

Klein explains that antecedent to either the mirror stage or entry into the symbolic order (for her, the depressive position), the subject is in an orbit of mother's body. He or she repeatedly returns in phantasy, to an inside state, to perpetuate the control or mastery over the separating colostrums, and to explore the internal mysteries that cannot be seen, touched, or heard through the senses. Meltzer defines this conflict as the aesthetic conflict, the conflict between the beauty of the world, mother's face, eyes, breasts, and lips assaulting the senses in a riot of colors, sounds, and kinesthetic experiences, and the fearful, dark shadows of the unknown caverns of mother's insides and her absences. Meltzer explains the beauty of her physical reality, part of the postnatal experience, may metamorphosis into a frightening Giaconda smile of hideous inscrutability, something that Leonardo da Vinci appreciated in his portraits of women's faces (Meltzer and Harris-Williams, 1988).

There is another step in the infant's postnatal relationship to mother's body. As the infant subject experiences and perceives mother's body and presence, the prenatal images that the fetus developed emerge, and are projected onto the percept of the Object. In this way, we can entertain the notion that the postnatal infant already has a repertoire of experience of life inside the body of the mother. The "newer" images of mother's body and mind are in fact made up in large part by the projective film of preconceptions and internal history.

It seems to me that Klein grasped the significance of the concept the labyrinth, as an exquisite universal template for pursuing the meaning of the infant's relationship to the mother's body, and illuminates the hazardous journey from the phantasied relationship to the interior of mother's body to their own rendezvous with separate mental life. It is at this crossroads that infants of both sexes struggle to discover and maintain differentiation. The search for the object of destiny, the odyssey of entering the labyrinth and returning from it may be filled with personal and cultural fears, admonitions, and signs of limitation in such a way that the odyssey is blocked.

The imaginary body is a complex entity created out of central memories of prenatal experience, powerful need of mother's presence, intense curiosity about the new outside mother and her unfolding complexity, her inside/outside dimensions, her presence as part of the infant's body, and her withdrawal from that space, laying bare the gap in which imagination and creative structuring of experience may take place, or conversely, opening up the presence of rips, wounds and infinite holes shorn of any markers of being (Bion, 1967a, 1967b; Grotstein, 1990a, 1990b; Meltzer and Harris-Williams, 1988; Tustin, 1981b, 1990).

If we bracket Klein's idea of the death instinct as the prime motivation for the infant's entry into the imaginary maternal body, we may propose instead, a need to experience aspects of the odyssey of mental life, made up of traumas, memories and phantasies of the past and present in a safe and manageable setting. With the assistance of mothering one's capacity to dream, detoxify, and eventually signify the contents of the inner world, we are in a position to appreciate the intense significance of the labyrinth for the human infant of both sexes.

One thrust of postmodernism is the deconstruction of the philosophy of presence seen in phallocentrism and named by Derrida as phallolocentrism. His interest, while including the contours of gender, is focused on the binary oppositions in Western logic and language. The idea that one aspect of the binary opposition is seen as superior and the other inferior; one visible, one invisible; one strange, one familiar, etc., is deconstructed by Derrida as a resistance to absence. He substitutes *differance* for difference. *Differance* is constructed on the notion of deferral, and within Derrida's logic, no concept, belief, or experience is ever definitive or complete, since meaning rests on elements that are not present as well as those yet to appear. One might say that *differance* allows us to give up the tyranny of physical presence and the axiogenic terror of absence. Absence associated with mother's interior is experienced as the power of life and death, which becomes persecuting and haunting in circumstances of binary opposition. In this way, we have developed concepts of masculinity and femininity, which perpetuate the rigid splitting of male and female identity, gender and sexuality.

As I see the situation in the wake of deconstruction of many of our most fervently held beliefs about sexual difference, there is for the present a bedrock template of the infant's experience of the mother's body prenatally and postnatally, which stimulates both preconceptions and realizations of mental birth (awareness), and thus deeply colors and shapes the concepts of female or woman. The conflation of life and death inside the maternal caverns, at the breast, and in the maternal arms and lap, is the profound metaphor around which culture and the individual build many belief systems and signifiers for sexual difference, and the relationship between men and women. Another dimension of the icon of mother's body is the refusal of sanctuary. After birth, immersed in the pressures of postnatal life, the wish to return to paradise feels denied.

Recent studies of fetal life and early postnatal mental capacities provide convincing evidence for brain readiness to make important discriminations in utero, and to receive on a psychosomatic level communications from the host mother. The evidence points to the infant's vulnerability to mother's states of mind; at the chemical level, mother's imbalance may be conducted through the placenta and umbilicus, producing a similar state of mind in the fetus. At the level of proto-mental life all the senses are in place and capable of organizing experience and likely including the reception of projective identification (Mancia, 1981; Osterweil, 2002). The anguish and comfort of mother's presence or absence is introduced through the sound of mother's voice. Maiello has conceptualized this capacity as the development of the sound object, a precursor to postnatal interaction (Maiello, 1995).

This newer work on fetal and postnatal experience brings us into the heart of the mythologies of the mother's body and presence, both evil and blessed. For the most part in cultural narratives, we find the ground of being associated with internal aspects of mother's body. Though we are able to demystify aspects of belief about women's capacities to protect and nurture mind, phobic reactions, denigration, tactics for control and dominance continue to haunt the minds of both sexes. The internal world and the unconscious are saturated with the terrors of failure to survive and when not able to be digested and signified are passed along for generations through violent projective identification. The present generation, the fetal or infant subjects, "inherit" beta element messages from their ancestors. A thought without a thinker is another way to conceptualize the nature of the messages. The intergenerational trajectory can lead from grandmother to mother to daughter, or from grandmother/grandfather to son to daughter. Within this intergenerational communication, unresolved anxieties about pregnancy, childbirth, mothering, and breastfeeding are distorted. These transmissions appear as nightmares that mandate the murder of life-giving thoughts and feelings, substituting instead, in Bion's way of thinking, -K links that destroy any hope of meaning and generation. The relationship of young women to their bodies, particularly their reproductive organs, is saturated with feelings about and beliefs in endangered eggs, fetuses and babies. Menstruation is often signified as a holocaust and brings shame about the lack of a phallus. Anorexia, fears of sterility, truncated sexuality and feelings of worthlessness are signs of the mandate's power.

The mandate or errands (Apprey and Stein, 1993a, 1993b) passed along to the male offspring, produce a fear and hatred of mother's body, and of their own masculinity centered around the phallus, and adoption of a predatory attitude with blind adherence to the belief in the superiority of presence. The ineffable experience (Bion's transformations in O) of reverie suffers mutilation and murder of the ineffable experience. Mother's and father's capacity for reverie to maintain a mental pregnancy and states of mind that welcome the new generation's mental life, or to dream the infant's agony, are threatened by the mandates from generations before and from failure to meet the emotional dilemma in the here and now.

We must ask how does the project, or legend or curse come to exert profound influence (Bion, 1962a, 1962b) on the minds of the offspring. It is true that emotional forces which remain deeply unconscious and often outside the structures that contain meaning are the stuff of abnormal projective identification, or to put it another way, the inner passions that propel the legends are partly unbearable elements in the mind that seek for meanings or containment (Bion, 1962a, 1962b; Grotstein, 1990a, 1990b; Klein, 1946, 1952, 1955). Maurice Apprey describes the creation of many cultural myths from this perspective: "In short, our entire civilization is shadowed and foreshadowed by one story behind the other" (Apprey and Stein, 1993a, 1993b; Bion, 1962a, 1962b; Feldman, 1987).

The story of Oedipus is such a legend. James Grotstein has also written of plural generational transference and countertransference legends. In his article "The sins of the father" (Grotstein, 1997), he describes the passing of unresolved, unbearable dilemmas or sins. The parental generation carrying the burden of thoughts without a thinker or pockets of madness seeks a messiah to rid itself of its hopeless agonies. Mother and father project their unresolved infantile neurosis into the infant, engraving the child with lifelong identity themes, which constrain its future unfolding as a self with a destiny of his or her own (Grotstein, 1990a, 1990b). The narrative of the little child Jesus and the savior who dies for our redemption function as a structure for the intrasubjective and intersubjective drama of sacrifice and salvation (Grotstein, 1997).

Customs and rituals, which code male and female gender, are often mapped in -K ways that do not bring the truth of the experience. Menstruation has evoked many rituals and beliefs as the blood signifying the sin of murder or mutilation. The taboos around menstruation demonstrate the presence of great persecutory anxieties. The belief that the menstrual blood is poisonous, dangerous and contagious carries the notions of the mandates of power to destroy potential life.

Similarly, the act of circumcision also is propelled by the mandate against unthinkable thoughts. The cutting of the phallus in circumcision is believed to protect the son from the dangers of incest and sets him on the pathway to the social contract. In "circumcision," Derrida adds another dimension to the cultural practice of circumcision. He focuses on the idea of mother's participation in the ritual against incest (continued merger), and protection for the alliance between Moses and God. In the biblical story of Elijah, mother does not passively give her son to the male order. Zipporah is the one who circumcises her son with her teeth by biting off the foreskin and thus repairs Moses' default, incapable of circumcising his own son (Oliver,

1993). She is responsible for this ritual, which inscribes the proper name on the boy's body, and is the guarantor of the mother tongue. In this way she marks the male body, makes it proper so that the alliance of the social contract can be renewed. Language is safely grounded on the bridge between dream, phantasy life, verbal and symbolic representation. Elijah has come to language because mother protected and created the bridge. She sacrifices an aspect of him for the integration of the semiotic with the symbolic (Kristeva, 1980b).

In this parable of Zipporah and Moses and their child, we see the extension of the maternal sphere into the realm of the symbolic order. However, the underlying anxieties that the Law of the Father will break down, continue in the insistence that women (mother) are a danger to the symbolic. It seems to me that the consequences of this failure to find the experience of reverie and transformation in O has left us with a legacy of material or concrete renderings of sexual difference. In this way, we are able to realize that physical experiences (i.e., pregnancy and birth) are also signs of deep anxiety about survival and are not limited to either sex.

The illness of the signifier

Without the inclusion of O, sexual difference appears in the conscious mind of both sexes saturated with stale but gripping imperatives. As discussed, the signifiers may well be weighed down with severe anxieties that remain largely unchallenged, or one could say, their power remains unquestioned and unknown.

Consciousness, as Freud understood it, was largely made up of the twists and turns formed out of negotiations to accommodate the unconscious or the drives. This insight marks the Copernican blow to the Enlightenment and Rationalism, and provides the Romantic strain with a pathway towards legitimacy. Freud suffered the consequence of straddling this division for his entire career. However, for us fortunate enough to be working and thinking today, he provided us with the pathways to understanding, and feeling the different aspects of the brain-mind and body-mind. In Freud's mind, consciousness is severely dethroned. He explains his new revelation in *The Interpretation of Dreams* (Freud, 1900). Consciousness, which was thought to be all, was in fact only a part of awareness that registers experience (Freud, 1900). Freud also warns us of the difficulty of tracing the unconscious thoughts to their deepest meanings. He explains – there is always a navel in a dream, which cannot be reached. Parents and analysts then are challenged to make contact with non-linguistic messages. Kristeva speaks with courage about the requirement to be sensitive to the presence of internal language.

When a mother endows her child with language, which is a process that society has deemed maternal, she is often all alone. Ideally, mothers give us meaning. We analysts are the ones who must discover signification. This means our role is more than maternal through our identification with the mother–child relationship; we recognize and often anticipate the meaning of that which remains unsaid. Our potential to understand the logic of the unsaid or buried alive is expressed in psychosomatic signs and imagery, and eventually in representational symbols and signifiers. However, we do know the experience of language, deceiving, misleading, and diverting us from realizations. Language and symbolism are the outcome of careful selection by the spinners of meaning (Barthes, 1972; Grotstein, 1980; Lacan, 1977a). Just as Freud mapped out the work of the censor selecting and arranging the forces and wishes from the instincts, Bion and Lacan propose the formation of meaning out of transformations of anxiety, and other intense affects into structures that convey messages from different levels of mental life, or are contrived to mislead or to dilute the impact of the gathering meaning. Bion and Matte Blanco believe that only partial doses of the essential emotional experience can be tolerated due to the vast discrepancy between ultimate meanings in the unconscious, and the limits of three-dimensional conscious thought and language (Bion, 1965; Grotstein, 1978; Matte Blanco, 1988). Freud, however, grasped the idea of vast inpenetrable truths, the navel of the dream, which could never be reached. These later writers, building on Freud's ideas, add other descriptions of the unconscious and its manifestations in conscious awareness. Their emphasis centers on notions of emotional truth and the evolution of the subject.

From their perspective, the signifying process contains many serious pitfalls. The concept the "illness of the signifier" points to these processes such as disavowal, splitting, projection, separating the emotional meaning from the verbal expression, and displacing the potency of the experience to mild and pallid substitutions for the signifier. We can readily grasp the similarity between Freud's notions of the development of neurotic symptoms and psychic pain as evolving out of the (divergent) nature and purposes of the pleasure principle and the reality principle, and the notions included in the concept of the illness of the signifier. The central shift from Freud is to Lacan's, Bion's and Matte Blanco's notion of the unconscious is found in the idea of the unconscious as a meaning-making organ, in contrast to the fulminating id concept. In this scheme, meaning and containment becomes the responsibility of the pre-conscious. Also, though Lacan's, Bion's and Matte Blanco's descriptions of the formulation of emotional significance include the ordeal of disruption, and the onset of fearful anxieties, they are not thought to emanate exclusively out of primary aggression. However we can see that the agents of distortion and dilution often render powerful emotional messages useless.

Suppose we return to our evocative signifiers man and woman, male and female. Lacan constructed a drawing and a small narrative demonstrating the process of designation. Two children traveling on a train pull into a station. Looking out the window, they each read a sign that they take to be the name of the station. The boy exclaims, "Oh look, we are at Femmes." The girl replies, "You idiot, we are at Gentlemen" (Lacan, 1957, 1977b). The diagram reveals two errors in thinking. The first mistakenly places the location of their odyssey by equating one signifier with another. The sign that demarcates the place for urinary segregation when away from home is confused with the sign that identifies the railway station. Second, the signifiers differentiate the identical pictures. Lacan's illustration is meant to give the reader pause as to what information is being conveyed, and through what means. In this case, language is used to designate and reinforce cultural practices, but through the device of the children's naivety. Lacan illustrates the potential for the superficiality of language and the use of deception.

We are able to associate other meanings to the appearance of the signifiers "Femme" and "Gentleman." One might be the use of figuration to suggest potential equality between the sexes or genders. Or the implication might be that while there is difference, there is no inequality. Lastly, feelings of jealousy, rage, and fear are "signified" out. Barthes shares with us his notion of the construction of social mythologies. He accounts for the slippage from language to myth by defining it as stolen language. Barthes understands the formation of the social myth as the conversion of the sign formed in the primary semiotic chain signifier, signified-sign into a second order construction, in which the meaning of the first is used as the basis for the myth. Thus, for example, the original sign that carries the significance of girl or femme is transposed into a structure made up of metalanguage. The concept "girl" becomes increasingly estranged from immediate experience. Meaning is drained away and replaced by the form of second order signification. The subject's signifying chain is transposed into a so-called signification structure that denies or seriously alters the personal experience of the unique mind expressing her or his subjectivity. In psychoanalysis, we are trained to understand the dilution of meaning or of desire as a many-leveled process conceived for protection against imbalance and anxiety. The different parts of the mind are thought to function in ways that facilitate physical and emotional survival, but in the course of growth and development may be diverted and become imbalanced. Mythological signification stands ready to join with personal anxieties, particularly those held by the surrounding family. Mythological structures scoop the existing emotions into their new form, providing support for the individual to escape from painful realizations of mortality, loss, and guilt among others.

In the transition from the sign made up of signifier, signified and sign to mythic signification, a solution is presented. For instance, the signifier girl or boy, part of a sign carrying unconscious, and undigested feelings about mother's body, flow into the symbolic order's arrangement of socially accepted belief systems. The myths of "womanhood" or "manhood" omit many of the complex dimensions of personhood. Bion's idea of the basic assumption is apposite here. Ambiguity and contradictory feelings as well as guilt and persecution are stamped out by zealous righteousness. Refuge from painful affects is sought within the system of beliefs in the basic assumption network of ideas, affects and suppressed desires. The feared aspects of the relationship to the meaning of mother's body are disavowed and projected out of the original chain of signification into or onto a new sign of femininity such as a sexual predator, or an evil embodiment of feminine power, or an angel with no desires other than to serve the family. The subject who carries both the old sign and the new one is also split and loses his/her relationship to their affects and their significance. The infant and child emerging into the realm of communication and symbolic discourse are immersed in the mythology of the current symbolic system. At the same time familial, intergenerational projective identification permeates the subject's attitudes about the self. We begin to see that there are diverse threads of belief and desire that are woven into our personal and social belief systems and attitudes for countless generations in dichotomous ways. Sexual difference is a crucial aspect of every culture, structuring and defining rules and rituals for survival and safety. Since mother is signified as the source of life and death, control of women in all their incarnations are common and fierce. The latter arise from several levels of mental functioning, which appear to be placed on a spectrum from sensory dominated presentations, icons, symbolic equations, and ultimately representations. The range from concrete, sensory signs to signifiers is determined by the implementation of psychic space. We are able to conjecture that development of the capacity for representation and signification includes the emergence of the ability to find psychic space as liberating in contrast to terrifying (Silver, 1981). Newer theories in semiotics and psychoanalysis bring to the surface the battle between meaning and action.

Klein's notion of projective identification leads us toward the fundamental origins of the distortions in signifying the nature and differences between female and male. The psychological need to enter into a preverbal communication system has been understood in evermore detailed and expanded ways through clinical experience and the windows of neurobiology. Allan N. Schore (1994, 2002), opens the vistas for us of the brain's active involvement with preverbal, projective identification or communication. He and others such as Maiello (1995), Mancia (1981), Osterweil (2002) and Piontelli (1988) elaborate on the presence of projective identification between mother and the fetus. The mind–body connection is believed to be the most dominant aspect of early communications between the mother–infant pair, because the presence of emotions in utero as well as postnatally is built into the brain-mind system. Schore (1994, 2002) explains that the right hemisphere, which is dominant for the first year and a half, is deeply connected to the limbic system and the autonomic nervous system, and is centrally involved in controlling vital functions supporting survival. The inevitable outcome for the failure of right brain to right brain communication is disregulation. Schore maps out the consequences of the failure of projective identification at the level of one limbic system communicating with the other, especially in critical emotional situations. The absence or disruption of this channel leads to acute states of disregulation. Burdened by biological primitive emotions, excitement, elation, rage, terror, disgust, shame and hopeless despair, the infant drowns in deregulated states (Schore, 1994, 2002). Here, we see the underpinnings of failure to thrive in infants, and the precise experiences leading to failure in the attachment process. Overloading leads to chaos, this in turn may lead to severe states of dissociation. Splitting away states of awareness enabled by powerful phantasies of loss of the mind that can think or perceive and register experience, brings on felt states of catastrophe, which become more and more biologically based as normal circuits that join together mental experiences from different parts of the brain-mind are blocked. Bion observed these chains of deterioration through his clinical work with deeply disturbed patients (Bion, 1967a). Bion (1967a) emphasizes a crucial difference between the psychotic and non-psychotic parts of the mind, whereas the object is felt to be attacked in the neurotic personality, the mind itself is believed to be mutilated in the psychotic personality. Bion gives the example of a patient who feels his mind to be seeping away like so much urine.

In normal bonding processes, the channels of preverbal communication are kept open by the welcoming warmth of body-to-body interacting. Feedback loops, envelopes of sight, sound and touch grow out of right brain interaction, and in turn, stimulate the growth of connections between different part of the brain (Anzieu, 1989; Fonagy et al., 2004; Schore, 1994, 2002). The newer notions stemming from the neurobiology of bonding and attachment suggest the map of the failure of meaning and significance to evolve. If the infant's mind is met with non-responsiveness or cruelty, she/he spins out of control pressed by emotional overload, leading to a hatred of awareness, and the development of various techniques and structures employed to ensure that emotional meaning is aborted; these include fragmentation, disassociation, stupidity and violence. Today we need to add the very real changes in brain functioning (Schore, 1994, 2002).

The repercussions we see in our clinical work are mirrored in society. Think of the generations of infants whose emotional life remained undiscovered. We might ask how many infants became distraught or ill. Think also of the pockets of abnegated parts of the personality that return in violence toward others, cloaked in high moralistic assumptions and religious fervor. Since self-consciousness is known to us, as an individual experience, only recently in human history, the tendency to project emotions into the external world, or into others was disguised for the most part. In contrast, painters and poets rendered the primitive emotional world visible in its many facets. In the present, psychoanalysis provides possible routes to the recovery of lost or buried aspects of the personality, and the emotions that accompany them as well as the release of the significant feelings that were overwhelming to the infant subject.

The complex of the dead mother

André Green's (1980) theory of the dead mother offers access to the disappeared aspects of the subject. He emphasizes that the invisibility of the internal world is held in place by the employment of negative hallucination. He explains that similarly to the crumbling of ancient civilizations, life suddenly ceases. But unlike the historian's explanation, of a natural catastrophe that ends the civilization, Green is talking about a pathological organization that overcomes loss by stopping the vibrations of life. This organization stems from absences or breakdowns of the maternal (paternal) partnering and the consequent lack of links between mother and offspring (Green, 1980; Sekoff, 1999). One source of the endeadened imago is the actual depression of the maternal presence; another is the infant's special need in participating in the interactions that create a lively sense of interaction of going on being.

Green (1980) is also exploring absence as a fundamental property of psychical life (Sekoff, 1999). The critical hurdle for the infant–mother pair is enduring the painful and unknown manifestations of disconnection. Green couches the struggle with absence in a vocabulary of the missing or unknown emptiness, non-being, non-breast, non-integration blankness, negative narcissism, psychical holes, and nothingness (Green, 1980; Sekoff, 1999). I think the sense of nothing, doubtful existence, or precarious going on being, is intensely related to the feeling of abjection; i.e., to have lost or never to have found the belief in one's own existence or being. The complex of the dead mother ties us to her certain deadness, the avoidance of the feelings of lack, loss and mortality is managed; for she is always there, unchanging since she never dies. The price for her empowerment is deadly, since nothing can arise spontaneously and bring new meaning lest we waken the dead. The fear and horror of woman's power is often connected to the concepts of pregnancy and birth, but in the dead mother complex, women are imagined to carry the authority to hold life as a hostage. The more massive the embrace is felt, the more life is arrested, and the more the risks of emerging from the dead mother are felt to be life threatening. Perhaps some of the processes of encapsulation related to psychological withdrawal and deadness can be understood in this way. As Green emphasizes, at a deeper level, nothingness is not bypassed but perpetuated. The infant and adult subject remains hovering over the endless chasm of nothingness.

In earlier and non-Western cultures, little value was given to individual experience, and for most of human history, mythology and ritual were founded on the idea that human personality and character stems from supernatural forces (most often religious). The psychic disappearance of many has gone unnoticed or thought to be anguish within the soul. Both men and women are vulnerable to the experience of abjection. However, as discussed above, Klein's concept of the manic defense, particularly as it is organized against vulnerability and dependency, designates mother as the helpless baby, through splitting and projection, while the subject imagines her/himself becoming the phantasied all powerful one. Though today we can acknowledge female omnipotence and grandiosity more readily than ever before, the more extreme formulation of the manic defense includes a further split seen in the belief that men are better equipped to think, speak, act and protect society than women are. The concept or signifier "woman" remains so profoundly associated with death and fusion that it calls for profound control over actual women. In the 1990s several schoolgirls in Saudi Arabia were burned to death in a fire at their school building. They were not allowed to escape because their heads were not covered properly. In the same spirit, women in the Middle East are still stoned to death for infidelity. However, the split includes the high price that men pay for their "superior" status as the warrior group.

I think we can readily see in contemporary images of women, particularly as presented in films, television, advertising and competitive sports, the destruction of the passive ideal for women. We are all familiar with these new signs of female vigor. We are privy to the competence of female athletes on the ice, court, boards and slopes. These women are compared not only with their male peers but also to each other. A common fictional representation, however, includes assuming some aspects of the male personae. The young woman in *Alias*, a current TV series, is designed as a female James Bond. Her remarkable self-defense skills are carried out by her extraordinary long and powerful limbs. Her fierce warrior incarnation suggests myths of Amazon women who are trained to use their bodies as weapons and can bring down male predators. However, it is important to acknowledge that "Sydney" (a name which spans both genders) is also sexually appealing to men, brings out the protective impulse in her colleagues, and has a large capacity for empathy, reminiscent of maternal qualities. What are we to make of these popular cultural icons? Of course, we know that the producers, writers, and advertisers believe that the viewing public will welcome a woman with Sydney's talents. The film, *Charlie's Angels* (2000), an updating of the old TV series, shapes the three women detectives in the mold of the Sydney-Bond character. Though still dependent on Charlie their male boss, they have developed much of their bodies' strength. Utilizing Barthes' understanding of social myths as a second or third order signification structure in which emotional meaning has been split away, we are invited to be convinced that the passive and inferior version of women has been transcended. The three young detectives are also invested with superior martial arts skills and are provided with some shrewdness and wit. Nevertheless, they remain under the tutelage of Charlie, who also keeps them in the dark, so to speak, by withholding his identity and presence. I think we can see that the demand for women's autonomy seems to be gratified but at the same time women's minds and ability to signify and think deeply have been left out of the portrayal of these "new women." In Chapter 7, on portrayals of women in recent films and television, the discussion centers on the appearance of new qualities and capacities in the women characters as well as revisitations of their old dilemmas (see, for instance, *Thelma and Louise* and *The Hours*). The major transformation needed to restore women to wholeness of mind and body is the realization of their capacity to vigorously contribute to the signifying realm (from cradle to the grave). The absence of this idea in significant cultural portrayals suggests the fear and anxiety that a powerful maternal force evokes. The following chapters carry on the search for the strangled or disappeared female subject.

Chapter 2

Female subjectivity

The interest in subjectivity is closely associated with the waning of faith in traditional belief systems. Interest in women's subjectivity follows as the deconstruction of given values release them from incarceration inside concepts of sexual difference that had marked them as limited, and inferior. These trends developed into a crisis in belief in Western culture in the movement known as postmodernism. The latter is the most recent expression of modern Western culture to move away from traditional and a priori belief systems. At the closing of the Middle Ages, the discoveries of Galileo announced the rejection of all finalist explanations of the universe and brought the idea of a hierarchically ordered cosmos to destruction. The notion of an infinite autonomous universe undermined traditional proofs of the experience of the existence of God, and forced the individual to seek God within her/himself (Roudinesco, 1990). These changes produced the anxieties of standing alone in a limitless universe, which had previously been felt as the wrath of God or the forces of Nature.

Enlightenment epistemology had also announced itself as an iconoclastic movement, but as we know, remained attached to particular Western philosophical traditions including: Reason, Rationality, and Empiricism. In this way, Enlightenment thinkers were able to maintain the illusion of an orderly universe. The Democratic Revolutions continued the process of demolishing the fervent and widely held belief in a priori laws and substituted the rule of democracy and equality, which themselves were unmasked soon after their birth, not only intellectually (Whitman vs. Poe or Longfellow vs. Dickinson), but were shattered by the various wars in Europe and America: the Napoleonic, the Civil War in America, and both World Wars. Modernism broke open the sanctity of appearance, and particularly the stability of form, first in European painting and literature, and then in the United States. Think of Picasso, Mallarmé, Proust, Woolf and James Joyce. Although these modernists do not set themselves the task of uncovering the underlying forces of meaning within the objects of exploration, they open the pathway towards free association, and move into the realm of different layers of meaning. Freud is the contemporary of many of these modernist figures, and they influence him as well as he influenced them; both are part of cultural and social shifts away from tradition, hierarchy and a worship of appearances.

The move toward deconstructivism was already underway in the writings of linguists such as Roman Jakobson and Ferdinand de Saussure. Linguistics broke away from the belief that a priori or divine laws that carried only one set of irrevocable meaning governed language. De Saussure characterized the linguistic signs in terms of the relationship, which pertained between its dual aspects of concept and sound image, or to use the terms which have made de Saussure famous: signified (*signifié*) and signifier (*signifiant*). He held that the structural relationship between the concept of the tree (the signified) and the sound image made by the word tree (the signifier) constitute a linguistic sign. It is a system of signs that express ideas (Hawkes, 1977). De Saussure stressed that the overall characteristic of this relationship is one that is arbitrary. There exists no necessary fitness in the link between the sound image or signifier tree, the concept or signified that it evolves, and the actual physical tree growing on the earth. The word "tree," in short, has no natural or tree-like qualities, and there is no appeal open to a reality beyond the structure of a language in order to underwrite it (Hawkes, 1977).

For de Saussure, language stands as the supreme example of a self-contained relational structure whose constituent parts have no significance unless they are integrated within its bounds. Language is a system of interdependent terms in which the value of each term results solely from the simultaneous presence of the other (Hawkes, 1977). Thus, for de Saussure, all aspects of language are based on relations.

A critical idea that Lacan was able to draw from de Saussure was the idea of the relationship of the words to each other in the spoken sentence. De Saussure looked at this as structured in an oppositional mode. For example, hat-cat-bat-fat. Also, the words, which are not chosen for the spoken sentence, constitute the sentence in its final form. Thus, de Saussure seemed to reinforce a closed, self-sufficient, self-defining nature of semiotics and language in which they look inward to their own mechanisms, not outward to a real world that lies beyond them. Signs, like phonemes, function not through their intrinsic value, but through their relative position. Since the total mode of language is oppositional, whatever distinguishes one sign from the other constitutes it. De Saussure thought that in language there are only differences without positive terms.

Lacan found considerable freedom in de Saussure's notion that there was no external demand that a sentence, a group of words, or associations be structured according to some pre-existing value. Instead, value came from within the arrangement of the signifier to the signified, and one sign to another. As discussed in Chapter 1, this freedom from tradition also contained a paradox. Lacan's theory of the Symbolic Order insists that culture defines values, which are injected into the individual before and at birth. Perhaps the site of the interplay between the two aspects of the paradox lies the notion that interpretation and meaning do not descend from divine or divinely ordained authority, but from the arrangement of symbols and signs derived from the mental processes of humankind.

The twentieth century has seen the formal recognition of the Other or unconscious. Freud's discovery of the unconscious led to concepts of other voices with will and agency that seemed to originate in unknown sources, with some awareness that they were part of the person experiencing them. Nineteenth-century writers were intensely interested in alter egos, doppelgangers, and monsters. The appearance of representations of other parts of the personality probably reflected the lessening of massive projection of split-off aspects into religious and supernatural characters; this caused more awareness of inner personal thoughts and feelings. Robert Louis Stevenson's Dr. Jekyll and Mr. Hyde is a splendid rendering of these transitional concepts. Freud, as we know, lost touch with the notion of alter subjects and buried them under his emphasis on the drives and the defenses. Although they reappeared in the notion of the super ego and the ego ideal, they were figured as outcomes of the ego's battle with the drives. Later, object relation theorists recognized the existence of other voices with their own alter subjectivity (Fairbairn, 1944, 1946; Klein, 1928, 1940, 1952).

Within the innovations of Bion, Lacan, Matte Blanco and Grotstein, the concept of the subject is described less as an instinctual matter that is driven only by the push toward survival (resting on the innate wiring for nurture or aggression). They emphasize the search for postnatal attachment carried out in the infant's quest to be respected as a communicating person who sends significant messages of his/her own (Fonagy et al., 2004; Trevarthan, 1980). The infant's need to project in order to express him/herself overrides the theory of the exclusive emphasis on somatic interactions as the groundwork for the development of vigorous mental life. Lacan's interests in language and meaning shape his contribution to changes in concepts, of the nature and function of the unconscious. The philosophers Martin Heidegger, Jean Paul Sartre and Immanuel Kant informed Lacan's study of subjectivity, as well as an infusion of Freud's dream theory, and de Saussure's work with language, and his concepts of the signifier–signified. Lacan's critical innovations are found in his idea that the unconscious functions like language, and his concept of the Other.

Let us begin with the unconscious as functioning like language. Lacan thought that the real Freud was to be found in his theory of the dream work. Lacan supposed that metaphor and metonymy functioned like displacement and condensation. He believed the purpose of the dream work was fueled by the need to re-find the lost object, "petite object *a*," the sign for the aspect of the mother of primary atonement. The infant, becoming aware of separation and the realization of lack, and infused with awareness of mortality, searched along a chain of meaning in the quest to refind a sense of wholeness and everlasting going-on being. Building from de Saussure's theory of semiotics, Lacan thought that the search for being and meaning was conducted through language (Nobus, 1998).

By inverting, de Saussure's signifier–signified relationship, the signifier carried the weight of the creation of meaning, which was determined by its position in the chain of words and its relationship to the Symbolic Order, as well as emotional forces. Deeper yet lies the role of Desire. The implications of Lacan's concept of lack points toward the experience of incompleteness, and the striving to overcome or mitigate the pain and immanent sense of danger realized by the impact of life and death through substitution and deflection (metonymy and metaphor). Lacan guides us through the danger of confusing need and desire. The needs of the body if withheld cause a sense of danger. However, the experience of desire eternally taunts the subject along the chain of signifiers. Part of the experience of emerging from the thrall of atonement is the awakening to the existence of desire. The desire of the newly forming subject is to reunify the subject–object pair. Thus, desire is felt to reside within the subject, but as he or she grasps that his/her desire cannot be gratified without the consent of the Other, a shift takes place in the mind of the subject that he/she is searching for the desire of the Other to gratify a sense of connection.

Lacan understood, drawing from Georg Hegel's (1977) *Phenomenology of Spirit*, that desire carried the lack or hole in the being of the subject, which could be satisfied by one thing only, the desire of the other (Grosz, 1990). At this point we are placed inside the enigma that the subject experiences him or herself as lacking, but in search of a sense of wholeness, and compensating for the loss of "petite object *a*," becomes beholden to the desire of the other. The subject finds him or herself enthralled to the Other. Lacan underlines this outcome describing the analytic transference as always filtered through the Other.

Lacan charted the function of "Otherness" as the dawning awareness of lack and he thought that the mirror stage brought this awareness forward. In the mirror stage the infant saw her/himself in the mirror and in mother's (father's) eyes as she/he might appear in the future, as a solid body that could hold her/him upright. The feelings of being were not yet joined up with the mirror image. In this way, the image became the "Other." Similarly the mirror image reflected back to the infant subject may fail to match the experience of the infant and lends itself to the creation of an alter ego. Both the mirror stage and the use of language split the subject from his/her original core self. Furthermore, Lacan depends on Hegel to understand the creation of desire. Hegel posits in the *Phenomenology of Spirit* that desire functions to fill the hole in being with the desire of the Other (Grosz, 1990).

Thus, we can conjecture through Lacan's theory of the Other that subjectivity is always filtered through this aspect of the self designated by the Other in analysis, but in the subject's inner life perpetually. We are accustomed to think of the Other as outside the subject, and imposing values from the point of view of a cultural consensus found in the Symbolic Order; that is also true.

Another dimension of the notion of the Other is also found in the culture and society in the form of an out-group that varies in the extremity of its out-group status culminating in the abject or the experience of excoriation (Kristeva, 1982). Nazism, apartheid and Arab–Israeli xenophobia are examples of extreme Otherness. Lacan includes all three forms of otherness as important elements in the constitution of the subject that lead to bifurcation in the subject and the construction of a false self.

Bion finds the etiology of subjectivity by gradually leaving behind the notion of the tyranny of the death instinct. We can follow the beginning of this trend in the articles that are collected in *Second Thoughts* (Bion, 1967b). At that time, he begins to realize that the infant's needs include the experience of attunement and reverie. In "Theory of thinking," Bion (1962b) lays out the deterioration of the infant's mind, when the mothering one is unable to contribute her capacity to dream and phantasize the archaic messages emanating from the infant's raw subjectivity, which as yet attain only tentative significance for the infant, except in terms of pain and fear, as well as ecstasy (Bion, 1967a; Grotstein, 1981; Tustin, 1981b). Bion begins to describe the process of dreaming in terms of not only managing intense overflow, but also birthing carriers of significance that are evolving in the interface between the deep fathoms of limitless meanings, and other layers of mental life that move toward the surface to mate with the artifacts of asymmetrical logic (Bion, 1967a; Grotstein, 1998; Matte Blanco, 1998).

For Bion, the architect of the ineffable transformations in "O" brings to awareness the vastness of the unknown and its potential power. The subject of analysis moves through concerns with frustration couched in terms of the terror of absence or of separation; to increase his/her ability to preserve the image of the primary object, and ultimately develops the capacity to have faith in its return without destroying its goodness. Part of this growth process includes an ability to transcend dependence on control of a tangible object, and to ride on the crest of faith that ultra-sensual experience brings. This transition is exquisitely challenging, as it deprives the subject of material reassurance, substituting the ineffable as the means to the richness and fullness of emotional depth and truth.

Thus, Bion takes us through the experiences of myth and phantasy and depressive concern, to the ineffable, and our relationship to being (Bion, 1965; Grotstein, 1998). Being breaks through the veil of signification from simple signs to iconography and symbolization, in the sense that the experience of being comes forward as feeling and emotions, which seem not yet to have been dreamt or demystified from the conscious point of view (Goldstein, 1995; Grotstein, 2000d; Silver, 1981). Thus, we are always struggling directly with all significations, which in a sense can only shadow the truth of the messages from the deep unconscious (Bion, 1967a; Grotstein, 2000a).

Analysis is a critical arena for this struggle. The individual seeks help from the analyst not only because of pain and various aspects of dysfunction, but also because he/she has lost or never made contact with aspects of him or herself. These might be thought of as the unborn or stillborn (Grotstein, 2000a). The analytic process balances precariously between containment that regulates and modifies powerful overflow, and that which avoids the meeting with the infinity of the unknown and unsaturated. Bion suggests that the analyst must reach states of patience and confidence as he or she journeys through the paranoia of the paranoid schizoid and the pangs and regrets of the depressive position (Bion, 1965; Grotstein, 2007). The states of mind of both analyst and analysand are mediators to the extent that they are attempting to make contact with wavebands of experience that are less confined in the familiar signs and certainly by the barriers of not wanting to know. In this state of mind, intuition becomes possible in that it brings the subject into contact with the ineffable and freshly evolved.

Bion emphasized the analyst's similarity to the mothering one who must abandon memory and desire or any familiar "signposts" that confine and reduce meaning. Of course, the infant, unlike the analysand, has far fewer veils to discard and is burdened less with convention and more with immaturity and helplessness. However, recent research points to risks that infants bring in terms of genetic loading or neural physiological deficits. In either case, the mothering one is challenged to endure the pulsing emergence of the unknown and unstable.

The danger that threatens mother–infant, analyst–analysand couple is to stay lodged within the currents of the paranoid schizoid position fighting demons, and approaching the depressive position, or to be trapped by melancholia and/or daunted by the overwhelming task of achieving reparation. The irritability and rage of the highly deregulated analysand ensnares the couple attempting to voyage into latent significance, and arriving instead at a battle made up of betrayal, violence, and hatred. Melancholia drives the analysand into spirals of repetition.[1] Within these circumstances, we must ask how are we to encourage the ephemeral and the unknown to emerge and survive. Violence and repetition block the arteries that nourish being and intuition. In the adult speaking subject, holes in the sense of being are covered over by a skin of words, practices, rituals, and creative endeavors; they are efforts to draw circles around the abyss of nothingness (Anzieu, 1989; Barthes, 1972; Grotstein, 1990a, 1990b; Sullivan, 1991).

---

1 See Freud's (1914) discussion of closed off internal dialogues in *Mourning and Melancholia.*

The maternal presence

In disparate cultures, over the millennia the woman's body has been coded as a critical signifier of death as well as life (Campbell, 1959; Klein, 1928, 1940). Women's bodies are described as parts, which are circumscribed, separated from personhood, sexualized, and denigrated in the effort to mask the powerful dread of the loss of the primary object. I am suggesting that women's subjectivity and speech are deeply affected by a chain of signifiers buried in the unconscious that attempt to disguise, avoid, and to mend the holes in the skin by attributing the fear of the hole to women and the designation of wholeness to men.

We must ask how are these biases transmitted to the female subject and how do they constrain women's utterances particularly those which stem from their innermost core? Various theorists have described the subject as originating at the infant's dawning awareness that his/her incipient mind is active and relays experience that originates within her/himself (Alvarez, 1992; Fonagy, 2001, Fonagy et al., 2004, Schore, 1994, 2002). Awareness of one's being and subjectivity, the subject defined here as the one who collects and organizes the data of personal existence, depends at once on the mothering one's supplemental capacities to nurture the infant's fragile and inexperienced mind.

But the site of body-mind experience is not the only source of the subject's origins. Here, we may rely on the explorations of Bion (1962a) and Matte Blanco (1988). Bion emphasizes that all mental life is potential in a vast array of preconceptions that will meet their mate in lifelong realizations (Bion, 1967a). The preconception for the breast is a fundamental endowment of this kind as are other aspects of the relationship. Similarly, Matte Blanco postulates infinite possibilities of potential meanings in the unconscious that predate life in utero or physical birth. Often, the great and infinite in the unconscious have been thought to be emanations from God. We might suggest today, more in keeping with our views of psychic reality – that infinite possibilities lie in waiting to pass messages through the sluices of the pre-conscious (Matte Blanco, 1988). Thus, we might add that the catalyst for the creation and birth of the subject is the idea in the mind of the procreators on the one hand, and on the other, the infinite messages that are pressing to be realized and interpreted.

The transformations from potential expressions of the subject, to their realizations in emanations from the individual internally, to aspects of the self, and externally to others, involve many layers of the mind and diverse modes of expression (Grotstein, 2000a; Schore, 2002); somatic and sensory signs are often thought to be the original marks of the presence of activity of the mind.

Now we are at the place where we can see that the coalescence of women's subjectivity is deeply affected at many levels of mental life. The preconceptions for realizing oneself as a potent living woman have already been altered by the violent prejudices connected with fears of awareness of a fragile and limited hold on existence. Mother's body, thought to be a place of death as well as the site of birth, is felt so intensely, that the realization of femaleness and the birth and nurture functions of the female body are distorted, and associated with the deeply held conviction that females of all ages are subversive to the Symbolic Order and the Law of the Father. Furthermore, women's internal voices (superegos, maternal and paternal presences) are created not only out of the many layers of the mind-brain but also out of the urge to create and overcome helplessness in a postnatal realm that feels so determined by others (Grotstein, 2000a; Klein, 1928, 1931, 1952).

Also the massive pull back into an unborn state into what is imagined to be the womb of protection from unexpected dangers, hurts and painful frustrations, shape, color and limit women's thoughts and feelings about their capacities and purposes as subjects from prenatal states to adult discourse, and seriously alters the Symbolic Order's recognition of the non-linguistic layers of signification constituting the creation of meaning (Kristeva, 1982). Lacan stressed that the subject's enunciation was made possible through the no of the father, the Law of the Father, which protected and maintained the space between words and letters controlling the drag into merger. The underlying misconception is that mothers encourage merger, and fathers stimulate the use of symbols and signs.

Women find themselves believing that they are not able to speak power-fully inside themselves, and to the external society in which they find themselves embedded. Within the internal reality of the women subjects with whom I have worked analytically, powerful inhibitions undermine their belief in the power and authenticity of their thoughts and feelings. I want to caution the reader and myself to keep in mind the analogous difficulties in men. They too "speak," feel and think from false premises. However, in this analysis I wish to focus on the internal world of women. Much of the difference has to do not only with the fear of "mother's" powers, protectively identified as weakness, stupidity and evil, but also with the processes of pregnancy, childbirth and nursing. Women's superego development and autochthonous interpretations of psychic reality are dominated by the failure of the family, culture, and the individual mind to "contain" the nameless dreads of the centuries before.[2]

2 Bion's deep understanding of the interconnections between intrasubjectivity and intersubjectivity has helped us profoundly to make links between these two areas of human relating and communication. Grotstein (2000d) and Ogden (1992) have elaborated on these connections helping us to find our way towards understanding psychic reality and the impact of the "Other."

I want to take up Klein's brilliant discovery and exploration of infantile phantasies with the theory of nameless dread in mind. I am suggesting that the "death instinct" appears as a tyrannical force in conditions of an infantile catastrophe. Female subjects are prey to a double assault from the "death instinct." One may be seen as the infant's own response to trauma and the other the projective identifications of the family and culture which carries the impulse to sacrifice. Klein brings to our attention this critical version of projective identification. As discussed above, the infant mind under circumstances of distress feels sacrificed to a cruel destiny and wishes to rid her/himself of that pain. The infant sends the feeling of sacrifice to the "Other," (M) (other) or mothering one. But in need of containment themselves, the parents use projective identification to unburden themselves; their offspring become the warehouse for their sacrificed infant aspects. The next generation, infants and children, are overwhelmed and take on the projected designation, or they hurl back a rejection of the parents' messages. Feelings of confusion, of not being able to help and feeling unappreciated, flare up in the parents.

In this closed system, the psychic reality of female infants and children are haunted by vengeful maternal imagoes that are felt to be the murderers of the subject's body and mind, particularly the reproductive organs. Unborn infants and eggs are felt to be demonic and vengeful in retaliation for the girl's wrath and hatred of mother's capacities for reproduction. The subject is deeply identified with infants and children stuck in the caverns of the maternal body; thus, claustrophobia, including fears of entombment, burial alive, and serious mutilation are major phantasies blocking their sense of being. Mergers with the dangerous figure are often translated into somatic suffering and parallel ideation of lack of self-worth and self-denigration. Alternatively, identification with the vengeful mother is manifested in hatred and destructive feelings toward helpless aspects of the self most particularly toward the infant ones. Menstruation, pregnancy, childbirth and nursing are staging grounds for the presentation of these inner dramas.

The subject who creates

Klein begins the reformulation of the idea of the contributions of the unconscious with her emphasis on phantasy. She provides us with the anecdote of an infant left too long in the garden who becomes hysterical and inconsolable. Klein explains that the infant was frustrated beyond endurance, and that accordingly was beset by a surplus of the death instinct. However, she also explains that the infant imagines that he or she has fallen into the grasp of the bad mother or breast. She explains that in the absence of the good aspect of the mother the infant imagines the presence of the bad and dangerous one.

Another example of the existence and presence of phantasy is given in her accounts of projection and introjection, and projective identification. The satisfied baby manages to create and maintain a balance between good and bad internal figures and the infant relating to them. In many other cases the imbalance tipping towards turbulence and chaos dominates. Surely, these were the patients that Klein saw; recall her young patients who could not play or who were unable to communicate. At this time, between the 1920s and 1930s, Klein proposed that the damage to the internal breast was believed in phantasy to be so devastating that a cruel and vengeful superego developed that prevented the child from developing freedom in phantasy, and consequently play. Hanna Segal followed this understanding and developed it in her paper on symbolic equations (Segal, 1957). Psychic space is thwarted to the extent that equations take the place of potential symbols. Klein (1928) felt that females of all ages were very vulnerable to organized oppression by the maternal superego because of their likeness to mother's body. The implication of this idea is that female phantasies are shaped by the identity of their mother's body with their bodies, and the functions that various aspects of their bodies perform (Klein, 1928). Klein spun out the further implication that males also suffered from persecution anxiety, but not exclusively associated with castration anxiety. However, as she moved into the more archaic levels of the Oedipus complex and linked infantile anxiety to its original sources, death anxiety or survival anxiety, she thought that the closeness to the whole drama of pregnancy, birth and survival intensified the female child's sense of responsibility and fear of retaliation. I think that the internal worlds of the female analysands discussed below will support Klein's hypothesis.

Recall that the patients that Klein saw, including her own children, were caught in a culture that was slowly emerging from the long dark ages of fear and ignorance about infants. Infant and child mortality remained excruciatingly high until the late nineteenth century. Furthermore, religious conviction and lack of knowledge about child development encouraged the perpetuation of the belief that if children and babies were human in their capacity to feel fear, they might be made to respect authority through training (Freud (1911) on the Daniel Schreber case). Today, these ideas live on in systems that wean the child from dependence on the parent's body by allowing them to "cry it out" ("Ferberizing" your child). Klein leapt into the modern age by piercing the experiences of dread, anxiety and the sense of persecution created by psychological processes, particularly, phantasy and projective identification of these phantasies. Her theory including the defenses of the paranoid schizoid position, take the position of the infant as suffering death anxiety, and paves the way for Bion's discovery of the need of the patient and baby for containment.

Bion moved away from the inevitability of "original sin" with his recognition of the container function of the "mothering one." At the same time,

Bion was broadening and deepening his concept of the unconscious. As part of these additions, Bion included the notion of unknown feelings and thought that came from other dimensions of the mind, including the infinite realms outside space and time (Bion, 1965; Grotstein, 2000d; Matte Blanco, 1988; Paul, 1997). Bion also points out that the evolution of the infinite into digestible forms takes place on the edge of the ineffable. He thinks that the acceptance of the full impact of a new realization requires the presence of "maternal" reverie, but he takes us further into our experience of the unconscious. Grotstein's transcendent position elaborates on Bion's concept of the unconscious as contributing meaning beyond meanings, which are always evolving. Think of speech, writing, and the process of signification as evolving over thousands of years.

In the transcendent position, we may assume that the subject has negotiated the paranoid schizoid position to the extent that he/she has added the depressive position to her repertoire. Bion reminds us that this relationship between the two positions is not a linear process, but is based on a constant process of integration, breaking apart the elements of new realizations, and waiting patiently for new integrations to form. Through adding the concept of the ineffable, Bion strikes at the heart of concrete or undeveloped realizations that are grasping, insatiable and shallow, and in which substantial security and dignity are scarce. The human mind suffers great mental pain in the face of the unknown; the space of uncertainty is confused with the gap of premature separation (Bion, 1962a, 1962b).

Transformation in O is the underpinnings for achieving the transcendent position, the name that Grotstein chooses to describe the state of mind that the individual achieves after moving through the other positions, and becomes able to tolerate ultimate experience (Grotstein, 2000a). He explains O is the ultimate happening, the unlimited mystery that only can be partially known through K when it becomes knowable. Once again, O can only be known as it descends from absolutes to becoming (Grotstein, 2000a). Also Bion stresses that O cannot be known through the senses or understood cognitively, but can only be touched through the experience of becoming. From this perspective, realizations may be felt in two dimensions. "The name of a concept constantly conjoins its unknowable nominal essence, 'the thing in itself,' with a phenomenal counterpart for normal, symbolic linguistic employment" (Grotstein, 2000a).

It is important to note that Lacan's notion of the unconscious as a symbol-forming organ is integrally connected to the symbolic order and culture, and gives less emphasis to the currents of the primordial stream. Klein, Bion and Grotstein, on the other hand, are committed to the belief that the unconscious is made up of primordial feelings, innate knowledge, instincts and emanations from the Godhead. We might translate the concept of the Godhead as infinite potential experience being orchestrated by the messiah within us, who guides us away from certitude, prejudice, defensiveness and duplicity, and leads us toward our appointment in Samara in order to encounter the truth of our experience (Grotstein, 2000a). We might look at the analytic process as the challenge to find the O of our inner life and to recover or reclaim our liveliness and our being rather than to uncover our attacks on life (the concept of original sin has played an important part here).

The subject awakens or is born

The concept of the False Self or the As/If Personality (Deutsch, 1955; Winnicott, 1960a), has described developmental scenarios in which subjectivity is seriously prevented from forming, and at the extreme is mutilated seemingly beyond repair. The signs of a False Self or As/If Personality disorder are: severe compliance, imitation, clinging and grave despair of not being able to count on one's self; feelings of artificiality and, worse still, states of deadness. More recently, Bion has added significantly to our grasp of the formation of False Self or As/If Personalities. He proposes that the subject is unable to form authentically due to the failure of the container–contained relationship. He adds that intersubjectivity is essential to the expansion of intrasubjectivity (Bion, 1959; Grotstein, 2007).

This notion of a reciprocal process for the nourishment of capacities to create signs and symbols that are faithful to emotional experience revolutionizes the concepts of basic beliefs that had made up much of psychoanalytic understanding. Bion begins to gather up and juxtapose the crucial elements of the internal world constructed out of biological need, the imagination and memory, and the reception and interpretation of the infant's (and individual's) experience. I want to emphasize here that every word spoken to the individual, every ritual practiced in the culture of the society in which the infant subject finds her/himself, acts as a powerful container/interpreter that shapes, distorts or enhances the core feelings/emotions of the singular subject from earliest awareness through the life cycle.

The nameless dread curses that we have seen in our patients passed down as toxic, indigestible basic assumptions – "I am not meant to amount to anything due to the assignment, errand or message" (Apprey and Stein, 1993b). The errand or assignment dominates and mutilates the person's subjectivity until an exploration of the split-off commands, and beliefs are revisited in the light of new thoughts and points of view.

Recently a young woman in her late twenties told me that she always knew that she was meant to be a failure. Of course, there are many ways to explore her convictions. As a Eurasian, "Linda" carries the stigma of her father's incarceration during World War II, and at the same time, she carries the inferiority of Japanese women. She is also the youngest child of four children, two of whom are Caucasian. Envy and jealousy play a large part in her failed self-regard, but I believe these feelings are also stimulated by the heavy tasks placed on her as the youngest child; she is to carry the nameless dread of her family.

Linda has been designated through projective identification, the identity of the one who is hated, scorned, and fated not to thrive. She elaborates, "I am not meant to succeed at anything." In place of passionate desires, a sense of hopelessness soon covers her like a shroud, and she feels herself to be buried alive. Alternatively, her despair grows to such massive proportions that she feels her only escape is suicide. Mother is coded in Linda's inner world as passing on her own infanticidal and hopeless feelings (Apprey and Stein, 1993b). Apprey explains that the subject often weaves these projective identifications into their personal mythology: "I am fated never to have children," and worse still, at a deeper level, "I can never have children because I have murdered the unborn babies in mother" (Apprey and Stein, 1993b). That concept is a complex entity made up of projective identifications of the infant/ child subject into the growing "image/presence" of "mother." If not detoxified it enters each new generation as a curse or a mandate. Another possibility is the belief that only one can live, or the contrasting belief is found in the command that one must fill in the tragic space left by a dead sibling. Apprey introduces us to the concept of an invariant pathogenic phantasy. He adds that the task of the analysis is to enable the analysand to break free of the otherwise pathogenic invariant phantasy (Apprey and Stein, 1993b).

A frequent and powerful obsessive thought that spins through Linda's mind is that life has no value for her; the associated thought is that she has no passport to a vigorous sense of existence. Alternatively, she escapes into outrage and superiority, believing herself to be brighter and more creative than most other people. However, Linda's dominant position under the rule of her invariant pathological belief system, is that she is a slave to some superior forces. In this version, Linda reveals her identification with the enslaving internal presences (Grotstein, 2000b). Tragically, she is severely handicapped forever, caught between the various aspects of her cruel dominating superego, and its victim.

This stream of phantasies or basic assumption unfolds powerfully, not only under the unconscious demands made by the familial projective identifications, but also in the absence of some aspects of bonding and attachment, and the capacity to signify. Looking through Bion's lens, the need for the parent's support of the infant's nascent capacity for dream work alpha is a major nurturant for the efflorescence of truth. We must ask then, can the parent dream the deepest experiences and meanings, and how would culture enter into this process?

As discussed in Chapter 1, in the section on "The illness of the signifier," the emotional truth and meanings commencing at birth or before are diverted and distorted for the purposes of defending against terror, or feelings of helplessness, and for enhancing delusions of power in the individual and in the group culture. However, cultural change does occur even with great difficulty allowing for awareness of children's emotional and physical well-being. These cultural shifts include attention to human rights, and the gradual wearing away of violent and persistent prejudices.

Thus we might understand the lessening of thoughtless indifference to the pains of human suffering as a step by step inclusion of more emotional truth, and less splitting and projective identification into the "other." The record up until the present portrays these "progressive" changes as fragile and unstable as the recent terrorist situation makes clear. Palestine and Israel, Bosnia and Iraq remind us of the precariousness of our civilization, and the continuing imbalances between the protection of life, and the hatred of life and growth. The capacity for trust and hope in the survival of the human family powerfully influences the health of the signifiers of our culture and language. Lacan has emphasized the symbolic order as mirroring back to the individual the meaning and depth of their emotional experience but filtered through societal and cultural prisms. He explains the signifier determines the signified (Lacan, 1953). Bion helps us with this circular process by placing the reception of emotional significance and experience at the crossroads of preconception to realization. If the parental mind dreams with the infant in a fully impassioned way, the infant subject is enabled to integrate their differing aspects, and may avoid the tragedies of disassociation. Winnicott adds that disassociation in society and culture allows war atrocities to exist alongside proclamations for the protection of human life. Similarly, the destruction of the environment and the planet itself is held to be unimportant through the dangers of disassociation (Winnicott, 1963).

In embracing a false or partial awareness of emotional experience, the individual subject commences the process of splitting off aspects of their experience than allowing them to be acknowledged and lived through. Johan Norman's (2001) work with the infant subject indicates the potential prevention of the continuing process of excommunicating the emotions that are felt to be unbearable, and the parts of the self who carry these emotions. Under poor conditions, the elements of subjectivity are strewn around, fragmented and stifled. The individual is confused about the truth and about the origins of their experience. Contrary to that situation, the subject is born and expresses her subjectivity by immersing herself in her experiences.

Another woman came into analysis seeking help with an ongoing sense of hopelessness and self-hatred. At the time of her commencing treatment, "Elizabeth" was in her early fifties and had raised one child, a daughter. That union was made out of desperate motives to overcome her family's terrible legacy, and predictably came to a sudden end. Later she married again, this time to a slick sociopath. Despite all these "errands" of destruction, Elizabeth was blessed with a gifted intellect, and a determination to go straight, i.e., give up on alliances that were doomed at the onset. However, she suffered from traumatic stress syndrome out of which she had created a legend of a curse, and a belief that she was guilty and responsible for the misery of her siblings.

The "real" that underlies her trauma is her grappling with her Irish alcoholic father, and a sanctimonious religious mother. Her inner pageant is played out as several, small, innocent children being tortured endlessly by an out-of-control and violent father with mother as a good Christian woman who could only advise forgiveness, humility and sacrifice. Lacan's definition of the real as that which cannot be signified, due to the overwhelming force and speed of the projections and real dangers, is very helpful towards deconstructing Elizabeth's inner reality. Along these lines, Elizabeth has been ravaged by persecutory feelings that stem from the mythification of her father's alcoholic rages and sadism and from her own sadistic father-like aspects. Actual violence towards the children's pets, the interior of the house, and the children themselves are the basis for many of her dreams and phantasies.

In another part of her inner drama, she dreads to become the sanctimonious female, the partner to the violent phallus, the Christian female who turns the other cheek, secretly murders males (little brothers as well as father), and at the same time kills off any awareness of danger and inner and outer hostility. At a scene of violent cruelty, unable to offer any emotional soothing, empathy, or reverie, the mother inside tells Elizabeth to pray and trust in God. The cruelty or indifference of both these internal presences make up a large part of Elizabeth's super ego that savagely attacks her and produces her melancholic and suffering side (Freud, 1914; Ogden, 1994). In the end, Elizabeth believes herself to be a disgusting person, and her male and female identifications not only are polarized, but also inspire contempt and terror. As you can imagine, her desire for various types of relationships feels hopeless. In keeping with the splits, her transferences to me have been polarized as well. The good me offers her an opportunity to escape from the old quagmire, but my goodness stimulates enormous envy since she feels she has nothing but grief. If I carry the other side of the polarization, I am felt to be violent, selfish and devoted to causing her suffering. That experience also stimulates enormous envy toward the imagined children who I do "care for."

Elizabeth is a subject ruled by an internal "chora." However, this chora is actively seditious and undermining, and detests emotional truth (Kristeva

1977; Meltzer, 2002; Rosenfeld, 1987; Steiner, 1993a). The analysis frequently is dominated by freeing other parts of her personality from the enveloping "advice" of her chora that cause her to lose most of her connection with her emotions that come back to her only in confused fragments, and vanish much like Hamlet's ghost-father. Therefore, the elements and pathways that make thoughts possible have been mutilated as Schore shows on the neurological screen, and Winnicott, Bion, Grotstein, Tustin, Rosenfeld, Steiner and Ferro lay out on the phantasy and dream screen. Though Elizabeth does not display any signs of a formal thinking disorder, often in her sessions she appears to lose her capacity to comprehend, and take in my comments. I think that at these times she is under the domination of her "chora" whose prime obsession is to attack all the links that hold together her mind and relationships. In Elizabeth's case, any sign that she might link up with another aspect of herself, or with me, brings great distress. She cannot bear relationships (links) between others and me. The idea of my linking up to others – husband, child, students and colleagues – brings on a deluge of physical symptoms: severe headaches, severe stomach-aches, an unstoppable craving for sugar and intense anxiety. As the spiral of envy spins out violently Elizabeth feels attacked, and attacking. Paranoia and suffering alternate, and the broken links seem to come at her as lashing her, and imprisoning her.

Fortunately, Elizabeth has been able to maintain a sense of hope, and while living through and revisiting horrendous versions of nightmarish interaction, has found and used alpha function and containment in the analysis, and with me, as the one who can offer reverie. Slowly she is gathering her thoughts and feelings and is able to think and speak from herself. In a recent session she remarked after meeting another patient of mine, "You make good babies." Elizabeth is able to feel more toleration of rivals for the breast, and the connection to mother. She does, however, spiral down into a bleak picture of her relationship to me when the situation between us gets rocky. The most debilitating beliefs reappear when it seems to her that I either have or will make more links, with another child or lover. The consequent hatred of those links and the fear and dread of the retaliation "due her," brings on an emotional storm, which is felt to attack violently all her desires to create anything. The storm of broken links and beta elements swings around repeatedly rising in a tornado-like structure, which seems to have no beginning, middle or end. How I am able to intercede and slow down the chaotic state of mind, feels very difficult to me, but my willingness to go through the underlying panic and frenzy while treating her situation with the utmost compassion and respect, seems to open up some channels of thinking, or at least to entertain another point of view.

The opening up process offers a release for emotions that have been buried, among them anger, rage, envy and nameless dread. Though this process involves great pain and disorientation, Elizabeth seems increasingly to be able to take responsibility for her autochthonous creations. In turn, as she lives through the vastly turbulent versions of her inner emotional life, psychic space becomes available and the conditions for reflection and thinking develop. For the most part, we have been able to steadily create meaning in a container–contained working relationship, but at the same time, we are faced with resisting the intense pull to believe the chora and its negating envious messages. I believe that the ability to overcome the drag towards destruction of mind and the links that hold together thoughtfulness and meaning, allows Elizabeth to begin to experience at the level of O; stale preconceptions, the need to please and propitiate the demons are lessening.

After a period of vital expression of her most meaningful desires, signs of backlash appeared. At first, it was subtle, but rapidly spiraled into deep paranoid pain, depression and hopelessness. Attacks on her self increased, alternating with disguised allusions to corrupt maternal authority (mine). The appearance of hopelessness carried along with it the curse against anything that she wanted and desired. The context had to do with a recent pro-fessional promotion of considerable prestige. Many people in her work environment expressed their enthusiasm and gratitude for her assuming significant responsibilities so competently, yet she remained mired in her feelings of inferiority. Some of these beliefs and elements of her life curse escaped out of the analytic frame. She handled her new responsibilities well, but under terrible strain and increasing anxiety.

Internally, she became anxious that her competency was deteriorating. This aspect of her work involved maternal-like interactions. In two sessions, after considerable exploration, her inner dilemma broke through. She brought a dream of a parade that she was involved in, somehow. One of the floats was of a queen on a throne. She had blue eyes and blonde hair. Her hair however was made out of ridiculous thick straw, and was piled on her head in strange shapes that were weird and unflattering. It was the most scathing image, since it figured as a pile of shit. We both recognized this. Elizabeth soon realized that the queen figure represented myself. She wondered why it was such a scathing presentation. I thought to myself, good, the idealization is breaking up. I said as much to Elizabeth, she nodded yes, but soon after became anxious and confused.

In the next session, Elizabeth became confused, and her hostility appeared as irritation, as if I was up to doing something tricky and hostile to her, and at the same time I was confused. When I called attention to her contradicting herself, she became angry and said that I was mixed up. I ventured to say that she had two opinions at the same time. Elizabeth became more confused and angry. In the next session, she remarked that she was angry with me because I was insisting that she did not know what she was talking about. However, she also remarked how well she had handled a meeting the night before. Suddenly, her state of mind veered radically; she complained of stomach pains and terrible increasing anxiety, as she burst into sobs of great despair. The sobbing continued for several minutes. I remarked to myself, that her crying felt painful, if not impossible, to bear. I thought that Elizabeth was overcome with several realizations: her hatred of men, and her envy and hatred of me as mother, who let her down by having other relationships, while failing to contain her well enough. Elizabeth also began to realize she contributed to that situation. I began to explore her terrible bind with her. As she felt fearful of abandonment, by a mother/me who was felt to have so many other preoccupations, mainly with father, and other babies – in conditions of no responsiveness to her nameless dread, Elizabeth emptied herself of her own potential. Her phantasy was that anything wholesome, useful or beautiful was believed to be in great danger from the destroyed and envied vengeful mother inside, entering into a second cycle of nameless dread and envy. I began to try to communicate her experience to her. Suddenly Elizabeth shot up from the couch gagging and throwing up. She squelched her vomiting and left the room for water, saying upon her return that she did not like the acid taste in her mouth. She spoke hesitantly as if she were a little child who was not sure she should desire attention and comfort. I realized that she started to take in some useful thoughts from me while we were also exploring the deep-seated belief that she had better not keep anything good inside of her. I shared these thoughts with her. Elizabeth agreed. I added, that her greed for sweet things became out of control now that she felt some growth inside of her and was based on her efforts not to devour the breast mother, or the thoughtful mother. Elizabeth became very silent and thoughtful and her anxiety had diminished significantly.

Certainly, we can understand this session as an approach to the depressive position with a passionate version of her fears and blocks. I think we can also see the strangulation of her inner most desires and the mutilation of her subjectivity. Elizabeth's internal reality was organized around an extreme split between male and female. In turn, the relationships between strong and weak, and hard and soft, not only were split apart radically, but also one side was obliterated. In the analytic sessions, they emerged as a "masculine," dominating, cruel, vicious, father persona, or a sanctimonious cowardly mother (Tustin, 1981b; Van Buren, 1993). As the analysis intensified, the banished selves became present. Elizabeth continued to experience only one side or the other or became very confused, though my responses to her attempted to take into account the presence of both sides. The sessions discussed are typical of a situation, where the partial integration and awareness of her emotional realities began to emerge from severe disavowal. The integration and violent rejection of her emotional significance came together and after some physical illness became her "O" experience full force.

These sessions allow us to see into the processes that freed and recovered her feelings and thoughts. Elizabeth and I were deconstructing the mother and father presences and the family curse that had set her life course, and began to find her subjectivity at the level of "O."

"Rachael" came to analysis in the most desperate circumstances. She was actively suicidal and as she explained, she wanted to end her life because she was losing her mind. Finally, Rachael had consulted with an admired training analyst who recommended that she break off treatment with her current therapist, who not only seemed over his head, but also was caught in the vice of the negative transference.

Most of her life she functioned as a survivor economizing on her meager resources to carry her through her attempts at a mock-up, false, self-personality in search of a life. In the early days of treatment, she was mainly angry, distrustful, and frankly paranoid. She developed a very negative transference to my office. My office had been freshly painted. Rachael thought that there were poisonous fumes in the suite. Thus, it was very difficult for her to sit in the waiting room without feeling somewhat like a person in a gas chamber. She chose to wait until the last minute to come into my suite. Of course, she developed negative feelings toward me; wouldn't I be the one who was poisoning or gassing her? Accordingly, she assumed that like the other therapists, I would not be able to help her, although she felt I had some better understanding of her difficulties in a different way. It was however, very problematical for me to have any sense of finding a way of breaking through this cynicism and extreme paranoia. Thus, I had to proceed with measured caution. Her cynicism subsided to the extent that we were able to make other kinds of contact despite her underlying fears and anxieties. At this point Rachael revealed that she felt very haunted. I must say that I was not surprised, since I felt a sense of weirdness and strangeness even when the extreme paranoia subsided. In this context, Rachael sometimes fell into states of numbness, disassociation and had a strong conviction that she had lost herself, or at the extreme, she had died. I later learned, that she felt herself to be floating in space with no ties to other people, or the earth, or that she was buried alive in a crypt. Rachael complained that her life was meaningless, and she could not accomplish anything. She often complained bitterly that whatever projects she undertook, at some point, she would become listless and inhibited, especially when the project might be carried out into productive action. She felt that the feelings of impotence worsened seriously after she contracted a life-threatening illness, since it was the same one that had killed her mother at early middle age. The illness strengthened her conviction that she was doomed by some unseen forces to die, to never achieve anything, to never find any feelings, or contact, or productivity. A dream, divided into three parts, including the associations she brought into the sessions, opened a window for us to see in more detail her difficulties in developing a sense of going on being, and the hope that she might be an alive effective person.

The patient has an extraordinary intelligence, and this gift has been undernourished, if not sabotaged, throughout her life. At the same time, Rachael does possess a strong desire to learn and expand her knowledge and experience. Shortly after my summer vacation of some two and a half weeks, Rachael had this dream. A strange, blond-haired, blue-eyed boy evoked very weird vibrations. When Rachael looked into his eyes, there was a feeling of being mesmerized by a weird and demonic presence. I recognized the figure as a composite of myself, partly evolved into a demonic presence that was felt to be controlling her mind. In my absence, she had held on to me by projecting her will, needs, and desires into me. Her use of projective identification produced feelings of becoming a zombie, since she gave over her capacity to think to the image of me. Rachael felt terrified with no normal, helpful me in her mind. The male identity also came from her intense envy towards her father and her brothers, and my partner on vacation, and the harm she wanted to do to them.

Her further associations led her to another portion of the dream. She felt that something was terribly wrong with someone, and they were not being given the help that they needed. These feelings were the cause of her deepest anxieties. She remembered, at this point, that there was part of the dream where she was in a kitchen looking for something, she opened all the cupboards, and in her search, she came upon a number of pigeons stored in a cabinet. Some were shut up, some were lying listless, and another pigeon had its head severed from its body. She felt horror and terror, and was undecided as to whether to close the cabinets back up and leave, or to alert someone to this terrible situation. Here, in the scene of the mutilated pigeons, we see the infant that had been encapsulated and sent off into Siberian psychic space, away from awareness, due to traumatic circumstances. It seemed that her infant self, and the memories and emotions that were contained in this part of her were now returning for review and help. In this regard, I felt the dream was a splendid breakthrough for her, given these ideas, and her continuing problem with passivity and numbness. Here, she imaged aspects of the disastrous outcome that takes place when no one is aware of a psychic catastrophe, and the burial and murder of the infant part of her personality. Rachael agreed with the meanings that I suggested, but suddenly said she was falling asleep, as if she were drugged. She said, she did feel mesmerized, but at the same time wished that I would hypnotize her, and then she would be able to break out of her impotence and doubt. She again complained that she was feeling drugged. I suggested to her that her drugged state of mind was related to the boy in the dream. Then she explained that she no longer had any language. She offered that everything she was thinking was in images without words. Rachael continued, "Even your words are being turned into images. It's as if I can't hear what your saying, I can only see images." At this point, I asked, might she be able to describe them. Rachael offered that to move from images to words was impossible, and that she often felt that there were things she was going through where she simply could not find the words. It came to mind that she was talking about a chasm without a bridge. Perhaps as she was engaged in the process of accessing and integrating long ago lost aspects of herself with the memories, feelings and emotions that have been lost as well she felt herself to be dangling over a chasm without a bridge. We might think of the chasm as the place where no connections could grow. The connections to reverie and interpretation were absent at the level of brain development, the implementation of alpha function, birthing dream, phantasy and transi-tional phenomena (Bion, 1965; Schore, 2002; Winnicott, 1951). Also wouldn't it be possible that this aspect of her never achieved what we might designate the capacity for language? The dream itself, and the dreamer's associations, seemed to be a vital part of a process of integration and exploration. In our further exchanges, Rachael revealed that it was scary and weird. She returned to the description of feeling drugged or mesmerized. I then had the picture of an infant trying to organize her experience without the use on phantasies or dreams, let alone words or concepts, who was critically alone with these experiences. Was it then that the drugged sleep state came over her? I returned to the dream, and the appearance of the boy with his demonic eyes compelling and powerful. We investigated his coloring and Rachael laughed, and said, "It is not unlike yours, is it?" I thought of the missing maternal me, having only just returned from a summer break. There was also a change that was necessary to make in her regular schedule, from one day to another, due to some obligations that I had, and she then brought in the coming Monday holiday, Labor Day. Now certain elements came together in my mind. The present context would be the holidays, gaps and the experience of unreliability which stimulated Rachael to feel abandoned as an infant, overcome with emotional forces to the extent that she would either break down and fragment, or turn to weird companions. As we are engaged in the analytical process, these experiences are felt to be newly traumatic, at the same time organized as emerging through the prism of the lost aspect of Rachael's self. First, she is faced with the absence of language, and second, Rachael was having an experience of losing her mind to an evil force. If no one was present to share infantile feelings, another figure took the place of the maternal container. In place of holding and reverie, a sinister power filled the gap but at the cost of losing any hope.

The sinister young man sent another message; he stood for rival males, whom she felt she had damaged and destroyed. Among these were mother's partner, who robbed her of her maternal relationship, as my vacation did, and any breaks in the schedule, and her mother's depression and illness and death. Rachael associated repeatedly to her mother's changing moods from gentle and concerned to removed and depressed. She often expressed compassion for her mother, who had lost her separate identity as a working woman, and was cooped up in a cottage with young children, with no means of escaping, and not able to develop external ties. At the same time, she experienced her father as cold and ascetic in regards to feelings, pleasure and money. It has been hard to assess or distinguish how much the father contained the infant's miserable rage from his own emotional coldness. The birth of her two younger brothers was felt to be catastrophic for Rachael. For her, each brother brought painful realizations of having to share a mother with whom she never felt a solid attachment.

In the following session, Rachael brought another dream, which had similar form and content, but was somewhat less violent and disturbing. The dream was that there were two boys hanging around on a street. These boys appeared to be hoodlums or homeless. She said that she was not sure what the connection was between her and the two young men, as she had been more certain in the first dream of the night before. They seemed not to be so dangerous, mesmerizing, or weird. She was not sure what they wanted, but felt she had better leave the scene for fear that they might become violent. In the next session, she brought another part of the dream. I consider it to have elements of transformation. First, there was no mention of having lost language, which suggests a beginning integration of splits, without the loss of sanity. However, I was worried that she had already begun to cover up the worst implications of the dream. My feelings were somewhat allayed when she said that these people were not as crazy as the boy in the previous dream, though they were not well off and could not get a grip on their lives. In this regard, Rachael offered that these people were not as psychopathic as the boys in the earlier dream. These men seemed to be misfits without psychotic features.

In the next session, Rachael offered the third part of the dream. She came to a morning session and said she already had a terrible day. The elements of her terrible day were the difficulty with her little granddaughter, who was cranky and rebellious, her upset with that, and the day before, with a younger granddaughter. She then had an episode in a gas station in which she was short changed. She described the woman at the cashier window as very stupid and stubborn. I then asked if perhaps she was feeling very shortchanged here, and like her little granddaughter, she was feeling very outraged and rebellious.

She then remembered this dream, which I consider a further transformation of the first two. Again, two men appeared rather derelict in their dress and activities. One had a motorcycle, the other was standing around on the street, similarly, to the first pair, and they seemed homeless and rootless. She associated to herself, when she was on the edge of poverty and insanity. Rachael added, that she was not sure of their intentions and felt nervous about being in their presence. However, she acknowledged that the situation was not as perilous as in the other two dreams. She then associated to a project that she wanted to undertake, and finally said, she had made a connection with the people who might facilitate this new opportunity that would improve her career. This would be quite a step up, and I thought to myself, a much better use of her intelligence as well as an opportunity to gain emotional satisfaction. But then she said, she lost interest and felt deflated, and did not feel like doing it anymore. Even if she were to make the connections, what meaning would it have for her, and what was the use. Finally, she added, after all, it cost a lot of money to get further training. A list of negative prohibitions came to my mind, and I thought to myself these were perhaps the legacy from the dire situation in which she didn't have thought at her disposal. Instead she felt mesmerized, sleepy, and taken into a zombie zone, in which she felt more dead then alive. Now, however, her complaints were couched in more than the usual sort of defensiveness. "Oh what's the use anyway, they wouldn't be interested in me, and I don't know why I want to make the effort, and no one would like me, I'm not very good at maintaining group relations," and on and on. I suggested around this time that she was cranky because she did not feel that I could help her in carrying out her efforts, and that she lost interest, feeling dropped. This was an old theme for her in any case. She felt very angry with me, and she wanted me to do something, especially since she felt that I did not understand some critical aspects of her experience. On one hand, we could say that Rachael expected me to do everything, and make everything right through some magic means. On the other hand, I really believe that this first dream revealed that she was pulled back into a state of mind in which she lost her wits, and was complicit in her mind with this evil character who would promise help, but in fact would endanger her mind. I interpreted something along those lines, which seemed to satisfy her, and she said she felt an opening was taking place in her mind. Before, she always felt stymied at a certain point.

The next sessions were devoted to the terrorist's attacks. Rachael displayed an entirely different state of mind. She discussed the situation from many points of view. She displayed a clear detailed account of the situation in Afghanistan, explaining the various groups there, and added an intelligent discussion of the Muslims. The question that came to mind was, was she reacting to the trauma and destructiveness by splitting off her terror and infantile feelings of destructive rage into the Taliban or had she gained ground in reclaiming her mind and her intelligence from the deterioration of the breaks?

I would like to add, that the dreams were an effort to address our attention to the underlying situations. I felt she was showing us and reliving the various catastrophes that led to the abandonment of her mental infantile self, and the deterioration of her will and capacity to think and to give into fragmentation, or a sadistic evil force, in the absence of the maternal or paternal containing function.

I began to be more convinced that the drugged state of mind, foreshadowed by extreme paranoia, was the expressions of a psychotic part of her personality that showed itself as both hostile and cruel to our relationship, and really vicious to her efforts to emerge from her drugged state, or to have respect and compassion for her infant-self.

The birth of Rachael's granddaughters signed profound changes in her attitudes towards growth, meaning and the plight of babies and children, who lacked the scaffolding of mother's reverie. Before these changes became visible, Rachael's perversity was often so extreme that I felt hopeless that she would ever develop the "milk of human kindness." Recall the dream of the mutilated pigeons shut away in cupboards, left to die. Several questions came to mind. How had she come to be so indifferent and cruel? And why was she able to change into a compassionate grandmother, patient and wife?

At the beginning of treatment Rachael was a psychic wraith barely clinging to any sense of herself. Her subjectivity was profoundly damaged and seriously underdeveloped. I think we can see that she had become quite ill as an infant and child. As her analysis progressed, she was able to drop many of her feelings of weirdness and of inferiority. Rachael gradually developed her own voice. She revealed that she was moving out of the mire of despair, self-accusation and perversity. In Rachael's family milieu, backwoods asceticism ran from her father's line. Early settlers that could be traced back to the eighteenth century, who had kept close to the land from which they found their living. Rachael's father at 89 years of age remains the epitome of the self-sufficient man. Emotions and concepts are banished as unhealthy intruders. Mother's line could be traced back to the eastern seaboard at least from the eighteenth century. They placed themselves in urban environments in which Rachael's mother learned a freewheeling attitude suitable for business and enterprise. During World War II, she enlisted in the Women's Army Corps. Before that, she had owned her own beauty salon. Rachael's parents met in the service and these two disparate types married and settled in a town outside the Los Angeles city limits. They were so poor that they lived in a tiny pre-fab house for many years through the birth of three children. Rachael feels that her poison gas fears originate in those days of cramped barren quarters living with the smell of oil pumping nearby and her mother's heavy smoking. She also mentions her mother's fall from opportunity, and open possibilities, as a significant cause of her early death.

However, Rachael is able to connect her own claustrophobia with an internal situation, more as an outcome of her unstable states of mind and body. These feelings are couched in terms of her overbearing father who keeps women prisoners; the pre-fab house, cramped and lacking boundaries (mother's body), and her mother's overbearing attention to her. Rachael no doubt suffered from the cramped quarters of excessive projective identi-fication. As discussed above, her attempt at expressing her desires and com-municating had become weird, reducing her to a zombie state without the benefit of a dream partner. In turn, I was taken over by the mesmerizing one, rendering me powerless. This aspect of the transference led to rich here and now experience. Mainly that she did not care if I lived or died. The coldness and indifference that she felt towards me captured her relationships with her infant self.

I think that Rachael had some special capacity to move out these dismal states. During the time of the dominance of the controlling, mesmerizing, and sadistic transference, she was moving into new states of mind. Evidence of this was felt in her sessions by a dramatic change from argumentative and concrete responses to me. Rachael responded increasingly with thoughtful-ness and creativity. She displayed her fine intelligence, but with compassion and some humor. Also significantly, Rachael began to hold down a job. The inner backlash was fierce. "Working would make her very ill; she would be the worst worker ever; fellow workers would hate her; the place of work would be toxic."

The remarkable change came at the birth of her granddaughters. Before the birth of the first child, Rachael had a plan to help her daughter care for her baby full time. She wanted to avoid long days in childcare for her yet unborn granddaughter. In both their infancies, Rachael made herself available, protected the nursing couple, and was deeply involved in their care. Occasionally bits of impatience and cruelty flared up. These were followed by regret and questions about the benefits of strict and angry responses to childish loss of control. Yet she felt unsure that she should depart from physical punishment as that might lead to trouble. That point of view led to thoughts like "they will turn into wild Indians, criminals, and what they needed is a physical punishment to control their evil tendencies." I felt as if I was not only in the realm of cruelty and retaliation, violent projective identification, but also in a time warp, entering the cultures of previous centuries which had not yet discovered that children and infants would thrive on tenderness, kindness and empathy; on the contrary, they were believed to thrive on hardening.

Tenderness did not appear until late in the nineteenth century, and often lost ground, as we know today. Finally the temptation to use physical punishment dropped from Rachael's emotional repertoire. The cases that I have shared here illustrate the subject's loss of herself, caught in the dilemma of surrendering to the concept of "male superiority" and the dread of the maternal imago inside. In the analytic work we have begun to free the subject from the culture's fear of mother as well as her own bias against men, who are felt to steal all the attributes of their being.

Though she continued to worry that she had no reliable mental stamina to keep up with her life and she painfully believed that her mind was still captured by the old demons, Rachael continued to develop a more trusting and positive transference relationship with me. Notably, she proved to be a wonderful grandmother supporting her daughter's mothering, and enjoying her grand-daughter's company. Frankly, I was surprised and remained on the lookout for splitting. Rachael brought her granddaughters one at a time to her analytic sessions. They were both lively and endearing and were able to make clear demands for attention and participation. For the purposes of this discussion, Rachael's deep love and concern for them as well as her capacity to be playful and relaxed portrayed significant changes in her inner world. Might we think that she had broken out of several mutilations of her mental capacities to develop concern for others? She had developed the capacity to interact with the maternal me in a way that mitigated her envy and rivalry. She has entered the program for advanced training and found herself to both enjoying it and at the same time, to be taken over with thoughts of inferiority, self-pity and envy. Also, she became ill the week before the program started. I suggested that becoming ill was a retreat from these conflicts and blocked her attempts at the growth of her new sense of herself and capacity to enter into experience with pleasure and vitality.

At the level of phantasy, she expresses her own claustrophobia as an internal situation, more as an outcome of her unstable states of mind and body. These feelings are couched in terms of her overbearing father who keeps women prisoners, the tiny pre-fab, cramped and lacking boundaries (mother's body) and her mother's overbearing attention to her. Rachael no doubt suffered from the cramped quarters of excessive projective identi-fication. As discussed above, her attempt at expressing her desires and communicating had become weird, reducing her to a zombie state without the benefit of a dream partner. In turn, I was taken over by the mesmerizing one, rendering me powerless. This aspect of the transference led to rich here and now experience. The coldness and indifference that she felt towards me, not caring if I lived or died, captured her relationships with her infant self.

Chapter 3

Saint Anne and two others

Configuration of the grandmother within the dreaming couple

I believe we can find in Freud's analysis of Leonardo da Vinci's *The Virgin and Child with Saint Anne* a psychoanalytic semiotic that yields many possible realizations about maternal reverie (Freud, 1910). It seems convincing that the Madonna, Child and Saint Anne, as they appear in Leonardo's portrayals, are visual signifiers of cultural themes evolving in the West from the early Renaissance to our own time. Freud's specific analysis and interpretations of Leonardo's images of the Holy Family are based on the idea that they signified the vicissitudes of Leonardo's infantile sexuality. Moreover, we are privy to Freud's excursions into an area of pre-Oedipal discourse that was not yet present in his theoretical explanations of what has later come to be understood as the classical Oedipus complex based on the phallic phase and its mode of discharge.

If we analyze Freud's theory of the mind in the first decades of the twentieth century, we find an autochthonous mind fueled by biological necessity. The dream work is described by Freud as arbitrating the inner contradictions between the pleasure principle and the reality principle, and later the drives or the id, and the ego. Mother and father appear in Freud's schema as the targets for satisfaction and discharge and important players in the journey from hallucination to real satisfaction.

Maternal (paternal) inherent capacities set in place for the transformation of archaic modes of expression into understandable communications for subject and receiver are notably absent from Freud's account. Terror, bewilderment, excitement and joyous affects are displaced and condensed into manageable forms or into disruptive structures, such as symptom and neurosis, without the participation of the mother offering states of mind, which we call today: her reverie, empathy, attunement and powers of signification. Freud's analysis of the dream work, however, discovers and illuminates the mind's capacity to realize inherent mythic structures of familial relations.

I would like to propose that Leonardo's painting and the cartoon of *Saint Anne and Two Others* present a particular realization of the Oedipus myth that looks forward to later psychoanalytic concepts that include articulation of more primitive states of mind. Thus, we might interpret Freud's analysis of Leonardo's visual renderings as a manifest to a latent content that might be deepened, as psychoanalytic probes would later realize, during the course of the twentieth century.

It is Freud's reading of the Oedipus complex as a phylogenetic inheritance, that in some ways looks forward to notions of the Oedipus structure as containing mythic themes, that extend the narrative of Oedipus into a web of relations between mother and baby, and between the generations.

Lévi-Strauss (1963) understood the Oedipus myth as structured on the laws of symbol making. He proposed that the Oedipus myth was found in every society in the world, and that its various mutations eternally signify relations between parents and children, men and women, and groups. Themes of power of men over women and within the generations dominate Lévi-Strauss's structural analysis. Bion also interpreted the Oedipus narrative as inherent scaffolding for learning from experience along the lines of sexual and generational difference, and at a deeper level as a preconception for patterns of inner growth, that spun out in patterns of intrasubjectivity and intersubjectivity. Bion proposed that the Oedipus myth at its deepest level is a preconception and/or the inherent capacity for realizing one's place in the psychosomatic relationship with mother's body, and later, with mother as an object, and still later, as a person or a subject with the family, forming the links of meaning to the family's inner and outer forms (Bion, 1962a, 1962b). Innate qualities, as well as environmental factors, sculpt the realizations even to the extreme of an infantile catastrophe, in which the preconceptual structure is shattered before its birth into realizations of awareness and experience. Bion warns us that in these circumstances we will find no preconceptual Oedipal structure, but only its debris.

Lacan's notion of a discourse of the Other, and the Desire of the Other, complements Bion's description of psychoanalytic mythmaking, and provides another access to Freud's notion of the phylogenetic inheritance embedded in the Oedipus complex and myth. Freud referred to the Oedipus narrative as a libidinal developmental journey, but he also suggested mythmaking processes in several texts, such as *Totem and Taboo* (1913) and *Moses and Monotheism* (1939). He defined the Oedipus structure as a phylogenetic inheritance, part of which was a group dream occurring repeatedly through the generations. Lacan innovated on Freud's theory of the unconscious and emphasized his theory of the dream work. In place of the unconscious as the seat of the instincts, Lacan substituted the mind's capacity to make meaning through a chain of signifiers propelled by the forces of Desire. Lacan's notion of repression differs from Freud's and his notions of the phenomenology vary in purpose and outcome, in the sense that primal separation from the mother of originary jouissance, forces the infant to begin the symbolic process, however primitive it may be. The failure to achieve this transition results in psychic death in that the person is closed in a spaceless dyad without benefit of the space of thirdness. Lacan also differs from Freud somewhat in his understanding of the Oedipus complex. As Lacan emphasizes the unconscious as a symbol-making organ charged by Desire or the search for lost jouissance, he proposes that a fall into the symbolic order is necessitated by the dangers of the continuation of merger states. He then provides us with the example of Freud's grandson and the use of the symbols "for/da" as the entry into the law of the father, the laws of time and space. We might say that for both Freud and Lacan, the Oedipal constellation is largely focused on male experience and the separation from mother, either the sexual mother linked to the dread of castration, or the mother (M)Other of primary jouissance, shattered by ultimate semiotic death. Crucially, as in Freud's sense of the mind's development, mother is not present as a participant in the transformation to a symbolic mind. She is a lost object.

Recall that Freud referred to the mother as an object of libido rather than a person with a mind who would participate in the development of the infant's mind. This lack has been attended to in some ways by infant studies, object relations theories, and feminist readings of psychoanalytic theory; they have brought forward the idea that much of the dynamic unconscious that enters into transference and character is made up of infantile states of mind, and the primitive imagoes created in the depths of experience (Cixous and Clément, 1975; Irigaray, 1974; Klein, 1946, 1952, 1955, 1975; Kristeva, 1980b, 1982; Stern, 1985). Following Freud, each in their own way, Winnicott, Fairbairn, Klein and Anna Freud, among others, came to emphasize the notion that mother's mature mental functioning imparts a scaffolding of meaning to the infant's experiences. They began to appreciate, that in the absence of interpretation or a "reading" of the primary repressed feelings, preverbal or even pre-linguistic experiences would fail to coalesce, leaving the infant to states of mind which "tell" only of the nothingness that remains in the turbulent void of pre-significance (Grotstein, 1990a, 1990b, 1993). In circumstances of long deprivation from mother's (father's) holding and signifying capacities, benign emptiness becomes virulent nothingness, or degenerates into chaotic states of mind that eventually affect the functioning of the central nervous system, as Spitz's (1946) studies of Mirasmus made clear.

The horror of the abyss of not mattering, known to our infant selves, is repeated in culture, and may lend an appreciation of the need for cultural myths, ideologies, and belief systems of all sorts. Without their efficacy as safety nets and as signifying structures, the culture or social group falls into a panic and fragments (Eco, 1979; Grotstein, 1990a, 1990b, 1993). The rise of Fascism, in the void created by the loss of centuries-old traditional structures and beliefs, gives shape and explanation to the desperate need of signifying structures in the group, as well as in the individual.

I want to explore Freud's reading of Leonardo's attachment to the kite-vulture as a mythological structure or discourse of the other presented as memory, and as seen in Leonardo's paintings of Mary, her mother, Anne and the Christ child. Though his reading of passionate attachment is couched in the vocabulary of infantile sexuality, Freud provides the culture with a narrative of the infantile internal world as represented in Leonardo's painting and cartoon of the Christ child, his mother Mary, and her mother Anne (Plates 1 and 2).

Freud contextualizes Leonardo's mental development through his parental losses, first his father, and then his mother. The first loss provides the background for Freud's explanation that a surfeit of oral libido was not only sublimated, but also fixated and unsuccessfully repressed, and later dominated Leonardo's capacities to represent and signify his internal scenes. Freud invites us to infer that Leonardo's creative solutions were gradually dominated by obsession symptoms and character traits. Both baby and mother bereft of husbandly and fatherly functions were pulled into a libidinal vortex of desire in a closed dyadic structure, which partly compromised Leonardo's capacity to use symbolic forms, and thus to move into a vital subjectivity and differentiated sense of self. Freud proposed that during the evolution of the subject Leonardo, an intense, confusional identification with mother, split his ego and changed his identity, subjectivity, and core gender identity permanently (Bion, 1962a, 1962b; Freud, 1910; Lacan, 1949, 1953, 1977a; Ragland-Sullivan, 1991). Thus, on the one hand he felt permanently attached to mother. On the other, he felt as if he might suffer annihilation by disappearing into her. Mother, on her side of the intersubjective field, turned her passionate attachment towards her infant son, grasping him with her desire, to the extent that he felt forever inside her subjectivity. The second absence, that of his mother, dictated a repression of severe loss, a sense of distrust and betrayal concerning women. Both losses contributed to a homosexual turn in Leonardo's libidinal development.

In this paper, Freud (1910) placed his imaginative conjectures inside the infantile or pre-Oedipal desires and phantasies of Leonardo. The discussions of the vulture, though mistakenly named, open to the reader the possibility of signification structures that "speak" to us in the language of desire and need. The bird is a signifier in the midst of a long chain of signification of attachment, desire, passion, and loss, and of love and hate (Lacan, 1953; Ragland-Sullivan, 1991; Silverman, 1983). In the painting *The Virgin and Child with Saint Anne*, we find three figures portraying the holy mother, her mother, and the infant Jesus. Mother Mary holds the baby Jesus, who moves forward to touch the lamb without regard to his safety. Mother holds her baby as if to steady his emergence into differentiation and the exercise of his mind. Behind her placement as the infant's context is the background figure of her mother, Saint Anne, lending strength and support (Grotstein, 1980,

Plate 1 *The Virgin and Child with Saint Anne*
Leonardo da Vinci
1510. Oil on wood, 168 × 130 cm (5½ × 4½ ft)
© Musée du Louvre, Paris

Plate 2 *The Virgin and Child with Saint Anne and Saint John the Baptist*
Leonardo da Vinci
1499–1500. Purchased with a special grant and contributions from the
National Art Collections Fund, the Pilgrim Trust, and through a public appeal
organized by the National Art Collections Fund, 1962
© The National Gallery, London

1983; Sandler, 1987). The skirts of Saint Anne and Mary intermingle and form one shape. Freud interprets the shape as the vulture signifying all the vicissitudes of the baby Leonardo's libidinal desires for his mother. He points out, especially in the London cartoon, which is similar in form and content to the painting, the shape of the vulture outlined in the folds of their skirts. The shape proves abundantly significant, suggesting as it does infantile phantasies of the breast, the maternal soft body, where one can find comfort, and even the placenta itself.

Opposite imagistic readings suggest themselves as well, such as the void of non-attachment, or the malignant possibility of lack, made visible in failure to thrive infants (Stern, 1985; Winnicott, 1958). The shape interpreted as a dark foreboding possibility, implies the intersubjective field in another manifestation, not only as the failure of empathetic attunement or container/contained of the baby's mind by the mother, but also as the place of projective identification of mother's unformed, turbulent and uninterpreted states of mind into the infant (Alhanati, 2002; Apprey and Stein, 1993a, 1993b; Cramer, 1986; Cramer and Stern, 1988; Fonagy, 1999a, 1999b; Fonagy et al., 2004; Grotstein, 1990a, 1990b).

The enigmatic smile of the various Madonnas reiterates this theme of the importance and mysteriousness of mother's face. Donald Meltzer (1988) explains a contradiction implicit in the noble experience of appreciating mother's beauty, a beauty brutally agonizing in its presentation of both life and death. Its powerful strangeness for the neonate, a recently arrived traveler to an unfamiliar land shadows the adored mother's presence. The aesthetic ecstasy of the sight of mother's face is disturbed, too, by its inscrutability. Meltzer explains:

> The mother is enigmatic to him/her; she wears a Giaconda smile most of the time, and the music of her voice keep shifting from major to minor key. Like "Kafka", s/he must wait for decisions from the "castle" of his/her mother's internal world. S/he is naturally on guard against unbridled optimism and arid trust, for has s/he not already had one dubious experience at her hands from which s/he was either expelled or escaped, or perhaps s/he, rather than mother, was "delivered" from the danger? Even at the moments of most satisfactory communication, nipple in mouth, she gives the ambiguous message, for although she takes the gnawing away from inside, she gives a monstrous thing which s/he must expel her/himself. Truly, she giveth and she taketh away, both of good and bad things. S/he cannot tell if she is his or her Beatrice or his or her Belle Dame sans Merci. This is the aesthetic conflict, which can be most precisely stated in terms of the aesthetic impact of the outside of the "beautiful" mother available to the senses, and the enigmatic inside, which must be construed by creative imagination.
>
> (Meltzer, 1988: 22)

Camille Paglia in her book, *Sexual Persona* (1990), provides us with a similar analysis of the Giaconda smile of Leonardo's Madonna. She reads the smile as a representation of the chthonic undertow (Paglia, 1990). She believes that many cultural signs of women are massively linked with the underworld, the Dionysian, or the mysterious unseen. Though she does not link the dark netherworld, the bowels of the earth, with infantile phantasies of fusion with mother's body, or disappearing into zero dimension of the place of nothingness (Grotstein, 1990a; Klein, 1945, 1946) she brings to life the anxiety of the unbounded infant and the male lifelong quest to abate it, and to avoid re-experiencing it by building a culture of the Apollonian.

Our focus on the pretty is an Apollonian strategy. The leaves and flowers, the birds, the hills are a patchwork pattern by which we map the known. What the West represses in its view of nature is chthonian, which means "of the earth," but the earth's bowels, not its surface. Jane Harrison (1962) uses the term for the pre-Olympian Greek religion, and I adopt it as a substitute for the Dionysian, which has become contaminated with vulgar pleasantries. The Dionysian is no picnic. It is the chthonian realities, which Apollo evades, the blind grinding of subterranean force, the long slow muck: the muck and ooze. It is the dehumanizing brutality of biology and geology (Paglia, 1990).

It seems to me that this description grows from the infantile archaic perception of matters of life and death with mother. Paglia interprets Leonardo da Vinci's *The Virgin and Child with Saint Anne* (1508–1510), as a representation of a chthonian link, which comes from Leonardo's reading of his repressed infantile mother. Paglia reads the two figures as invidious "twin sisters" who represent "one archaic personality that has partheno-genetically cloned itself" (Paglia, 1990). To my mind, this is the infant's phantasy reading of the complexity of the maternal imago. The good mother may be taken over by the mother of failed bonding, who needs no one but herself, and becomes the belle dame sans merci.

Another perspective on the Saint Anne portrayals is that of the history of the maternal reverie. Contemporary theory familiarizes us with the notion that the growth of the infant's mental health is inextricably linked with mother's mental and physical presence as context and support for the tangential forming self. In Leonardo's Saint Anne portrayals, these functions are represented, her body as background and as foreground (an intersubjective guardian), and as the embodiment of important linking organs: the breast, nipple, face and the placenta, are represented in the shape of the bird (Bion, 1962a; Grotstein, 1983; Klein, 1945, 1946, 1952). Thus, Leonardo's paintings and Freud's translation of them open the way toward personal and cultural realizations and interpretations of the mother–infant relationship.

The appearance of the figure of the Madonna and child in medieval religious iconography anticipates the birth of the idea of the consoling

mother who accompanies her child through all the joys and agonies of her/
his life journey. The Renaissance in Italy was a time when the Madonna
began to take on an increasingly human and less iconical style (Kristeva,
1980b). The metamorphosis from Byzantine formality to human likeness
reflected important transformations in Western culture's grasp of the
meaning of human life from one thought to be a prelude to a higher form,
to one defined as human existence.

God's departure into a more distant heaven in the context of the age of
exploration and the changing concepts of the earth in space, brought
forward by Copernicus, opened out the vista of this world. The human gaze
no longer looked exclusively heavenward, but looked across the plane of
everyday life. Concepts of time and space grew out of immediate experience
in distinction to the future perfect time of the afterlife. The discovery of
perspective, i.e., the view of the object through the subject's perception and
consciousness, added a new dimension to the notion of space in which
distance unfolded as a place where adventure, immediate experience, and
radical change might be discovered.

Copernicus' discovery that the earth was not protected by a heavenly
canopy but was a planet moving in space challenged the privileging of the
afterlife. The voice of God, partly released from the church hierarchy, was
now heard from within a subjective space. Certain notions or realizations of
an inner dialogue filled with intense dramas and passions formed, and made
it possible to understand the origins of disruptive feelings and personas
as residing inside the self, rather than originating only in external forces,
and especially supernatural ones. Importantly, idealization of supernatural
figures, with the accompanying phantasies of living under or inside their
authority and intentions, were challenged as the exclusive guide for the
purposes of human life. Put into the language of human individuation, we
may note that a clearer sense of inside and outside was felt consciously
(Anzieu, 1989). During the Italian Renaissance (the time of Leonardo's life
span), secular justification for the meaning of human life encouraged the
appearance of notions of human nature as the underpinnings of societal
and familial interactions.

Concepts of children were changing, too. The idea that internal growth
and development were part of the transition from infancy to adulthood was
understood in new ways, and led to ideas of nurturing and training that
were far more psychological than Western culture had previously thought
out or woven into its ideologies, or other value structures. We can place the
great interest in the Madonna, and particularly her increasingly human
look, in this context.

The themes taken up in Leonardo's paintings and cartoons are also
known universally in cultural history. The Christ myth expands the trope of
mother and child to encode the Christ child as a sacrifice to humankind
who, by assuming the function of containing the abject, unspeakable states

of mind, became a savior for God's children. The legend of Christ, like that of Oedipus, is structured around several basic themes of family life. The author of the narrative, God, places the child in the midst of a central human malaise, the precariousness of achieving and maintaining sane, thoughtful and regulated states of mind (Bion, 1962a; Grotstein, 1980, 1990a; Kristeva, 1980a; Lichtenberg, 1989).

Christ's sacrificial death may be seen as the necessity of the child to replace his/her parents, or the adult generation, by assuming the function of containing the suffering of the infantile parts of the mind, while giving significance to mental experience as well as protecting the infant from the pain of meaninglessness. We might interpret Christ's sacrificial death as necessitated by the agonized plea for organization, regulation and significance.

Bion explores in his "Learning from experience" (1962a) the transformation from sensual experiences to those based on the awareness of psychic reality. He provides the analogy of the feeding breast, and the infant's digestive capacity, to the giving of love and significance to the infant, and the digesting of mental experience, by the infant's psychosomatic digestive capacity. Bion asks what the mother does when she loves the baby, and what transforms sensual experience into feelings of love and care. How is the infant able to begin to signify the experiences of love and care?

Bion proposes a watershed in mental development brought about by mother's reverie working on baby's sensual data. Mother's capacity to dream the infant is potential and supports the infant's capacity for dreaming and thinking. As the baby's mind is challenged by the absence of the beloved and needed object, "maternal reverie" acts as a ground of support to provide the scaffolding of strength needed to manage the disturbances and changes attendant upon crossing the boundary into the realm of abstract experience. Bion suggests that the first thought evolves from the mating of a preconception with a negative realization, that is, living through the experience of the idea of a "good breast wanted," in place of closing down the mind around the experience of the "bad breast present."

What follows when the infant's preconception of the object that is needed is met with a negative realization, depends on antecedent and simultaneous interactions taking place between mother and baby. Bion states that mother's alpha function breathes life into the infant's potential for organization and signification.

Anzieu explains the precursors to thinking and secure being as found in the development of a skin ego. In the same way that the skin functions as a support for the skeleton and muscles, the skin ego fulfills a function of maintaining the psyche (Anzieu, 1989). The biological function is performed by what Winnicott calls "holding," i.e., by the way the mother supports the baby's body ego. The psychical function develops through the interiorization of this maternal holding. The skin ego is part of the mother, particularly her hands (Anzieu, 1989).

Anzieu goes on to explore the maternal presence as the ground of being, the guarantor against an inner void preventing the solidity of being. Contrasting the need for a skin ego with those of sexuality and nutrition, Anzieu draws on Grotstein's concept of the background presence of primary identification. The latter is the figure who contains and provides cohesion and context for the being of the fragile subject, and who gives meaning to the infant's existence through her capacity for reverie (Bion, 1962b; Grotstein, 1990a, 1990b, 2000d). Without the scaffolding of belief in external and internal boundaries (skin ego functioning and awareness) that hold together the self evolving out of the data of experience in a way in which meaning can accrue solidly, the infant part of the mind (or preverbal part) is left to flounder and throb against its sense of meaninglessness and exclusion (Anzieu, 1989; Bion, 1962a, 1962b; Grotstein, 1990a, 1990b; Paul, 1997; Tustin, 1981b, 1990).

Only recently in human history has the notion of mental bonding been consciously understood as a crucial aspect of survival and well-being for the human infant and child. Now we are able to add the notion that the human subject cannot develop a sense of continuous being without the appropriate responding partner attending to her/his fragile but potential sense of being (Anzieu, 1989; Grotstein, 1990a, 1990b; Schore, 1994, 2002; Stern, 1985; Tustin, 1981b, 1990; Winnicott, 1958). Without the mental bond, the infant is at risk for physical death, or various parts of the mind are endeadened, exiled or compelled to continually fend off emotional significance, which is felt to be too agonizing, and eventually is believed to be the enemy itself. In the Christ narrative, the child takes on the burden of gathering all the bits and pieces of the discarded aspects of mental experience. Mother Mary is, from the very roots of the narrative, placed in a compromised position as the foil for God's purposes. Christ is shown to be in jeopardy and fated to be sacrificed from the moment of Mary's designation as the vessel for God's design. As she consents to the incarnation, she seals the fate of her unborn son much like the patriotic mother who sends her son to war. Her participation figures the failure of the parental function to protect offspring from external and psychic trauma. The idea that a sacrifice is necessary, in order to save humankind from evil, is the manifest form for the signified: the terror of impotence, at the loss of sanity in circumstances of mental abandonment. In the drama of Christ, the child must assume the functions of the parental mind and offer him/herself as the messiah (Bion, 1962a, 1962b).

Critically, Jesus' sacrifice also signifies a darker version of the shape in Leonardo's *The Virgin and Child with Saint Anne*: the parent's need for relief from his/her endeadened, unmeaningful and partially aborted unborn self; the parent's infant self, like a homeless orphan, longs to become a foundling but feels hopeless about that possibility and unwittingly projects that part into the infant, who then tragically becomes the parent's messiah, and forever loses his or her own identity theme (Fairbairn, 1946; Grotstein, 1983; Tustin, 1986). Saint Anne's function is to offer the outcome of the growth of the mind brought about by living through the upheaval of catastrophic realizations. These are the birth of thoughts without a thinker, wild thoughts, thoughts that arrive from the infinity of the unconscious or the unthought known (Bion, 1997; Bollas, 1987). The grandparents' capacity to tolerate the thoughts without a thinker is a critical aspect at the heart of cultural change and the growth of the individual mind and critically spares the new generations from the destruction of the mind that can think. Evolution of emotional truth replaces sacrifice.

The idea that mother is dominated by the wishes and demands of God, the father, powerfully suggests the failure of coupling in the discourse of familial and sexual relations. Joseph's ambiguous role doubles this theme. Thus, another reading of the Christ narrative is its recounting of a tale of a divided or split family. Mary is prevented from protecting her son from his ill-fated destiny, father is a peripheral character, and the paternal God places his son in a position of fearsome responsibility and danger. In this reading, the Christ child is sacrificed in an effort to insure the sanity of the rest of humanity under circumstances of parental failure or of mythic structures, which can represent this experience. The aspect of the configuration that mother is dominated by the wishes and demands of a patriarchal god goes beyond the significance of male/female relations as dominated by male authority. Freud's discussion of Leonardo's work, *The Virgin and Child with Saint Anne* (Freud, 1910), is based on the observations of Oskar Pfister, who emphasized the dark shape, or the area of the blue cross, as a symbol of motherhood. The vulture's tail appears to touch the infant's mouth, representing various aspects of oral experience which Freud designated oral fixation. However, the part of the shape that reaches toward the foot, shown clearly in this figure, outlines the figure of a phallus. How are we to interpret this sign in the configuration? One possibility suggests itself readily, that is: the phallus gives life to the infant.

Looking at the symbol in this way challenges the notion of the virgin birth, or the delusion that one is born from mother alone. More evidence for this interpretation is set up by Julia Kristeva in her essay "Freud and love: treatment and its discontents" (Kristeva, 1986). Kristeva proposes that the infant finds an early profound encounter with lack or emptiness by discovering in mother's unconscious what she terms "the father of individual pre-history." For Kristeva, this figure represents the legacy of mother's pre-Oedipal desire for the phallus. The presence of the archaic father of mother, introduces the infant to lack, and allows him or her to fill it with narcissistic phantasies. The encounter with mother's father in mother's unconscious frees him or her from the sole desire for the mother, which does not allow for realizations of emptiness or lack, and mental experience beyond sensual fusion. Looking at this delusion suggests that the

Christ child's family portraits portray conflict between fusion and mental growth. Leonardo's portrayal of Christ with Mary and Anne (*The Virgin and Child with Saint Anne*, 1508–1510) reverses the reading of sacrifice to some extent, revealing a little Christ as dependent upon Mary, and Mary upon Anne, who supports her. Freud's (1910) reading, which is actually a reading of Leonardo's painting for its infantile themes, also omits the sacrificial aspects of the Christ narrative and focuses instead on Christ's desire for his mother, signified in the painting and the cartoon. Freud imbues this child with powerful desires that seek to be gratified rather than pointing to his ultimate doom as a sacrifice. Perhaps we can interpret Freud's choice as reiterating the history of childhood. It marks the evolution from concepts of infancy and childhood saturated with images of sacrifice manifested in high mortality rates, infanticide as a common practice, and lack of recognition of the infant or child as a feeling, experiencing human being, to images and thoughts of the child as the immortality of the parents.

The birth of concepts of infantile internal life as part of the human life cycle, and of the baby as a feeling, thinking person, who requires love and care in order to survive, has been slow to escape from splitting or repression. Of course, both mythic interpretations remain, but the older idea that the child is not a real human being until he or she reaches adulthood, is no longer accepted. Before the twentieth century, the older notions of infancy and childhood did not yet include articulated realizations that the infant or child had a subjectivity, or was part of the discourse of the other in the parent's experience. Life was cruel, not many infants survived, and many responses to the infant were in the service of denying its physical helplessness and vulnerability. As the medieval period progressed, letters, diaries and paintings told of tender concern and love of parents for their offspring, however, always under the shadow of an early death (Ariès and Duby, 1988, 1989). As early modernist culture developed, particularly in the seventeenth century, incipient individualism and secular notions of human rights appeared. Associated with these ideas was a new appreciation of children. The belief that life in this world was possible and might be satisfying, if not pleasurable, led to the conviction that one's offspring had a future on this earth, and that future was the guarantee of parents' immortality now spelled out on the plane of generational relations.

Revised concepts of child nature were nurtured through burgeoning Democracy and Republicanism, after the political revolutions of the late eighteenth century in America and Europe. The rights of the individual transformed the understanding of the meaning of human life. Also, a more gracious and healthful life was possible for many, as the industrial and technological revolutions brought comfort and gradually overcame the likelihood of infant and child mortality. Increased privacy (more rooms and toilets, for example), affluence and permission to pursue earthly happiness and freedom, all allowed the realizations of vulnerability, playfulness and the human infant's need for consolation, understanding and support, to replace indifferent or stern religious attitudes toward the little ones, and towards child nurture. As Leonardo's discovery of the internal and external parent–child relationship, and as Freud's reading of Leonardo's work suggest, significant transformations in cultural themes and mythologies of these relationships were evolving from the late medieval period, well into our own era. I believe we are able to demonstrate that such transformations also help to set the stage for the discovery of psychoanalysis and for changes within psychoanalytic theory and technique, which we see today.

In the shape of the bird that appears in Leonardo's Saint Anne works, we may decode the emergence of the signs of infantile attachment and bonding. The bird connecting the two women may be interpreted as mothers' capacities to back, hold, think, feed and detoxify (these two latter functions have already been offered in utero). These themes are part of early modern culture that spawned the theories of internal space and latent sources of meaning. Implicit in the painting and cartoon is the representation of the epiphany in Leonardo's mind of a constant conjunction drawn from his own unconscious and conscious mental experiences. The former is a constant coming together of emotional elements in a way that an emotional realization takes place powerfully and is named (Bion, 1962a, 1962b). In non-pathological mental conditions, the constant conjunction fills benign emptiness with new meaning. In disruptive mental states, pseudo-meaning is desperately stuffed into the horror of a void in which meaning cannot accrue (Grotstein, 1990a, 1990b). Leonardo's realization seems to have arrived out of his own meaningful experience and out of his interpretations of humanist themes in his culture. The new realization formed out of an emotional experience, and out of a chain of signifiers coming together, was that of the human infant dwelling in his/her body in the here and now, with his/her still somewhat otherworldly but flesh-and-blood caretaking mother (and her mother). Freud also had an epiphany. He sensed the layers of internal mental life, and was able to abstract the concept of the dynamic unconscious in relationship to the system consciousness.

Freud's discoveries about the nature of the functioning of the human mind, psychological development, and of the causes of mental illness rode on the wings of the Romantic Movement, revolutionary politics and social upheaval, which were bearing new concepts of human rights and the sanctity of the individual. Individual experience became important as a fresh concept in the nineteenth century in Western cultures.

Romantic poetry and painting gathered up the scattered fragments of personal emotions not filtered through religious structures and rituals, particularly the phenomenon of grace. Passion, love, pain and anxiety were separated out from the enclosure of religious ideology. Will and individual choice were protected and encouraged by the growth of Democratic and

Republican philosophies. Even so, Freud's discoveries of the inner dimensions of mental life moved through several tentative stages. The "Project for a Scientific Psychology" (Freud, 1952), maintained connections to the theoretical paradigms of the nineteenth century. In the study of the phenomenology of mental processes, these processes were conceived as linked to brain anatomy and the functioning of the nervous system.

Literature, philosophy and theology speculated on the less tangible aspects of mental life, but the formal discipline of psychiatry had little to say about the intangible aspects of affective life or of mental illness. Freud's "Project for a Scientific Psychology" was written out of his effort to straddle the old notions of the principle of constancy and discharge and a feeling theory of the mind's functioning.

Theories of dreams and neurosis were implicit in the project as he worked out explanations for mental pain and illness. Also, Freud's interest in hypnosis and catharsis displayed his transitional position. In the former, states of mind might be altered or induced by the influence of another person's will; in the latter, the therapeutic partner helped to release dammed up energy which had been stored in pathological fashion, because of trauma or difficult arrangements between the censor and the drives. Eventually, Freud understood the rich dimensionality of internal space as made up of images, feelings and thoughts as well as energetic forces. In the process of carving out the internal world, Freud found infantile phantasy. Though the child's desires and passion plays were couched in the language of infantile sexuality, coursing through the libidinal stages, he in fact had discovered primitive states of mind. While it is true that the infant's experience remained somewhat sketchy for Freud, he had begun to signify and integrate formerly mute elements within Western culture that needed to be articulated within the discourse of the time.

The key idea in such texts as *The Interpretation of Dreams* (1900) and *Studies in Hysteria* (1893–1895) was of the inner and unconscious aspects of experience. Another crucial notion was the undeveloped mind that moved not only from infancy to adulthood (this concept was very new in conscious discourse), but also from primitive, uncivilized states of mind, to civilized, sublimated and moral ones. The child was the leading player in both of these new narratives, and they continued and elucidated the trend towards comprehending and appreciating the infant and child within the individual person, and within cultural signs. It is clear that Freud understood the development and construction of the internal world and laid the ground for an understanding of the analytic relationship.

We can observe that Freud's analysis of Leonardo is a semiotic structure for including the Madonna and child in the psychoanalytic text. Thus, in Freud's hermeneutic reading of Leonardo's visual renderings, we see the suggestion of the maternal figure as a holding environmental figure and as a container for the infant.

As suggested earlier, Mary is backed and doubled by Anne, who then provides weight and depth to the tasks of holding, soothing and containing the infant in his/her immaturity and vulnerability. The notion of Saint Anne or the maternal grandmother is interpreted by Freud to represent the three maternal figures in Leonardo's memories: his mother Caterina, his stepmother, Donna Albira, and his paternal grandmother, Donna Lucia. Freud understands the entangling folds of the combined Anne and Mary figure as signing a condensation of the various relationships during different periods of Leonardo's early life. Caterina belonged to the first five years, and the women of his father's household entered his intimate relations when Leonardo left his mother's house, and that relationship as well (Freud, 1910). At most the two figures Mary and Saint Anne signify the presence of the grandmother. Freud only hints that the person of Saint Anne is part of the child's emotional life. The little boy does not look to his grandmother directly for emotional interaction and comfort. But the abstract meaning implied by the overlapping of the two bodies (the folds of the skirts) looks forward to the significance for the child of a chain of continuity that guarantees his/her origins. He emphasizes the shape in its suggestive relationship to a mythology of primary maternal images, the Egyptian Goddess Mutt, a supreme maternal power that transcends ordinary conception and is impregnated by the wind. Freud had happened upon the figure of the phallic mother, and largely attributes this theme in Leonardo's creative imagination as stimulated by the absence of the boy's father, and by the more universal theme of the castration complex (Freud, 1910). However, the function of the background-holding-containing function that Saint Anne signifies is not noted in Freud's analysis. As discussed, Saint Anne's presence implies generational backing and holding emerging in conscious life during the sixteenth century.

We may also consider the notion that Saint Anne represents an early image of the psychoanalyst. Leonardo's renderings of *The Virgin and Child with Saint Anne* offer three different readings. The first is Leonardo's, which offers us a view of the emerging concept of the human family hatching out from otherworldly mythologies. The second is Freud's discovery of infantile sexuality and the dynamic unconscious. The third is our contemporary psychoanalytic reading, which emphasizes the development of the human mind as it unfolds in the context of maternal (familial) reverie or self-object relations. Infants with as yet undeveloped, unorganized and unregulated minds are exquisitely dependent on the caretaking adult, but since this need had not been consciously recognized until the twentieth century, infants have been subjected to indifferent and inappropriate treatment. Not that this is a settled matter, but today both lay people and professionals take infantile states of mind and the conditions of immaturity seriously.

The painting and the cartoon do not portray Mary and the baby Jesus engaged in the earliest enface interaction of the most intimate kind. Yet, the little Jesus makes visual contact with mother, but in the context of his reach for autonomy Mary saves the baby from falling, the two are portrayed as pulling in opposite directions, suggesting the vigorous holding that is often required to bring the infant through the conflicts between autonomy and dependence. It seems suggestive that the realization of mother and babe is the offspring of a constant conjunction (Bion, 1962a) that may be recognized or read but has not yet evolved into its deeper dimensionality. Bellini's Madonna also portrayed new realizations of mother–child relations, from a different vision; mysticism appears on the canvas with luminous chromatic unfolding, but without any eye contact. Mother firmly grasps her infant, but her presence is compromised by her concern with faraway thoughts. Her gaze seems compelled by unseen powers, suggesting her possession by spiritual powers pulling Mary away from her infant's corporeal existence. The weight of the fullness of the signified, in this case the infant's agony and ecstasy at the breast, is caught between the old religious universe of discourse and the emerging secular one (Kristeva, 1980b; Van Buren, 1993). Centuries later, the flesh and blood infant hatched from the capsule of otherworldly iconography.

In Leonardo's portrayals, eye-to-eye contact is present though earliest infancy is not yet depicted in these works. Lacan has put forward the idea that the subject's chains of signification are the scaffolding for the development of identity and a sense of being (Lacan, 1953; Ragland-Sullivan, 1987). He suggests that psychosis and the development of mental problems are related to the incapacity to use language and to enter the symbolic order. As we know, Lacan maintains that the law of the father is the means to depart from the original jouissance and for avoiding confusional states. However, he does not analyze the efficacy of the relationship between mother and baby. In this way, he assumes that the fragility of being is moved over to the responsibility of the father. Klein, Tustin, Kristeva and Grotstein have approached the phenomenology of being from a different vertex; they propose the sense of ongoing being in the early days of life to be tangential at best. Tustin and Grotstein explore a situation in which the sense of self is endangered by a serious flaw or break in ongoing being that in good intersubjective circumstances is prevented by an effective maternal presence. In accord with Winnicott and Balint, they theorize that a premature rupture of early symbiosis, bonding and/or skin-to-skin contact, leaves a hole felt to be black and filled with nothing, a void in which being and meaning have died or have never been born. They propose that the black hole is felt by the infant to be the site of mother's betrayal and her withdrawal from their bond.

Tustin emphasizes that though there may be a failure on the parent's part to enter into the rhythm of safety, there may also be an inability on the part of the infant, due to innate factors such as hypersensitivity or minimal brain dysfunction, to bond with mother and to thereby receive benefits from the relationship. She describes the ensuing hole as felt to be a rupture in the skin. Grotstein describes the black hole as a state of mind or lesion in mental processes: both emphasize jeopardy in the sense of going on being. Grotstein explains:

> I posited, following Bion (1970) and Tustin (1981[a], 1986) that these patients had suffered an infantile or childhood psychical catastrophe in which they had "lost their innocence" (Blake, 1812) – by which I mean that they had lost their sense of protected ness in a world of fairness. In short, "God had died," along with their personal world of meaning. They thereafter felt adrift, derelict on a sea of randomness. They could no longer "go on being" (Winnicott, 1960[b]), defaulting instead into existential discontinuity and "nameless dread."
>
> (Grotstein, 1990b: 391)

I believe that Tustin and Grotstein's discussions of being all point to the need of a signifying maternal presence who provides the "God" functions of a background presence of stability (a frame of reference, a feeling of ground support underneath and behind), a sense of safety which allows for the growth of a sense of fairness or justice, the signifying capacities that lead to meaning, and all of which in harmony create an alive, hopeful subject. I believe that many of our disturbed patients suffer from the trauma of a fragmented Oedipus myth and a discourse of the other which communicates only turbulence and meaninglessness.

Recently I have had the opportunity to see several patients in analysis who were parents of infants or children with whom they experienced very troubled relationships. I believe that each of these people suffered from the trauma of failed attachment or, to put it another way, a discourse of the other that communicated only turbulence and hatred. In each case, the patient had great difficulty bonding with his/her child, and as the analysis unfolded, it became clear that the patient was an emotional orphan himself or herself who powerfully experienced Saint Anne and Mary as having died, and consequently felt his or her own infant self to be dying or dead, or in the black hole. Each of these patients carried a family myth of mother or father cursed by their parents, and only able to pass on a family legend of hatred between parents and children (Apprey and Stein, 1993a). Thus, the patients as parents suffered painfully from the conviction that they were woefully inadequate in their capacity to parent, or from the reverse set of feelings, of wanting to get rid of their offspring, at times even to kill them.

One analytic task, then, was the location of these relationships within the mind of the patient via the analytic couple. Since they experienced themselves as never having had the realization of the background presence, nor the emotional experience of being powerfully connected to a holding, empathetic, containing maternal presence, we waited together to experience some form of these realizations. Until this process got underway within the analytic relationship, these patients experienced their pain and difficulty as residing in the child-out-there, and within their parent-selves in the present. Thus, while the noxious relationships were located, signified and given life, new intersubjective fields took on life as well. Also, as the psychoanalytic process filled out, and these patients began finding and employing parental functions in me within our interactions, their internal relationships became alive in the analytic exchanges. At the same time, the internal and external infant, or child–parent relationships were ameliorated.

The female trinity and the Pieta in mother–child phantasies

A young mother, who had recently had a baby with serious birth defects, presented one of these poignant parent–child situations. The whole birth was burdened with tragic aspects. The pregnancy itself was cursed with the danger of miscarriage. One of the patient's parents was found to be suffering from a terminal illness while the patient, "Jesse," was bedridden. At the actual delivery, Jesse hemorrhaged, had an emergency Caesarean section, and very nearly died. When she entered treatment, not only was she massively depressed and suicidal, but also she had many times packed her bags and very nearly left with her other child, age 3. The new baby, "Ann," continued to have severe medical difficulties, and entered the intensive care unit (ICU) many times, both for emergency reasons and for several reparative operations. Though Jesse was crushed and near breakdown at times, she ingeniously learned the medical procedures required during emergencies. Furthermore, she set up an ICU at home. Nevertheless, despite her great courage and ingenuity, she found it extremely difficult to bond with her baby and often turned her care over to others.

As we worked together, I began to see the crucial aspects of the patient's internal world in the transference and countertransference, which made clear her idiosyncratic experience of her baby daughter. Jesse revealed a severe split within herself between a hapless infant and a precocious, brilliant, adult self. She used her superior intelligence to conquer most obstacles that crossed her path, but at the same time she was merciless with her baby self. At these times Jesse would report that Ann had an episode of life-threatening dimensions. Certain circumstances seemed connected to medical problems and/or procedures that Ann needed to undergo. However, it appeared to me that the little girl's worsening condition was also related to her mother's states of mind. Mother appeared to be disavowing her own infantile states and projecting them into her baby daughter, making Ann the representative of her own split-off baby self, particularly her dead baby self.

My hypothesis became clear when Jesse's husband needed to go away on business. Just before he left, Ann had a severe crisis, and her father postponed the trip. A short time later, Jesse, not being able to tolerate the absence of her husband and the experience of being left with her critically ill daughter, decided to accompany father on the trip. She was absent for five days. Upon returning home, Jesse was tortured by fantasies of Ann as a rejected and dying baby. We worked at length on Jesse's identification with her own mother, who had great difficulty containing her children's emotional states. She remembered her as chain-smoking, talking incessantly on the phone, and rarely staying at home with her children. We also worked on Jesse's massive identification with an indifferent mother, and confusion with little Ann as the rejected, defective and dying infant. These dreadful feelings came up in the transference towards me as any separation time approached.

Further analytic investigation evoked screen memories, phantasies and dreams that gave shape and form to the inner abandoned infant. Memories and phantasies appeared of leaving her body in the crib. It seemed that states of disassociation followed on futile states of rage related to an emotionally absent mother experience. Jesse remembered a "scene" in which, abandoned in her carriage temporarily, she saw a murder or beating take place. Related to these prey–predator feelings was the constant presence of a lion that haunted little Jesse for many years. The lion sat and stared unrelentingly at her when she was put to bed. When she attempted to share her plight, she was told that the animal was in her imagination. Her family's inability to detoxify and deconstruct the monster imago left Jesse under the rule of her predator for many years.

When the infant Ann was born, Jesse relived many of her ancient horrors, particularly when real defects appeared which genuinely threatened her infant's life. Jesse fell into a severe postpartum depression. At last, she sought help for her suicidal feelings. I became increasingly struck by how emotionally isolated my patient was, and that part of her lived out of her body, desperate behind a wall of distrust or alone with the animal. Later, she volunteered that the only way she might end the persecution by the wild animal in her room was by swallowing him. In this "remedy," we see the effects of passing from generation to generation the trauma of infantile abandonment, if not on the streets of an ancient city, in the home of an affluent professional family. Within Jesse's subjective experience, the generational legacy or discourse of the other was of infanticide.

Further analytic work on Jesse's identification and incorporation with a beast-father in a powerful sadomasochistic symbiotic relationship began to uncover and reveal the tortured, unbounded, hapless infant that was entering into her image of, and subjective interaction with, baby Ann. I hypothesized that in addition to her birth defects which put her on a "G-tube" and caused her to stop breathing, Ann seemed caught in her mother's agonized projections of her utter horror at the failure of bonding and of the fragility of her existence. Analysis proved to be ameliorative for both mother and child. As the analyst, mother-grandmother, father-grandfather (the background presence-me) (Anzieu, 1989), functions gathered up the patient to the analytic container-holding and signifying mother, her terror and feelings of violence not only lessened, but found their way into the hours rather than into her infant daughter's subjectivity. Also, the analytic bonding was provided for Jesse, and little Ann received the benefits of a mother who felt contained by her "mother" and could reasonably bear her pain, terror and difficult identifications. Recall that her mother had died suddenly reminding Jesse of her abjected self with all the attendant feelings.

As suggested, Jesse alternated between a maternal aspect that was distant from the baby's emotional reality and a father who haunted her endlessly, and was experienced as a devouring predator to her sacrificial infant self. The primitive emotions are clear, especially in the signifier of the wild animal, but what is equally readable is the absence of maternal functions, which would transform the most elemental feelings of prey–predator imagistic scenes into tolerable experiences and meanings. As my function as grandmother increased, Jesse's alpha function and ability to dream her internal torments increased. The lion, her predator icon metamorphosized into manageable upset while her prey predator nightmares were lessened by a sense of safety for herself and for the little Ann.

"Beth," another mother, came to treatment because she had recently been left by her husband, who had moved in with another woman. They had fought for years but without surcease or satisfaction. Beth was near breakdown when I began to meet with her. I felt that the marriage had been holding her together, and her constant rage and anger covered her extreme fragility. Another aspect of Beth's psychic reality appeared in her relationship with her adolescent daughter. The daughter, "Melinda," had tried to destroy every relationship mother had. She believed herself to be the good woman in her father's eyes, and mother's boyfriend's, while she created a monster in her mother. Melinda felt that she was the only person who could save her father from her evil mother. The new complication that arose at the beginning of treatment was father's new relationship with an attractive, successful woman. Beth had always felt inferior because she had not fulfilled her dreams and ambitions. She was in fact a highly trained person, though she withdrew from her profession due to inner feelings of inferiority, and a savage conviction that she could do nothing well. From this position, she felt intense envy of her husband, and her boyfriend's, abilities in their chosen field.

She described another aspect of her suffering as her relationship with her demonic adolescent daughter. Sometimes they escalated into physical fights, with hair pulling and wrestling. These fights contrasted with the socioeconomic position of the family, which was upper-middle-class and well educated. Both parents had advanced degrees, and mother was soft spoken and very articulate.

Analytic work over many months revealed a very clean, tidy and self-reliant baby girl who had been toilet trained at under a year because of the pregnancy of her mother. The next child arrived when Beth, my patient, was a little over 1 year. Within the internal world of my patient, a compliant but wounded self interfaces with both a mother who weans precipitously, without regard for her baby's feelings, and her own outraged baby child-self which explodes into anger at any hints of restraint and control. Beth was very unaware of these feelings with the analytic mother-me and railed at her boyfriend or felt exceedingly misunderstood by him as a substitute for the "detached, unapproachable me" who appeared in my absence.

For many sessions, Beth had difficulty making any emotional connections between her emotional wounds in relationship to her internal mother and father, the feelings she had about me when I disappointed her by my absence or my lack of perfect attunement, and the stormy feelings she felt surging up towards her daughter, Melissa, and her fiancé, "Lewis." Many times, she experienced me in the transference as leaving her to take care of herself, though it seemed not to be me at other moments. Beth did begin to associate incidents in her early life with these feelings of rage and hopelessness. She remembered being left in the hall on the first day of kindergarten, to find her way to her room. The terror and outrage that developed within the child-her in relation to her mythic internal parents, as well as the external circumstances (many children in a short space of time), were in an extreme state of disavowal. Her relationships were dominated by either an effort to control the harshly weaned baby inside through her control of Melissa, or an angry, resentful girl who railed at her fiancé at the slightest infraction of those rules which she felt were necessary for her dignity and safety. Beth began having a series of dreams that revealed her attempt to organize her chaotic, angry, and raw feelings into life themes. In one dream, Lucille Ball played a large part.

Beth's associations were to her fiancé, Lewis, remarking that the best lay he had ever had before his relationship to Beth was a red-haired woman. Her daughter, Melissa, and her ex-husband were both red-headed. I suggested that her associations to the dream made clear her concern with several couples, which put her in the position of outsider and left her with feelings of painful jealousy. Beth has blonde hair; red hair signified her outside status and/or lack of special privilege. She soon had another dream in which worms were coming out of her chest. One was sticking out of her skin, and she could see it moving under her skin. Beth had several trains of thought: something was getting under her skin; also, she associated these worms to earthworms, which in turn brought to mind a man from India who had visited the firm in which she worked. He had recounted the serious health problems in his country, which included the presence of worms and feces in the drinking water. Beth also remembered seeing a picture of a man with a worm coming out of an egg he was eating. She next thought about her daughter borrowing her clothes without permission, crossing boundaries, defying her mother's authority, and treating these representatives of her mother's body and sexuality with contempt.

Melissa had recently found her mother's contraceptive diaphragm in mother's bathroom drawer. Beth experienced this as another act of invasion and an utter disregard for her feelings. However, she began to see that Melissa represented herself as well, feeling excluded by the breast and the couple that produced infants. I told her that and added that the "red-hairness" signified her excluded state, she did not have red hair, as well as sexual passion and fiery feelings of resentment. The worms and the contaminated water signed her feelings of always getting a raw and dangerous feeding from mother. Beth had created contaminated and unwholesome milk that came from a breast, which was itself poisoned. I suggested to her that her dreams carried these themes and images because she was fearful of my breast feeding, made bad because she imagined me as having everything, leaving her with only bad milk and very bad feelings. As her mother-analyst, and as grandmother, I attempted to detoxify her old relationship with the breast-mother and the copulating couple by exploring her feelings, of terror, abjection and her consequent envy.

As we worked on these phantasies and emotions, Beth began to soften. She was much less irritable with her daughter and the fights subsided and disappeared. She also felt much less persecuted by a damaged and vengeful image of her internal mother. Soon we had interesting proof of these internal changes. More stealing followed the discovery of the birth control device, but Beth thoughtfully remembered that her daughter slept in her bed after an argument over the "borrowing." Beth began to remember that she had slept in her parents' room until she was over 1 year old. Her associations led to the hypothesis that not only did she witness her parents' intercourse, but the conception of her little sister as well. The sister born when Beth was a little over 1 year old was felt to displace Beth, who soon had to share her room and all her special baby toys with the new baby, "Carrie." Beth and I hypothesized that at that point she felt that she was no longer a baby and had to become the clean, tidy, grown-up girl. Where had the feelings of angry jealousy and messiness gone? The dreams and images suggested to me the snake in the garden that entered prematurely into Beth's image of the maternal breast. My absence and empathetic failures stimulated the surfacing of these screen memories and dreams.

The first was that of sharing her parents' bedroom. The second may have been the arrival of her sister, but there were more difficulties. Her parents practiced a religion that stressed only positive feelings. Following these religious doctrines meant that negative feelings were due to weak will. Father would explain to the children that if they were troublesome, there were a trap door and a chute under the table, and he could open it and get rid of the bad child. For Beth, this meant the disavowal of all her negative feelings. It was better they go down the chute than she herself. The dream of the worms suggested that the snake in the garden was not only the phallus appearing early and possessively, but her own projections into the paternal phallus and into the maternal breast, none of which had been contained, detoxified, or signified. I thought that the worms and feces were signifiers of her projections now coming into me for reprocessing. At times I was felt to be a harsh, demanding parent who demanded premature maturity from her, causing her to kill or mutilate her true baby self. At other times I was experienced as a flexible, containing mommy/daddy/grandmother and as someone who found her to be lovable, shit, jealousy and all.

The internal reprocessing and restructuring came into the treatment through the improved relationship of Beth to her daughter. One night mother sat up with Melissa most of the night, while she cried broken-heartedly at the divorce of her parents, and their re-partnering. Rather than protectively identifying with Melissa as a jealous, naughty baby or child, Beth identified empathically with Melissa's pain. They had stopped fighting physically some months before, and now a new field of mutual exchange was developing, which reiterated the one developing between us within the transference and countertransference phenomena. Melissa continued to feel less depressed and angry, as her mother's increasing capacities to mother, helped her to feel attached. Beth has begun to appreciate her baby self, which has been buried throughout her life, and is developing a maternal self who is maturing as we work.

I believe these patients' analytic experiences are revealing of the function of the background presence (Grotstein, 1983) in a generational context. Saint Anne is a signifier and a metaphor for the beneficial and critical structures that evolve out of benign projective identificatory processes between mother (father) and child. Saint Anne as a signifier represents the functions of bonding and interpretation that continue through the generations, or fail. Her metaphoric value, in addition, lies in her connections to unorganized and uninterpreted material within the repressed.

Saint Anne read as signifier also reveals to us aspects of the history of childhood and the history of psychoanalysis. For millennia the infant part of the personality was unknown and heavily coded in conscious life in the individual and in cultural signs. For that matter, the internal world, or the discourse of the other, were known only through its external analogues. Anxiety and despair were interpreted as possession by an external spirit or by the loss or uncertainty of some sign of safety or salvation. The patterns found in attitudes toward infants and children and the emotionally disturbed or eccentric tell of the fears associated with the inner world of the psyche. Paradoxically and tragically, the externalization of inner states delayed realizations of secular, psychological consolation and bonding. Though many infants and children received good enough mothering (parenting), of course many did not. The paintings of infants being tossed into the river (Ariès and Duby, 1988, 1989) and accounts of those found abandoned in the countryside, as the Oedipus narrative recounts, display the difficulty of many parents to "humanly" bond with their child. Child abuse reminds us today of the continuing and universal aspects of these difficulties. I hypothesize, then, working back and forth between individual history and the history of parent–child relations and allowing them to illuminate each other, that each of these analysands were born into psychic families in which Saint Anne was not developed, nor the maternal capacities that shepherd the birth of the infant's mind. On the other hand, analytic pairing has reawakened and revitalized the capacities to contain, regulate, and signify intense states of mind in these patients and in their children. *Saint Anne and Two Others* is a metaphor for the analytic process.

The bond that extends from grandmother, mother and grandchild is powerful both in its life promoting and anti-growth elements. As discussed, unresolved feeling of nameless dread assert themselves in the grandchild as well as in the offspring of grandmother. The hope that grandmother's reverie is strong enough to detoxify generational nameless dread is well grounded in the fact of cultural change and the growth that can take place in the analytic group, as in the cases discussed, grandmother, mother and child.

Chapter 4

The daughter's body, Part I

The site of the haunting

We have been exposed for millennia to a received wisdom that holds that women who are menstruating are dangerous, and that the toxicity of the menstrual blood is contagious. In many societies over time and around the world, menstruating women are segregated and shunned. One interpretation, well presented by Leonard Shlain in *Sex, Time and Power* (2003), links the evolution of menses in our species with a dawning sense of time and eventually mortality. Women connected the monthly appearance of menstruation with the cycle of the moon, twenty-eight days, the duration till the next onset of menstruation, the signs of pregnancy and the birth of the baby, nine months later. Women realized these signs as markers of duration. The discovery of time led to concepts of future and past and ultimately awareness of mortality. Men's fear of the appreciation of the limits of one's life became entangled in the signifiers of women. Females were believed to be the exclusive keepers of time, the length of the life cycle as well as the givers of life. Resentment and envy may be understood to be the outcome of these beliefs. From this position men usurping the new forms of communication, language and writing may be figured as a remedy for an imbalance of power.

The concept of menstruation associated with the reality of mortality and birth as a human phenomenon was managed over time by the splits between body and mind. The origins of Christianity have been organized in this way. The Immaculate Conception, Christ's Divinity and his commitment to the ascetic life were constructed on the disavowal of the powers of women, the fertile couple and the integrated place of sexuality. Mary Magdalene was characterized as profligate woman; the Gnostic Gospels presented another version constructed on the dignity and essential importance of women as participants of the new religion. However, these were disavowed and remain controversial.

Bipedalism, the evolution of the larger brain and the appearance of the menstrual period are the signs of a dramatic departure in evolution. The most dramatic changes occurred in the females of *Homo sapiens*. Childbearing and sexual relations evolved suddenly leaving behind the characteristics of hominids and *Homo erectus*. Estrus that permitted conception every day was replaced by the complex system of menstruation, a blessing and a curse. Vulnerability to disease and infection, cancer and endometriosis entered the narrative of women's life cycle but so too privileged them with new conceptions and the power to withhold procreation at the time of fertility. Shlain believes that this power set up a fierce antagonism between the sexes adding to the tendency to believe that survival lay in domination of left brain qualities and the lack of toleration of infantile experience (Shlain, 2003).

Melanie Klein's discovery of unconscious phantasies and their connections to the signifiers of mother's body opened up new concepts of the unconscious. Actually Freud had already found the dream work and the idea of psychic representations and internal presences but Klein made an important shift in emphasizing survival or annihilation anxieties over the management of the instinctual quest for satisfaction structured in the Oedipus complex and infantile sexuality. Klein's interpretation of phantasies about the inside of mother's body and what the infant subject imagined they had done to it, creates a dramatic context for cultural and personal feelings about menstruation as a taboo and as a curse. Let us investigate the effect of menstruation and concepts of one's own body through the internal experience of several young women.

We are led to ask what are the phantasies of becoming a woman and how do they affect the pubescent girl? Or for that matter the female infant from birth or in utero. Voyaging inside the unconscious myth of internment inside the mother's body we find ourselves stumbling into Melanie Klein's phantasies of the paranoid schizoid and depressive positions, an experience that might be likened to Alice's falling into the rabbit hole, pulled down and away from any sense of terra firma and the known, familiar and third-dimensional. A struggle to get away from overwhelming emotional pain, really the fear of dying, drives the infant to break the boundaries between his/her postnatal body, and the body of mother who seems somewhat ominous for having boundaries unlike the "inside the mother" experience of prenatal experience. The infant immersed in projective identification with mother, imagines her/himself to be crashing into another dimension out of time and space, as he/she enters into the labyrinth of the maternal body.[1] Turbulent though this experience might be

---

1 Many fairy tales or, euphemistically, nursery tales provide narratives of a child in grave danger, on the verge of losing their life. Little Red Riding Hood, Sleeping Beauty, Snow White, Hansel and Gretel are snatched from certain death by magical means. The parents are portrayed as ineffective, negligent or cruel and sadistic. The film *Spirited Away* (*Sen to Chihiro no kam: kakushi*, 2001) presents a child's fall into another dimension without help from her parents, who are magically overcome by greed and turn into pigs. The little girl survives by her own wits and the help of peers who are not attachment figures.

for the frightened disrupted infant, the more extreme versions are more characteristic of non-attached infants; turning and twisting down blind corridors, ultimately strewn with dead bodies, babies, fetuses, mutilated body parts, blood, ghosts, and demons, signs that vividly display the failure of reverie and the dominance of images of chaos, death and a landscape of horror stories and nightmares.

The several dreams from a ten-year long analysis, not yet finished, have a special merit in tracing the recovery of a mind from shock, trauma and family instability. The familial endowment physically and mentally offered this young woman a dark, burdensome past which included poverty, child abuse and generations of depression. The Dreamer's parents had been orphaned at a very early age by the deaths of their mothers. The dreamer's immediate family was large, with six children, and marked by a struggle to remain intact, but with great cost. This effort on the part of the parents kept the children from a life outside the boundaries of societal law, but left them very limited in their struggle to achieve a good development and a satisfying life.

When the analytic voyager, let us call her Ephigenia, arrived at my office she was plagued by extreme anxiety and depression. Ephigenia had a new baby boy whose birth had brought her into intense crescendos of anxiety centered around his well-being, and the fear that she would not be able to protect him from whatever forces lay in waiting to destroy him. One of her presenting problems was nightmares and/or night terrors. Ephigenia had been plagued by these night terrors since early childhood, and more likely, infancy. The night terrors version of her nocturnal theater of the mind left her awakened by extreme terror and anxiety, but without a vestige of a dream. The nightmare version simply communicated anxiety and terror. However, there were occasionally dreams that left her with some content, but mostly dominated by anxiety dread and terror. These dreams gradually began to leave a remembrance of a man breaking into the house. What she also recalled was that he was trying to kill her. You will be able to see that these nightmares were more breakouts of emotion, not yet well linked with meaning. They were more an evacuation or a happening without will or agency, or any link to other kinds of causal factors.

As the analysis continued, the use of metaphors or symbols of any sort remained in short supply. The analysand, Ephigenia, could not respond to interpretations about her internal states. She seemed to express herself in terms of everyday happenings associated with difficulties with others who were to blame for her discomfort. She experienced my efforts of interpretation of the inner world as assaults. Therefore, this approach seemed to bring to the foreground the very things that she so feared, which were intrusion, and exposure to dangerous and un-empathetic interrelations. I realized over time that this approach needed to be rethought and I began to understand that this situation was related to a major severance between her emotional life and her conscious mind, with its concerns and reasoning. Constant danger and lack of a soothing containing environmental mother had shutdown the congress between experience and awareness and peaceful reflection. At birth, her collarbone was broken due to a forceps delivery, and you might imagine that the origin of the man coming to kill her originated in the forceps experience. She needed to be casted even before coming together with her mother. After birth, she developed eczema, curtailing further the bonding and attachment process.

As you may know, Bion has provided us with extensions of Freud's theory of the dream work. Bion makes important distinctions between the part of the mind that can dream and the part that cannot, this last being connected to psychotic or undeveloped life. Bion's basic reiteration of the dream process differs from Freud in its understanding of the unconscious and a fulminating Id with drives. Bion has presented us with understanding of the capacity to dream and mythify as innate, but in need of protection and assistance. The capacity Bion refers to is alpha function that nourishes dreaming and mythification. The information and stimulus from the body and the mind is searching for awareness and meaning. Information from all the sensory channels is available commencing in utero though limited in its functioning. Maiello, the Italian psychoanalytic psychotherapist trained at the Tavistock Institute, has proposed that the infant's channel of hearing and sound develops an object relation with the caretaker (mother's) voice. However, Bion does not consider the sensory channels less then mental. He posited that dream, phantasy, and myth are layered from deep innate preconceptions, and their evolution, into images. The images that can be linked give rise to organizations of emotional experience, which are in turn, gathered into my themes or dream elements and compressed into compromise formations. Here, the work of compromise is motivated by the danger of too much awareness at once, without the protection of the mothering ones assist. Bion emphasized the vastness of the unknown, the unsaturated, and the limitlessness of the unconscious. The motivation for the dream may be understood as a structure for presenting meaning from a different logic and different dimensionality. For him, the failure of the dream process is connected to the failure of the dream partner's capacity to take in the emotional turbulence and meaning that overwhelm the infant, if not met with maternal reverie.

As discussed, Ephigenia came into analysis with a history of life-long night terrors. She presented with panic, unregulated states, and symptoms of what we might call post-traumatic stress disorder. For the first few months of the analysis, the night terrors persisted as raw evacuations of dread. I soon was confronted in the sessions with the futility of verbal interpretations that one hoped would illuminate her difficult feelings of irritability, rage, as well as the painful relationships, external and internal. My offerings seemed to bounce off her back to me in currents of despair. Thus, I soon realized that the reverie I would need to offer would need to be silent reverie, something akin to Winnicott's notions of primary maternal preoccupation. While I was going through this period of primary maternal preoccupation, I began to feel that I was not doing the right thing, and that I should be able to do something better or different. This feeling tormented me to the extent that I often felt that analysis was useless, and should be given up.

One of the patient's persistent themes manifested in her associations was the welfare of her son. Though she had difficulty for some time connecting her sense of endangerment with her son's, she gradually was able to feel the worry in two ways; that it was about her internal infant and about her infant son, and she began to be able to see some of the elements of her displacement of her own endangered baby/infant self. She continued to have profound anxiety about separation from him and these feelings were provoked at the time he began to start preschool, and then kindergarten. The night terrors continued over the years but began slowly to take on the elements of dream, bits of plot appeared and the ghost-like phantom presence became a man who was breaking in. Here, we began to see a narrative plot of personas set in an emotional context of great intensity, although the emotional tenor retained the quality of raw anxiety with little evidence of the dreamer's agency. We still are able to see that the very dream itself was beginning to be an outcome of the subjects' efforts to put her dilemma in a known structure. Psychic space started to evolve, and some beginning ability to represent was displayed. I must say, that the patient rarely recognizes representation in the sessions.

Also, there is a close, tightly built barrier that came between us. I often felt kept out, and left out of the process, and that I was at fault, as I discussed earlier, especially in the sense that I should have done better to open up the underlying meaning of the patient. Now, I am given the experience that I do not have the means to communicate and feel. I am more then left out, I am severely blocked. In this sense, the left-out feeling is transformed into the experience of static mental life. Might I say that I am inside a place in the mind that is endeadened, and that serves to preclude meaning and awareness, and I would ask the question, "Am I also the infant trapped inside the encapsulated area where no awareness is allowed to take place?" A rather peculiar dream appeared in the middle of the analysis, and broke up the usual pattern of the man breaking into the house, in order to murder her; she would awaken, wondering if she was dead. In this version of the nightmare, her mother rushed into the room looking pale as if she had seen a ghost, and with great anxiety and terror announced to Ephigenia that her father had just murdered her downstairs. Ephigenia became paralyzed with horror, but managed to hurriedly pack a few things and flee the house. She told me that the dream about her mother was a fuller narrative of a recurring murder in the bedroom dream, but was also more horrifying. We had been exploring her experience of my recent vacation, and how she felt abandoned at this time to her ghost-like dream murderer. Now, her father was designated the killer. It is important to note that Ephigenia did die in her dreams, breaking the rule that no one dies in a dream. However, there remained a surviving part as is dramatized in the nightmare of her murder by her father, and a part that suffered a part of her death, or near death.

Another aspect of her feelings of acute endangerment seemed to be connected to eczema that lasted throughout the first three years of her life. I felt that on the one hand she developed the eczema as a hard shell by which she was protected from a brutal experience of the "real." If you recall, Lacan explains the latter as an encounter with that which cannot be signified "digested," for example, when the infant is exposed to an experience that is overwhelming. Thus, Ephigenia longed for a skin container that was present and adequate. The truth was that she felt her skin remained undernourished and very distant due to her shell enclosure. As I interpreted her dilemma, Ephigenia became calmer, she told me that she knew that when they uncasted her it left a terrible rip in her underlying flesh. I continued to call her attention to her underlying skinless state. Over many sessions, this particular panic subsided, and there was a development of some sense of an undamaged and more resilient skin. However, there remained the dilemma of the tough shell coming between her and experience. The shell has often been accompanied by a wild animal internal character breaking out, to guard her from the me who threatened her shell, and the infant within: a part of her that had been cut off from care, due to the many traumas she had endured and the resultant encapsulated enclaves, which left her feeling hopeless. These forces were projected into a father me and returned as a murderer. After the birth of her son, she included him in her nightmares and developed a terrible generalized anxiety about his differentiation. She was so terrified in those nightmares that she awaked to find herself screaming and traveling across the room. Added to the usual, "Oh no not me" and "He's trying to murder me," was a feeling that the murderer was trying to murder her child as well.

I propose that Ephigenia's nightmare or night terrors were messages from the disturbed non-signifying more psychotic aspects of her mind in which she believed that her continued life was a mistake that could not be rectified. As the growth of dream work alpha continued, we can see the existence of a cruel killing superego. You recall that I was not able to give interpretations about such internal relationships since as they were felt to come from "outside" they were experienced as projective identification in reverse, something like a missile returning, laden with her exiled feelings and breaking through her already fragile or thin skin. In the gradual transformation since her dream we can notice that she was in one sense changing from inside. How are we to understand this? Along these lines, Ephigenia brought a dream that revealed the internal existence of another aspect of her internal pantheon. She awoke as usual in the dream panic exclaiming in the familiar way, "He's trying to kill me." But this time she walked into the bathroom that happened to be lined with mirrors. She looked into the mirror and saw the murderer, and it was she. She became so upset that she struck the figure in the mirror, breaking it, and doing some injury to her hand and her wrist. She was astonished later to find out that she had been bleeding. In this dream, Ephigenia dreamt about an aspect of her that was saturated with violence and action and without thought. Previously, I had attempted to make such interpretations, but they were rejected quite violently. Here we see the dream as recognizing the existence of an aspect of herself as the killer or stalker. After these two dreams, I was able to interpret her father and herself as aspects of her superego-like characters, and to suggest to Ephigenia that they were distillations of her experience via projective identification, and the return of the projection without help of the container—contained relationship.

I began to introduce the possibility of transference phenomena that hitherto was almost impossible to explore. I suggested that I was experienced as the male stalker, which she had previously internalized with rage and fear of this threat, and turned it against her. This development also led to a tremendous lack of self-esteem. Now, I was also able to realize the existence of a very disturbed Oedipal triangle with resultant fear and inhibition on her talent, creativity, and ability to work. I called her attention to these possibilities with some effect. After this, she produced a dream in which there were many eggs strewn around. Ephigenia began to pick them up and return them to the mother. It was not clear what sort of a mother it was, an animal, or a person, for example. We discussed the many feelings she had about not having a second child: the fertility treatments that had not been effective, the fear of the substances that were being pumped into her, her husband's lack of support, and what her feelings were regarding the large number of siblings in her original family, as well as her hatred and dread of parental interference. To tell the truth, I felt very uncertain as to what inroads these remarks had made. Here, in the dream of the eggs was my answer. Contrary to my feelings of impotence and the skimpiness of her replies and low-key emotional stance, change had occurred, namely the existence of egg babies, and her own infant self who needed help.

As you may imagine Ephigenia continued to suffer from somatic symptoms: asthma, stomach pains, headaches and generalized body pain, but the most enervating and disruptive set of symptoms emerged as premenstrual syndrome (PMS). Ephigenia repeatedly described her premenstrual and postmenstrual cycle as discrete and opposite states of mind. In the former, she was irritable, negative and despairing as well as paranoid. In the second portion of her cycle, these symptoms were largely in abeyance; a more positive outlook replaced the despair and paranoia. In the postmenstrual part of her cycle she was somewhat released from the enthrallment of the expectation that a child or infant was in imminent danger. Furthermore, her husband whom she experienced as an obstructive saboteur enraged her; this persona offered only criticism and condemnation taking on a posture of stupidity and disinterest at the slightest sign of need for help.

Utmostly, Ephigenia suffered the torment of the undead in the premenstrual part of her cycle. Clearly, she was vulnerable to the changes in the balance of her hormones. Already depressed and melancholic, the onset of menstruation plunged Ephigenia into despair, hopelessness and paranoia. The chemistry contributed heavily, but the phantasies of disturbed, attacked eggs and fetuses intensified her internal dramas. Blood, signed insecure attachment and destructive interaction. Contact was felt to be a ripping and tearing experience, probably signified by the forceps. Menstrual blood has been signed by Ephigenia as the outcome of annihilation of the contents of mother's body and her own.

As Ephigenia gained some psychic space, allowing for the growth of the capacity for reflection, she was able to notice two states of mind, and the attitudes, which accompanied them. A dominant theme that has emerged is the struggle for connection and communication. Not only had attachment been severely curtailed, but also the flowering of dream work alpha. If you recall, Ephigenia could produce only nightmares at the beginning of analysis. Signification, symbolization and the regulation of emotional life were intermittent at best and often thread-like, uneven and impossible due to the dominance of beta elements and the fragmentation of the links of emotional experience (Bion, 1962b).[2] The content of the nightmares and eventually dreams also suggests the nature of male–female relationships dominated by violence, enslavement and cruelty. Coupling in creative and fertile intercourse is only dimly perceived. The elements of maternal/paternal reverie are fragmented, scattered or mutilated, producing unfulfilled longing for partnering that is cooperative, mutual and productive (Bion, 1962a, 1967a; Gooch, 2002; Klein, 1928, 1946, 1952). The sessions are filled with frustration, anger, despair and futility that coupling is beyond reach. Repetition and the absence of symbolism protect the traumatized subject from emotional realizations, but seriously impede growth and healing. In this regard, transference interpretations slip off the face of the hard shell of emotional deadness, while linking and communication are blocked off.

Ephigenia's predicament is connected to blocking awareness of the internal world, particularly the inside of mother's body; her phantasies and associations indicate the aftermath of a holocaust. Infants ripped untimely from the womb, babies destroyed and mutilated, eggs scattered and broken, mother drained, melancholic and victimized.

Furthermore, she began to respect her parents' fertility and had more tolerance for her siblings. You might imagine this shift shown in the dream, brought on a reaction of paranoia, anxiety and hardness in her receptivity. The latter was often couched, and still is in the sessions; mostly in relation to difficulty with her husband that she entirely believed to be due to his pathology. Yet, her dreams reveal that the dangerous man that almost killed her had been somewhat transformed. Also, lately she has looked at me as a separate person for whom she has feelings.

As discussed earlier, how are we to comprehend these changes in her and in our relationship? Though she continues to relate to me in the sessions often as a thing to evacuate into, there are intermittent flashes in which she relates to me with affection, or at least as a person. This is especially true if we laugh together over absurd situations. My hypothesis is that over the many sessions, while I have felt left out, inadequate and haunted, our relationship at the level of one unconscious to the other, has been forming a dream network with newly born alpha function in which she begins to feel and think. Significantly, Ephigenia increasingly speaks as a subject born from the reassembling of her core subjectivity, and the demise of the cruel links that dominated her mind.

---

2 Schizoid withdrawal in the sense that I am using it here may also be thought of as encapsulation, or a schizoid position in which little experience is fed by other points of view, internal or external and in which only highly subjective references are considered to be right and authoritative.

"Alicia," another woman, patient entered analysis in her late twenties suffering from considerable anxiety. Her fears and unease seemed to be connected with intense demands for perfection, in tension with self-doubt and denigration. Alicia is the only child of a well-educated and financially well-off family, but one marked by suffering and tragedy. Alicia is the first-born and the only survivor among several miscarriages, and the death of a 1-month-old sibling. Her premenstrual moods are marked by severe worry, depression and anxiety. Explorations of her phantasies at the onset of PMS and menstruation itself reveal dread and terror of mutilated and dying creatures. Consciously, Alicia had set up projects for the rescue of helpless ones, and the prevention of their extermination. The horror of extermination has haunted her throughout her life. Alicia has experienced some relief from interpretations that explore the relationship between her mother's failed and tragic pregnancies, and her belief system that holds herself responsible for the tragic outcome of her parents' attempts to have other children. The autochthonous creations that include lethal envy, jealousy and rivalry on her part, as the causal agents (Grotstein, 2000a), are marked by severe worry, depression and anxiety. Explorations of her phantasies about the onset of PMS, and menstruation itself, stimulated terrors of mutilated dying creatures.

A further penetration into the sources of her anxiety has recently become known. The worry over the contents and condition of her mother's insides were complicated by the family lore that told of Alicia's prize goodness and mildness. Mother was apparently depressed at various times, particularly at the time of failed pregnancies, but also at the time of Alicia's birth. The contribution of the family myths were drawn from a *Mayflower* heritage on mother's side that had translated into a social-psychological program of emotional control, and extreme sensitivity to lack of decorum. Alicia was sent to a girls' high school that was devoted to WASP values that moved her forward in that mode, including coming out as a debutante, and attending the "right" college. It seems to me that mother's depression may in part have been a generational resistance to these values, but not a complete one, understandably.

As Alicia moved along in her mental development, genuine concern began to emerge for her first child. At the time of her first pregnancy, her love and concern for him were scattered and split off, as were feelings about her own infantile self and experiences. Extreme anxiety, fears of non-existence and persecutory guilt shattered her sense of self and provoked states of morbid dread. All of these were covered over by the employment of polite, gracious manners on the one hand, and frantic activity, spiced with the belief that she should be able to do everything and be everywhere at the same time on the other. As we investigated her underlying beliefs, myths and dreams, Alicia began to experience authentic and deepening feelings about the endangered infant inside mother's body, and inside hers. About the fourth month of her second pregnancy, primary maternal preoccupation began to flower. Her pre-pregnancy worries were centered on her belief that she could never be pregnant with a second child, or if she were able to conceive, the pregnancy would be terminated; some of her phantasies involved a phallopian pregnancy, birth defects, and the threatened imminence of miscarriage. These were felt intensely, but almost in a delusional way, i.e., that these outcomes were inevitable and were part of a curse that she either inherited or instigated. Persistent work on the old certainties, and protection of the newer feelings that she could offer the fetus a safe environment in which to grow, yielded confidence in her pregnancy and in her primary maternal preoccupation. At the beginning of these transformations, I felt anxious, bewildered and irritable. I realized that Alicia was in pain and bewildered not only because she had disavowed her feelings of painful potential loss, but also because she was suffering from the birth of hitherto unknowns. As I became more tolerant of the shifts taking place between us, I was able to translate emotionally to her the feelings of a viable pregnancy. Alicia then became free to relate to the fetus inside of her. She named the little growing girl and began speaking more openly with her and to me about her future life with "Andrea." The various exchanges about the shifts in attitudes about the pregnancy and future life of the fetus seemed to me to function similarly to the generational errands and messages that contribute to transformation or the destruction of mental growth. Leonardo da Vinci's work on Mary and Jesus with Saint Anne as the grandmother comes to mind. Leonardo's rendering of the three, particularly in the cartoon, symbolizes various forms of projective identification taking place between the three (see Chapter 6).

At seven and one-half months, Alicia began to feel considerable pressure at the neck of the womb. Her hasty trip to her obstetrician confirmed that all was not well. The fetus was placed in a breech position and her feet were pushing insistently at the cervix causing considerable softening and dilation. Mother was put on bed rest. Two days later, we had a phone session in which her major anxieties were focused around the notion of forced dependency. The images that she described led me to imagine an infant trapped helplessly in her crib, trying not to bother anyone and feeling overwhelmed by her feelings. I offered this possibility to Alicia and also added that her need to do everything at once, and be everywhere at once, were efforts to shut out her feelings of need, fear and nameless dread. By the next session, she was able to come to the office. The crisis had subsided, Andrea had turned around, the pressure and thinning of the cervix had diminished. Alicia remained hopeful; however, by the end of the analytic week some of her worries returned. I couldn't be sure of the origin of Alicia's worries, but I felt a strong conviction that the end of the week's sessions was playing a very significant part in her feelings. I offered this to Alicia, and got a strong reaction from her that indicated to me that I was on the right track, "Oh, just a minute! I do not know about that." I thought that I had articulated her worst fears and penetrated her shell of self-sufficiency. I pressed on, "I think you want to believe that you have no need of a mother or grandmother me, and that Andrea is felt to reflect your feelings by not waiting to come out. She is felt to be strong willed and wants all her doubts resolved concerning when and how." Alicia began to relax and said to her prenatal daughter to be patient and to wait out the full term since it would be better for her. I hypothesized that the anxieties about the success or failure of the pregnancy were connected to Alicia's mother's many failed pregnancies. Persecutory guilt and a belief in a family curse fueled Alicia's manic-like attempts to avoid any unresolved feelings, and to remain straddling two alternatives, or to believe that she might be able to do both. One primary conflict centers around work and mothering – to give up work or not.

"Christina," another female analysand, became pregnant in a second marriage. She had one child already from her first marriage. This child, a daughter, was 13 at the close of the pregnancy. My patient, Christina, became increasingly disturbed as the due date loomed. These states manifested in rage, irritability and hatred of the child's father. At the same time Christina began to avoid coming to her sessions. She cut down from three to two, and then finally to one. Additionally, these were frequently conducted on the phone. Inquiry into her avoidance of any personal contact with me, or more accurately, of our coming together for analytic work, led to either a harsh response or to spacey confusion. The raging states, directed at the fetus's father (her partner), broke out violently, and at more frequent intervals. During our sessions, she repeated in a deadly hopeless tone her frustration with the situation, with her husband, "Allen," who was a baby, required constant attention, and complained endlessly. Christina also complained without surcease, that Allen could never empathize with her. The hopelessness and deadness of her communications stimulated me towards a realization that I was witnessing a scene in which the fetus is experiencing dread of the outside post-umbilical realm as turbulent and unreliable. I also imagined her newborn exposed to the intensity of her archaic trauma, if Christina did not give up her repetitious hatred and blame. Additionally, her subjective renderings of her prenatal and postnatal experiences released a Pandora's box of phantasies that placed her as a violent and destructive agent in her mother's illness, as well as fears that her own life was precarious (Grotstein, 2000a). The old internal configuration of internal characters or presences were made up of these phantasies and fears, and as discussed, were myopically constructed on a limited emotional portrayal which remained only bad and hopeless.

Critically, her feelings for her unborn child were still endeadened as the due date drew near. Christina called me to enlist my help against her raging hatred directed towards the child's father, her husband. This was the context for the last session she had in the office before her delivery. The session opened with a continuing diatribe against her husband Allen. Despair and hopelessness poured out, at first not directed at me, but towards an internal presence that was felt to be obstructive, impervious, or dead. I likened these feelings to an infant's reactions to a mother, really a conjured internal maternal container, who could only despise the infant's emotional experiences. As the session moved on, after my interpretation, her rage and negativity became directed towards me. I then had a powerful and tragic image of a little baby boy, ready to be born, placing his hand to his head as if faced with weighty and impossible decisions. The boy's agony was communicated to me as "How can I be born when my parents are so upset?" His feelings felt so powerful to me that I could hardly control my tears. I then said to Christina, "Have you spoken to the baby?" She allowed that she had not, because she was so preoccupied with her anger and frustration. She then placed her hand on her swollen belly, and spoke to the worried fellow inside. She told him that she was awaiting his birth, and would be happy to be with him.

Perhaps we might conclude that she was reliving, through her pregnancy, her life-long agony whether she should be emotionally born or to give in to psychic death. I imagined a newborn infant who felt helpless and in despair in the care of a manic-depressive mother. I offered this interpretation to her. At first, she responded with irritated refusal. I then moved on to her conviction that her husband was felt to be the hated and lethal environment. The certitude with which she experienced the ongoing friction between Allen and herself suggested to me not only the limited dimensionality of her thoughts (Bion, 1977b; Grotstein, 1978), but a basic assumption mentality that would allow no alternative views or fresh ideas to emerge or even to exist.[3] My

3 The term "basic assumption" is used by Bion to designate a narrow and closed construction of an emotional interaction that shuts out emotional complexity and other vertices.

mind felt shut down and I suffered from a sense of stupidity and/or intimi-
dation. In desperation, I searched my thoughts for some realization of the
dread that Christina warded off so intensely. I offered the interpretation that
repetition, albeit within the new family, was felt to be less painful than the
possibility of escape from the ancient drama inside her. I had been puzzled as
to what role I was assigned given her consistent avoidance of her sessions. I
offered that I represented another type of a maternal figure, one that might
lead her out of the nightmare labyrinth. Her dread then might be seen as
exposing herself to her archaic trauma if she gave up on her repetitious
hatred and blame.

Critically, none of these women spoke very much about their sexuality. Their
sessions were filled with concern about their feeling of being haunted by old
imagoes that separated them from comfort or delight stemming from their
body, and from sensual relationships with others. As discussed, the experience of pregnancy was loaded with feelings of being haunted by presences
that cursed their childbearing capacities. Also, menstruation was figured as a
terrible curse for the most part by each of these women. They seemed
particularly vulnerable to their hormonal shifts due to the existing dread
about the meaning of blood pouring out of mother's body. Their own
physical discomfort seemed to prove not only their expectation of persecution for hatred of mother's powers, but also the cultural signing of menstruation and pregnancy as dangerous, and associated closely with mysterious
and frightening forces. Ephigenia, not surprisingly, had little comfort with
her sensuality and sexuality, linking them as she did with terror and abuse.
Towards the end of her analysis she found sensuality and passion for the first
time. She described a new relationship as being a perfect fit, and felt very
trusting and friendly with this man. Think back to the dreams of the
murderous intruder. How far she had come! At the same time she continued
to have negative, distrustful and hateful feelings about her "husband." I
thought that her descriptions of the "new man" were similar to a transitional
object in that sensuality and sexual delight were embedded in a very playful
and non-combative ambiance. Her relationship to me had become more
trusting and appreciative, allowing playfulness and sensuality to color her
relationship to me (primary maternal imago), and to the new man. Significantly, Ephigenia had begun to achieve the acceptance of twoness, thirdness,
and coupling as a mental capacity allowing her to cross the boundary of
fearful singularity (Bion, 1965; Ogden, 1992; Tustin, 1981a).[4] The "real" of

---

4 Singularity in the sense that I am using it here may also be thought of as encapsulation, or a
  schizoid position in which little experience is fed by other points of view, internal or external
  and in which only subjective references are considered to be right and authoritative.

her traumas and her autochthonous creations of her emotional experiences had begun to lose their grip over Ephigenia's internal world. In this transformation from singularity to otherness, twoness and thirdness, a to and fro rhythm developed between us. I propose that coupling became possible for her as her deeper interior reality was changed by her analytic relationship. Is it then possible to see evidence, for the notion that the brain changes with analytic reverie, holding and containment? Schore (2002) is persuaded by brain window evidence that the brain changes as emotional patterns change.

Also, there is another way in which we might view difficulty with the concept of coupling. Realizations of coupling are made possible not only by the acceptance of maternal and paternal functions and their alterity, but also by the breaking down of original barriers set against the messages stemming from emotional significance. In the deepest way, the arrival of emotional significance is quarantined away from lively alterity, or cloistered like a nun, who is protected from any intercourse with alterity (Grotstein, 2000a; Meltzer, 1992; Tustin, 1990).

Alicia's difficulties with similar protective barriers are set in an internal reality that is far less disenabling than Ephigenia's. Yet, her thoughts and phantasies betray a limited capacity to tolerate otherness of several types. In Alicia's internal world, the scary phallus still remains with father. He often has appeared as a critical persona who values the correct way to proceed through life. He values prudence about money matters as a high priority. At a deeper strata, father's phallus is suspect due to the many failed pregnancies. Also Alicia's ideas about the dead or dying eggs and fetuses are that her desire to possess mother exclusively had ruined her mother's capacity to have successful pregnancies. In the sessions, Alicia displays urgent curiosity about other facets of my life; however, these forays are largely cut off from her awareness. A major split between the lady-like girl, and disavowed feelings of jealousy, envy and rivalry, has haunted her all of her life. She trembles at the realization of her violent feelings, plagued by her internal, paternal judge, and her own belief in her guilt, her potency, sensuality and sense of agency are severely curtailed. Also, since males are defensively designated as lesser beings compared to females, coupling is underestimated as well. Sexuality plays a complex role for many women who feel fragile and unsure of having a core self and an ongoing being.

Christina had found herself looking to a series of men to provide her with security and unconditional love. Each man, including her daughter's father, was eventually found to be seriously lacking in these capabilities. A de-idealization led to deep despair, and a return to the cruel crazy mother, which threw her into an acute, hopeless depression, that extinguished any other thoughts in her mind.

This last step brought on acute negativity that controlled her mind and was impenetrable prohibiting any change in her perspective. Prince Charming continued to be placed in the role of the curse breaker or the one who could break her enthrallment, experienced by Christina as replacing some elements of her fickle or non-existent background presence, and a guarantee against her terror of falling into nothingness. Sexual pleasure continues, as yet, to be diminished by hatred and fear of the early mother. Sexual conquest is subsumed under the desperate quest for some sort of attachment or to stave off the terror of abjection.[5]

"Sophie," another analysand, associates mainly to her desire to find a good partner that would be suitable "husband material" and provide her with a family. At first, she presented a sad and insoluble dilemma, which she described sorrowfully as she was doing something "wrong." All of her female friends were doing well, were married, and had a family, or at the very least were expert at finding a male partner. In addition to her belief that she was responsible for her "walking" alone, Sophie had profound confusion about how she might attract someone. For instance, Sophie admired a friend who frequented hotel lobbies or upscale bars and was able to attract several men to her side. The friend successfully accomplished her goals by going upstairs to the man's room. When asked if Sophie would like to join them she felt uncomfortable and refused. Yet she continued to admire her friend's prowess. Sophie shed some light on her dilemma as she explained that in contrast to her friend she was extremely passive.

Other sessions revealed that she felt a desperate urge to find a man of her own, a man who would treat her kindly, respect her, and protect her from deep anxieties. The context for this deep and obsessive longing was depicted as a very disturbing picture of her mother who Sophie characterized as critical, unconvincing in her love and interest in her daughter and violent. Further sessions revealed that her father was also violent towards the little Sophie when enraged with her behavior. This confusion was intensified when her father was suddenly assassinated. Living in a country with a Fascist regime made this horrific event somewhat predictable but also very shocking. Sophie felt torn between hatred of the forces that murdered her father and reproachful that her feelings of hatred of the violent father killed him off in the end.

Sophie opines at each session that she only wants to find a good partner and create a family. She repeatedly recounts various encounters with men

5 Abjection is used by Kristeva to describe a situation in which the subject experiences themselves as a lost soul, forever damned to float in a limitless universe with no guaranteed connection.

that never came to fruition. Some of these relationships are long term, others never come to anything but the manifest emotional complaints center more dominantly around her anguish that she drives men away somehow, that she is missing something or she carries something which is poison to any relationships that she might attempt to develop.

Sophie seems very accustomed to sex. She is a very attractive woman with an unusually well-formed body. She explains that all her life men have sought after her but that now she is more anxious that she cannot find the right sort of man. She also fears that men are not as attracted to her as they were. She worries that she is older and not as compelling as she was and of course she is concerned that her childbearing years are coming to a close.

The important difference with the other daughters discussed is that sexuality is a centerpiece of her life. The splits have formed along different fault lines. Sexual pleasure is important and gratifying to her and has provided a great deal of self-esteem but her sexual appeal and enjoyment has been dampened by her felt anxious animosity between the sexes. Complementarily is hard won if not impossible. Sophie's sensuality has fallen under the threats of violence within diverse phantasies. Sexual pleasure is used in ways that disguise anxiety and threats to her well-being. Sophie hopes to blot out the sadism that haunts her both from cultural and personal sources. She does this by combining sexuality with the yearning for a sensual and caring relationship that ultimately will become a wholesome family with children. During her analysis these strategies have become more palpable and disturbing to her. Recent dreams convey these shifts. In several dreams she is attempting to find a house. The occupants living there are strange and associated with unwholesome people, perhaps engaged in illegal or perverse activities. Sophie does suffer in fact from an ongoing sense of culpability. She is also impressed with the richness and lavishness of these houses. In her waking life, Sophie is torn between what looks good and what has intrinsic value. Of late Sophie's dreams have included presences that are kindly, generous and care taking. The latest dream more clearly indicated a maternal type.

At the same time that dependence on sexuality is decreasing, her thinking is becoming clearer. Previously her sessions were filled with fragments loosely associated and obscure. At first I had wondered if her accent and different musical patterns were keeping me from feeling the meaning and emotions of her associations. Now I understand her more deeply with less mystification. The dreams, her style of communication and clarity suggest a trend towards respect of my maternal functions and her own. The persistent doubt that the parental unit might produce and protect the infant's existence is lessening. Thus her belief in nurture over precocious sexuality (excitement) is unfolding.

Mother's body and mind are beginning to be appreciated, as is the parental couple that surrounds the daughter with a sense of safety and stability. These trends brought on a backlash that included the return of her cloudy, confused attempts to reflect on her feelings and imbedded her latest attempts to couple. I felt fairly convinced that the ideas that blocked her new thoughts including faith and hope, were spewing out of a very negative, traumatized but deceptive, devious aspect of her. This is her psychic retreat developed to protect her from the cruelty and the pain of damaged bonds but encapsulating her mind in the religion of the negative. Sophie made several attempts at developing a relationship and or coupling. All of her attempts fell apart. She had many rationales but I became aware that traumatic memories were used to break any links. On the other side Sophie felt deep regret and despair that she could not forge any relationship, that she was a bad person who deserved no comfort or understanding, only punishment. Sophie was possessed by her hopeless baby that was traumatized not only by parents who were suffering themselves but also by part of her infantile mind that held her fully responsible for her badness. As the analysis progressed she began to realize these ideas were shaped to avoid any sense of being helpless in a family that seemingly was not aware of her nameless dread.

Another theme that has emerged recently is the treatment of daughters and women in her native culture. Violence and dominance as well as an inferior status are also felt by Sophie to hamper any growth of her self-respect.

"Lia," another woman in analysis with me, was born to a similar culture as Sophie's; she felt herself to be hated by her mother because she was a girl child. She felt that her father was kinder but of little help because he didn't take her seriously. Her wish to get an education and go to medical school was ridiculed and criticized while her brother had the respect of the family. She also developed a sinister psychic retreat that fought our work continuously and battered her unceasingly. I think that we are able to visit the psychic retreat with Sophie and Lia and come to appreciate living under the rule of hate and envy. The group has been named the mafia by Meltzer (1992), Rosenfeld (1989) and Steiner (1993a) and demonical possession by Grotstein (1979). The work of freeing the daughter's subjectivity is arduous, incarcerated as she often is. Sophie is horribly entangled in the lies and strategies of the self-hating conscience that is felt to control all the power and keep her in a threatened and subservient position. At present she is confronting the perverseness of this advisor but is not able to make sense of her needs and desires.

The daughters of holocaust survivors that I have worked with analytically have had extremely disturbed mental functioning but more than that they have lost contact with their own sense of agency. As daughters raised by parents who lived constantly under the shadow of death they suffered from emotional projections of the blackest of cynicism and hopelessness. The dark cloud that hovered over them emitted such virulent and hideous imagery and sensual vibrations that any efforts at communicating to the patient were pathetic and bounced off the various protective shields that they had established with increasing ferocity (Bion, 1967a).

"Rebecca," entered treatment with a great many doubts about pursuing the etiology of her depression, poor functioning in personal relationships and in her profession. My impression was that she had exhausted her colleague and friend who had kindly but naively attempted to provide solace to her friend in the face of perpetual streams of agonized pleas to be released from what I later identified as an emotional re-enactment of torture, imprisonment and the threat of extermination.

Rebecca was 47 years old when she began treatment. By training she was an academic with a PhD in the humanities. However, since she regularly cast a net of paranoia wherever she worked, she never progressed and was let go. Since this pattern was not at all known to Rebecca, emotionally or consciously, she repeated an intense cycle of idealization, disillusionment, increasing paranoia and finally the attempt to rid herself of the whole unhappy situation, filled the person or persons in her present environment, personal or professional with feelings of violent hatred or of losing their mind. I not only listened to the accounts of these cycles but also was involved in them as part of the transferential-countertransferential field. However, Rebecca held this pattern of internal object relations rigidly away from our ongoing relationship in the sessions. She spoke endlessly about the new object of choice vacillating between dizzying optimism for ecstatic merger (atonement) and repetitive protests of poor or cruel treatment. I began to feel that these "relationships" went on in a limbo place constructed as delusions or hallucinations in the sense that they seemed without any inclusion of awareness of otherness, either internal or external.

Also there were other signs that Rebecca was locked down in a world of demonic anxieties and the more she tried to escape from the threat of the jailor, the more anxious and frenzied she became! She had let me know that the only way she could tolerate living in her skin or standing any sense of presence was to focus entirely on the goodness or badness of the chosen one. Since it could rarely be known as myself I attempted to live out with her the anguish she suffered in the "language" of her distraught undreamable emotions. I want to distinguish clearly that Rebecca could not yet turn her proto-feelings into feelings that were amenable to some meaningful organization. Instead they came at her like a tornado destroying everything in its path. Rebecca fled from these forces by acting out her delusional phantasies about the ideal or demonic character.

My first encounter with this release safety valve was her taking up with the manager of my building. I left my office after her session to find Rebecca and this man huddled together in a cozy tête-à-tête in the courtyard outside my front door. The relationship spiraled into an affair. I found myself becoming furious and feeling pathetically impotent. I, of course, took refuge in my faith in analytic technique. I interpreted the meaning of the office manager in all his shadings and dimensions. At moments Rebecca seemed to listen and consider; however this moment was tragically destroyed in a split second. Eventually this liaison lost its charm in that they had little in common except for the hallucinated link to mother's body. Also he was a refugee from a Fascist regime and had lost everything, his family, his profession and properties. Rebecca's relationships did not end because of her increasing insight into her unconscious feelings. She usually drove the person away due to her impossible demands and the dread fear that she was devouring them. Since her experience of what the two people meant to each other was so entirely out of the other person's range of experience, they lost interest or were driven to hatred. Critically, I myself didn't feel that way, which worried me because I knew that all this intense search for salvation remained extremely disavowed for Rebecca.

Another ritual meant to shield her from the feelings of the holocaust that lived on inside her inner reality was a strange kind of hedonism and sensual satisfaction. Rebecca would withdraw to her present residence that she had outfitted with every possible convenience and comfort. She would darken the house by drawing heavy shades, play music that she loved and drink the best of wines. The ritual may be read as a withdrawal to an elegant and plentiful womb that kept out the "witch" mother. The latter emerged infrequently and was hidden deeply but also was partially present in the character that disillusioned her. Also since her mother of provision was poisonous and unpredictable, she turned to her father for supplies she needed to hold on to her fragile sense of sanity. Her predicament led to the ending of her analysis; she could not bear to give or receive anything from me, thus the exchange of money was horrifying. Consciously she brooded constantly that supplies were running out; she believed that people were stealing from her and since she couldn't keep a job her worries were exacerbated. She was frequently let go because of her extreme attitudes towards people at work. Truly, she was also greatly relieved to be freed from her obligations and able to return to her retreat, a place where she believed she might escape all demands on her.

Another scene that we visited was made up of her parents' depression and anxieties. Rebecca rebuked her internal parents for being so caught up in their mental states. She accused them of making her life a living hell with their continuing complaints about their states of mind and miserable lives. She also understood and felt compassion for their holocaust history. Rebecca's parents were Viennese Jews. Everyone in their families with the exception of themselves, Rebecca and mother's mother died in the camps. Rebecca felt that they grieved endlessly for their murdered loved ones, leaving no shred of peace or happiness for her. She felt deeply convinced that her mother despised her having been born and that she deserved no happiness or satisfaction. She felt she was a child of her mother's guilt. A major outgrowth of Rebecca's identity theme as the one who had to atone for the deaths of the others was her inability to be born psychically let alone to have children of her own. Her womb became a burial ground for her murdered family, her mother's unborn children, hers and the stillbirth of her unborn self. Rebecca carried at the heart of her being utmost dread and terror. Rebecca's personal holocaust undoubtedly sprang from the grief and depression of her parents as well as her own rage and fear of living without much solace. The whole family lived under a reign of terror, the terror of the demonic attack on the life instincts.

We have learned in the last years of the twentieth century more about the etiology of the anti-life forces of the individual and the group. Psycho-analytic thinkers, commencing with Freud, began to understand that undischarged libido was not the fiercest foe of human health and peace but the stimulation of the wish to end life and escape its pain and dread. Klein, Bion, Meltzer and Grotstein interpret the surrender to death over life as derived from the fragility of life and the awareness of that possibility in the human infant. Klein had taken up Freud's explorations of the death instinct as developed in *Beyond the Pleasure Principle* (Freud, 1920) and *Civilization and its Discontents* (Freud, 1930) and emphasized the awareness of death brought to the surface by birth and manifested as death anxiety. In her theoretical and clinical observations Klein emphasized the powerful response to ward off the feelings of being attacked from inside. As we know, this led to her theory of projective identification, thus her infant was not described as passive but suffering from the introjected imago colored by the death instinct hurled outside the self. Bion modified the fate of the infant, threatened by the fear of dying by adding the container's role defined as the mature mind of the mothering one to accept emotionally the fear of dying. As discussed the absence of emotional containment, or reverie leaves the infant (patient) with tumultuous feelings of endangerment that gain in increasing velocity and power reaching tornado-like storms, fragmenting the mind and soma and scattering the bits and pieces through violent disavowal.

Another critical factor in the triumph of the death instinct is the over-whelming certainty that one is helpless; ironically, passivity of an extra-ordinary power pulls the living tendencies into a vortex of deeper pools of nothingness (Bion, 1967a; Grotstein, 1990a, 1990b). The collapse of the personality gives rise to the fierce drag into the black hole where no life can exist, and where no one knows that the individual has disappeared or "died" (Bion, 1967a; Grotstein, 1990a, 1990b).

In my countertransference experience with Rebecca I felt that the black hole was her utmost nadir of anxiety. She had been drowned in her parents' holocaust horrors as well as those of her surviving grandmother, with whom she shared a room. She sometimes was able to explain to me that she was the new hope for the family in the new world but was also severely criticized for not realizing their hopes. As discussed above, Rebecca functioned at very poor levels. Everything she attempted was swept away by the work of the negative (Green, 1986). She had no faith that she could survive carrying the utmost annihilation anxieties of the family and being overwhelmed by her own chaotic emotions that were not allowed direct expression outside the inner concentration camp.

I experienced a similar emotional drama spun out by Linda. If you recall, her father was interned in the Japanese camps in the United States during World War II. Hatred, deep resentment and outraged passivity saturated Linda's internal world and the transference manifestations in the sessions. Linda hated her parents with special virulence. Her feelings and phantasies were based on the extreme conviction that her parents were deliberately out of touch and sadistic. At times she very much identified with these figures and shifted from a suffering depressed victim to a raging murderous figure filled with violence and images of vengeance. In this state or incarnation Linda could not tolerate a single response from me. She found any gesture or utterance on my part as utterly dangerous and furthermore as an attack that would destroy her mind and its contents. We can assume with reasonable con-fidence that her responses when in the violent aspect of her inner world were shaped by the lack of appropriate responses to her infantile anxieties. How-ever, there are other dimensions shaping Linda's experience. She is caught within the whirling dervish of confusion and basic assumption mentality. I have the conviction that when she is so violent emotionally she is inside the ghost-presence of the murderous dictator who is dedicated by psychotic hatred to the annihilation of the victim. These terrors are in large part her father's undigested terrors. Her family and culture in her paternal line is burdened with unconscious undreamt catastrophic anxieties. Linda feels that she is the designated carrier of the banished anguish and anxieties and that her existence and presence stir up endless reactions of hatred and envy for her innocence. In this way Linda feels herself to be the helpless victim. In the sessions, her transference and my countertransference or counter-projective identification alternates between the two, i.e., the murderer and the infant.

Since the onset of Linda's analysis, we have lived through several of these incarnations. Each time I fear for my life as if attacked by a wild animal with whom there is no means of communication. Ultimately, I feel as if I will be mauled to death and have horrible phantasies of fending off the predator with any means possible. Linda is living this out with me and becomes the infant left to die alone with the wild creatures of the primeval jungle stalking her. The phantasies of prey–predator are part of the special genetic endowment of *Homo sapiens*, to recognize the battle between life and death (Shlain, 2003).

I think we can also apply Paul Williams' (2004) poignant and accurate hypothesis about the phenomenology of *invasive and intrusive objects*. He makes a useful distinction between them in this way:

> *Intrusive objects* may be motivated by a need to occupy or become a feature of the subject for reasons that include parasitism and sadism. *Invasive objects* seek to expel unbearable, primitive infantile conflicts, using, for the most part, powerful projective mechanisms. Expulsion is compulsive and violent. *Invasive objects* do not primarily colonize or strive to become a feature of the subject. They transform the subject into a repository or quasi-container in which to lodge unsymbolized mental states.
>
> (Williams, 2004)

I think we can see the presence and operation of the two possibilities that Williams (2004) presents but I think in cases of early trauma involving the traumatization of the parents that the invasive object prevails.

Linda feels that an intrusive judge dominates her whole life and she also feels occupied by an invasive presence. The former is associated with her father, while the latter is linked with her mother. It seems likely that both parents suffered significant trauma (mother in a more personal domain and father the target of social hatred and prejudice). Both internal versions of her parents are felt to be against her feeling and signifying her own thoughts and feelings and thus her commitment to life. They appear in the sessions seizing our interactions as they have always usurped Linda's psychic reality. Under the tyranny of the internal pantheon the subject Linda has lived with despair and suicidal thoughts.

Recently, Linda has latched on to the maternal functions provided by mental bonding. She still suffers from irritation and anxiety that she will be misunderstood and accused of terrible wrongs. In young adulthood Linda developed many of the symptoms of obsessive-compulsive disorder (OCD). Unconscious anxieties and phantasies take the shape of OCD rituals and compulsions. She includes contamination worries within these preventative measures. In the early days of our meetings Linda could barely tolerate any contact with my furniture or the toilet facilities connected to my office. She shuddered to think of the former occupants there. She phantasied that germs were left everywhere and that she would never get rid of them. Immediate showers upon returning home were somewhat relieving but worries continued in the idea of contamination as a never-ending battle.

Medication had been given by a former therapist and was helpful in lessening her compulsions and instability. I asked that she be re-evaluated by a psychiatrist known to me. She complied and continued on with medication. But at the same time Linda's internal world took on new patterns and emotional coloration. Also she gradually terminated the use of her medication. I am powerfully impressed with the development of a protective thoughtful me in the sessions who is giving the old *intrusive and invasive objects* considerable competition. My confidence derives from the positive relationship she has created between us. I noticed a softening of her attitude towards me: I was no longer figured as exclusively judgmental. She began to lean her body against my furniture and stretch her arm along the top of an upholstered love seat. She also moved closer to me on several occasions. At the same time, I feel cautious that the other attitudes towards interaction with her feelings and mine are in hiding waiting for a chance to annihilate the spirit of mental bonding.

If we think of the holocaust inside as developing into a kind of post-traumatic stress disorder, we can appreciate the formidable function of the analytic container to release the daughter from self-denigration, fear and devaluation of her reproductive powers and confusion about "mothers" offering protection of daughter's emerging subjectivity and her contributions to the next generation. I think that the hatred of psychic experience accompanied by the murder of preconceptions, destruction of alpha function, and the abortion of "O" is supported and perpetuated by nameless dread which in turn undermines the survival of reverie or of dreaming away the terrors of unsignified emotional experience.

Chapter 5

The infant subject in vivo

It seems important and logical that in the history of psychoanalysis, the origins of the human personality should be found as commencing at earlier and earlier times. Freud's descriptions were radical for the time, but tiny infants were not included in his analysis of human development. Freud emphasized the opening of the Oedipus complex at 3½ years as the crucial watershed for development. Though he referred back to the influence of the oral and anal stages, he had difficulty tying the notions of identification and introjections of objects to real infants. Klein and Winnicott placed the origins of character and mental life from the first moments of existence and postulated that experiences in utero played a role in the creation of personality and character.

Recall the absence of real infants and children in the artifacts of human culture for millennia. In more recent history, after Locke, who declared that babies and children were individuals and needed preparation for the new life of the individual, infants and children were defined in cultural artifacts, religious and educational, as creatures that needed training to overcome their wild animal tendencies. Empathy as we might identify it would not appear as a forceful influence in childrearing until the middle of the twentieth century. Instead, hardening and training filled the minds of parents who feared their own emerging individuality especially as loss of control. Democracy, political revolutions and religious reform formed the context for these fears or provoked the emergence of inner struggles between what would be called inner desires and the forces opposing their gratification.

Nowadays, infant studies (Trevarthen, 1980), neuropsychology (Schore, 2002) and attachment theories (Fonagy et al., 2004) bring to light the enormous capabilities of very young infants in forming communication systems or taking refuge from trauma through hardening or disassociation. Recent work on attachment theories points to the utter necessity of biological and emotional attachment to insure good development for the infant's mind and brain. Schore, Fonagy, and Target emphasize biological and developmental consequences of the failure of not only attachment, but also the absence or failure of the container (Bion, 1962b).

Following those new-found trends points to the infant with a subjectivity of their own. In recent years, Johan Norman has followed these new ideas and has contributed to our understanding and recognition of infant subjectivity.[1] He has made profound contact with infants of a few months of age who had already been forming pockets of detachment from their mother and from their emotional pain. By intervening with his reverie and interpretations, Norman has worked at forestalling permanent disavowal of aspects of the infant's personality and emotional experience. One poignant example comes to mind: an infant was in despair as was the mother because mother had suffered a dread fear of taking care of her infant, and having a relationship with him. She felt that such a relationship was impossible for her. Norman absorbed and interpreted the infant's bewilderment and misery, and prevented further development of the numbness and self-hatred that was already being formed. He explained to his wee analysand the emotional truth of the situation. Mother has been afraid to take care of you, and you have felt that you could not be with her (Norman, 2001, 2004). Norman takes great care to explicate the role of the non-lexical elements that reach the infant's subjective self. He adds that infant research makes clear the infant's ability to remember, discriminate, and read the partner's emotions and most importantly to resonate with the partner's reverie.

Another case of this kind came to my attention recently. "Anne," a woman analyst who sees mothers and their babies and/or families, was brought a 9-month-old girl infant. The baby had been adopted recently from an Asian country. She had been placed in an orphanage from her earliest days and for the first nine months had lain in a crib, receiving only the necessary attention to sustain life. She was brought to the analyst because mother and father were very inexperienced parents. Also they were into middle age and set in their ways; a crisis in the health of one parent had prodded them into feeling that their lives were somewhat barren and self-centered. The baby had recently come to live with them and they were shocked that they felt so overwhelmed. The infant herself seemed burdened with anxiety though she was eating and sleeping reasonably well.

As the session progressed the infant sitting on the analyst's lap looked deeply into her eyes and then thrust her tiny fist into the analyst's mouth. The

---

1 Since the writing of this chapter Johan Norman has passed away. Speaking for many colleagues as well as myself, I wish to honor his pioneering work in furthering our emotional contact with infants and their families. His imagination and courage led to the possibility of interventions of the most significant kind in the prevention of years of mental pain and confusion.

analytic partner in this drama felt an intense rush of feelings with images of blackness and isolation. She felt as if she were in a nightmare of severe abjection that seemed unbearable and without end. Later the therapist reflected on her experience with the infant as sharing with the little subject not only her present sense of lostness but also the earlier nine months of isolation and loneliness. The thrust of hand into mouth is richly redolent with the outpouring of emotional crises. The loss of mouth to breast, the mother herself, body and mind and the terrible burden of mental life in isolation. Anne, the therapist, felt close to losing her own sense of existence and felt acute waves of mental pain. The infant had intuited the capacity of Anne to provide contact and relief. We might suggest that the infant had somehow held onto her own potential for mindedness and recognized it in Anne and set up the beginning of a container–contained possibility. Anne was also able to help mother to realize her little daughter's presence as substituting for the reverie and container–contained relationship that she had never found. Mother sought out her own therapist and the family continued to avail them of the family/infant work.

Alicia, a mother in analysis, brought her newborn baby to some of her weekly sessions, ostensibly because of babysitting difficulties. At time of writing, I have known this baby girl from the age of 6 weeks to 6 months, and in some respects in utero as mother came to analysis throughout her pregnancy (see Chapter 4). The little girl, "Anika," is a happy baby who has little difficulty nursing and enjoys all the aspects of her relationship to her family, although she has had some difficulty with constipation. Around 2½ months, Anika became very interested in me. She would sit poised on her mother's lap after nursing. At birth, she made prolonged eye contact with her newly found external mother and presently latched on to the breast, happily and vigorously. Anika was reported by her mother to be easily and happily satisfied by the intimate cooperation between the two of them. When she accompanied her mother to some of the sessions, she fed comfortably and slept or played. As she became older, she focused on me from the perch of her mother's lap, smiling and exuding enthusiasm. She deliberately evoked eye-to-eye contact between us. In another visit, she began to make insistent sounds toward me, and I was stimulated to enter a dialogue with her, suggesting to her that she felt that she too wanted to be included in the exchanges going on in the room. She also used her body and arms to express that she wanted to get something across to me. We continued and Anika seemed somewhat satisfied. However, when her mother picked her up at the close of the session she protested vigorously, not with crying, but with special sounds of regret.

At the next joint visit mother asked if I might hold her baby, so that she could go to the bathroom. I nodded in the affirmative and said to Anika, "Hello again, I am Dr. J. Mommy needs to go to the bathroom, and I will stay with you until she comes back." Anika seemed delighted with this proposition; she smiled with pleasure and good humor. I placed her on my lap and she immediately began touching my body and patted my breast. I responded that I wondered if she wanted to see if I was some sort of a mummy too. I think her experience was somewhat confirmed by the next visit. She sat on mother's lap as usual, but this time she looked at her mother and then at me with a look that seemed to imply "Oh look who's here." Anika repeated this a few times and I felt that she was grappling with three. I said as much to mother and child: "We are all here together Anika, mother, and Dr. J." The next visit was the following day because of baby coverage difficulties. This day I felt that Anika's will and desire were emerging forcefully. She "spoke" loudly and insistently, stretching out her arms. Both mother and I sensed she wanted something more. We felt that she wanted to come over to me, and I invited her over. She immediately began to investigate me, once more patting my left breast. I felt that she was organizing her experience, making it her own out of her own subjectivity. I have the feeling that Anika finds herself able to express her desire.

As discussed in Chapter 4, during the course of her pregnancy, Alicia and I had investigated her underlying beliefs, myths and dreams concerning her pregnancy. We were able to challenge and dispel some of her doubts; she then began to experience authentic and deepening feelings about the endangered infant inside mother's body, and inside hers. About the fourth month of her second pregnancy, primary maternal preoccupation began to flower. I interpreted this to her and sensing Alicia's unease and discomfort as well her pleasure, I added that though she found herself powerfully empathetic and involved with experience of her unborn daughter, these newer emotions and the newer meanings and feelings that now flooded her seemed disorienting; but even more significantly put her in fierce conflict with other ways of feeling anxiety and uncertainty. We know this in our analysands as omnipotence that has grown hard and largely unchallenged maintained by extreme splitting, disavowal and hallucinatory or delusional certainty. In Alicia's case to be responsible for everything that crossed her mind, and the belief that she could fit in all these responsibilities with no concern for actual time or physical location, were efforts to shut out her feelings of need, fear and nameless dread.

I have formed a hypothesis that goes like this. What if Anika were carrying mother's nameless dread? Mother suffers from anxiety. The anxiety is mainly centered on dread that uncertainty and ambiguity may appear, and she will not be able to rid herself of the frustration or uncertainty quickly enough. Though Anika is a happy baby who feels bonded to mother (father and siblings as well), and often seems free of anxiety, she certainly has impressed me with her desire to use me in some way. She seems to have an urgent message to get across. Or as she matures, does she want to join in the dialogue, or is she coming to grips with differentiation? Yes, quite possibly, but my deeper feeling is that Anika wants help with some contradictions. In any case, does the analytic setting provide her with the opportunity to project her inner world so that it might be read? Mother's anxiety about being able to have a second baby, since her mother could not, colored Alicia's pre-pregnancy phantasies as well as those during her pregnancy. She dreaded mother's rivalry. At times, I became the less fortunate one who was unable to have a second child, and was felt to want to sabotage her pregnancy. I remembered Anika's forceful and active efforts to terminate the pregnancy more than once. This idea led me to ask is there a residue of the belief that she was never to have been born? Does the persistent difficulty with constipation suggest that an aspect of her remains confused about her psychic emergence? Is it that Anika knows me as the voice that helped to keep her safe inside the uterus until she was mature enough to be born? I think that the infant's present subjectivity must be met as well as interpreting to mother the meaning of her anxieties.

I think it is very interesting and moving that Alicia has been struggling with these very themes throughout her life and analysis. You may recall, as discussed in Chapter 4, that Alicia felt very torn up by contradictory allegiances occupying her mind much of the time. The larger question that has occurred to me after the birth of Alicia's second child is, "Were the daughters in Alicia's family meant to carry their fetuses full term?" And secondarily, "Were their wombs a safe environment for the fetus to grow to full term?" My next thoughts centered around Alicia's powerful and pervasive tendency to brood over the future as a set of problems that involved a contradiction that seemed unsolvable. Though they changed in the particulars, the emotional dilemma remained the same. I became concerned that Alicia remains undecided about the conflict, forever trapped in preservation. I have often had the image of Alicia straddling a threshold, stretching her legs as far as possible in two different directions.

Being the only survivor in her family of origin has placed an unquestionable burden on Alicia's sense of entitlement, and sense of purposefulness. I thought, in tracing generational messages from both the maternal and paternal sides, as presented by the patient, leads her to extreme uncertainty about the meaning and direction of her life. As a mother of young children, she is genuinely concerned to fulfill their needs for an emotionally attached and concerned mother. But her complete devotion to this realm of experience leaves her obsessed with neglecting her work life, and as she imagines that outcome, she will be forgotten and lose her opportunities to advance and find respect for her work in that realm.

If we follow this conflict, it appears that Alicia is very troubled by the necessity of ending or modifying primary maternal preoccupation. Similarly, in our relationship, she has great difficulty deciding when and how we might meet. Her indecision includes the number of sessions vacillating from five to two or none. Alicia seems to be in a painful process of emerging into the realm of experience. She is moving into an awareness and tolerance for the unseen and unknown and the formation of signification that takes place in time and space. Alicia finds these new vistas very threatening. I think it is essential to add that the absence of mother/father's tolerance of emotional ambiguity and pain in Alicia's internal reality plays a large part in her "either or" worldview. She is most uncomfortable if I do not present an interpretation immediately.

Recall that Anika seemed to have some difficulty waiting to be born at the best time. Now at 7 months, she displayed an almost immaculate split. During the day, Anika seems easily satisfied, and focused on the task with good-natured cheer and endurance in the face of loss or frustration. If a toy moves out of her reach, she moves on to another focus. The question crossed my mind, was she too easily resigned? Her happy, bright demeanor cast that possibility in some doubt.

At the same period, mother arrived looking somewhat overwhelmed and announced that she was sleep deprived. The emotional situation remained unclear, but Alicia let it be known that Anika was awakening every two hours. In this session, mother was irritable and anxious, and Anika was not. Her eyes sparkled with life, as she directly engaged my gaze. She had traveled a little and reached the ottoman that belonged to my chair and began pulling herself up with great pleasure. Her mother, Alicia, remained agitated and not interested in Anika's activities. I thought quite understandably since mother was carrying the worry and anxiety, while Anika was free to experiment with her developing mobility, and engage me for mirroring and encouragement. At this moment, I began to have a hypothesis. Although the forming realizations and thoughts without a thinker were not yet clear to me, I was able to track the shared anxieties between mother and baby. Anika held the one who was free to implement her desires. Alicia carried the confusion and sense of inhibition about realizing and accepting the emerging truths formally strangled by the tyranny of hyper-control.

A few sessions later, Alicia announced that she finally felt the freedom and conviction to formulate the desire that she wanted to stay home with the children, and it no longer seemed feasible or helpful to work. The thought that crossed my mind is she cutting off other competing possibilities and limiting her horizon to one domain? On the other hand, is she allowing herself to realize her deeply felt desires? I also remembered some recent shifts in some other analysands who dropped the urgency of their external commitments as a breakthrough occurred carrying into awareness concerns about their child or their child self, usually disowned and kept out of awareness except through painful and disenabling signs and symptoms.

The next session began with Alicia remarking that she was exhausted since she had only two hours' sleep. She explained that Anika awoke several times during the night and that her older brother Louis had also awakened, an occurrence unusual for him, and lastly the troubled dog Eloise needed to be let out. It occurred to me that mother herself was the troubled and disturbed sleeper in the context of my upcoming summer vacation of two and one-half weeks, and new awareness or realizations of loss, sorrow and regret.

Alicia had associated that week to the possibility of a third child and I attempted to explore this idea with her. Alicia said that once again she felt the attempt to have a third child was fraught with danger. I was then able to interpret that she remained very concerned about the fetus or infant's survival. I tied in the idea that Anika had been impelled to escape early lest she would not survive and now in the night she re-experienced the fear of being terminated unless she remained alert and awake. I added that the desire for a third child, though based on a complex group of thoughts, was also connected to the belief that she had to overcome her guilt and shame by producing healthy babies; Anika remained under the shadow of the curse of the unborn babies. I remarked to Alicia that I thought that she remained worried about the infant's survival in her and in Anika. I reminded her of Anika's wish to escape the uterus prematurely.

The disassociated baby

We have been considering the emergence of the infant subject participating in the analytic session with the analyst and with mother. I would like to draw attention to the influence of the infant who is stranded inside the adult subject and yet attempts to make her/himself felt and responded to. The subject has little knowledge of the existence of the infantile self but complains as the adult about poor treatment, exploitation and abandonment or isolation. In extreme circumstances, the subject identifies heavily with the victim part of the personality and feels him/herself to be passive (helpless and hopeless). The victim persona is a traditional pose for females but in psychic reality and in the domain of intergenerational projective identification carries the burden of suffering the fear of dying and the responsibility for the survival of the species.

A major crisis has surfaced in an ongoing analysis. I have seen "Anna" for ten years for the most part five times a week. The contexts for the powerful upsurge of emotions were my summer vacation, which was somewhat longer than usual. At the same time, Anna all but finished her dissertation. These two contexts gathered around having too much and too little; both set off a fear of catastrophic change. Anna herself suggested this. I agreed with her. The belief that she was a *have not* centered on a wretched self-concept that she was the unchosen and unloved one. Aside from injuring her faith in her own value she was ruled by a primitive conscience that fed her the conviction that she was worthless because she was envious of her parents, her sisters and her brothers. This conclusion ignored the evidence that her father was extremely abusive and her mother was confused with him (unconsciously). Thus her deepest feelings were of terror, dread, hopelessness and helplessness. Envy did play a part in her in her feelings of being empty and worthless; however, this recent crisis showed further complications and obstacles.

The recent crisis was felt by the patient to stem from work. Before I left, Anna had felt increasing pride and satisfaction in her work situation. At my return Anna was intensely upset, believing that she was only doing harm to her clients. Anna worked in a setting which housed, counseled and protected women who were pregnant without a father partner. Also these prospective mothers had little financial means. Anna broke down in her first session after the break. She fully believed that when her clients had their babies she could no longer work with them. Upon further exploration these feelings were based in a delusional belief that she would do some harm to the infants. Anna wasn't sure how or why this harm must take place. I wondered if Anna was operating under a curse that prevented her from helping her patients. She felt powerfully identified with internal forces that destroyed babies and little children rather than protecting them.

Thoughts went through my mind that she was also suffering from catastrophic change. And so, I wondered if her anxiety about growth was being projected into the patients. However, further along, she mentioned her father and his unpredictable storms of violence and cruelty and I began to put together the idea that she was afraid that this presence "inside of her" was endangering her growing self and also her therapeutic babies. I knew that one of her difficulties around my vacations stemmed from the fear that I would have the babies and that she would be set aside. Complicating matters she wished them no good and that something might happen to them. Related to this was her belief that if these other babies were born, she herself as an infant, a baby or a child in the analysis would have to be set aside, overlooked, or murdered.

Several possibilities crossed my mind over many analytic session, one was that she wanted to drive them out of their analysis, so as to save them from the father in her mind, who has turned up in the analysis as destroying his children, physically and mentally (which is evident in their adult development). Anna's guilt about her siblings torments her and prevents her from having confidence in her feelings of reverie, understanding and love. So, one possibility would be to get rid of her clients to save them. Another possibility might be the hatred of the new babies, these are her grandchildren so to speak and there may be a feeling that they are not safe with her, as their subjective grandmother and as the recipient and agent of underdeveloped reverie, she would inadvertently harm them.

Utmostly, I think that her wish to terminate her benign care of her clients helps her to forestall the awareness of the danger that children and babies are prey to. In so far as she's identified with her own experiences with her father, it is difficult for her to overcome the sense of impending disaster. In so far she has become more attached to me as providing reverie in the analysis, she has hopes that she will develop and grow into all her potential. It seems to me that Anna remains ensorcelled by dark powers and has difficulty holding on to the hope of transformation. Anna swallowed up by her identification as the offspring of malignant coupling is enhanced by her belief in the wrath of the psychotic, alcoholic paternal figure and the passive sanctimonious mother figure whose capacity to fight danger is insidiously split away.

Thus, I found myself in a similar predicament with the children presented by the patients and their children, who desperately needed to make use of the possibility of reverie in the face of the burden of the nameless dread of their parents and grandparents concerning profound anxieties about survival and sanity. Recall that Anika had actually come to the sessions and had communicated her wishes to express some unresolved feelings. I felt that these had been transformed into somatic difficulties; waking frequently in the night and frequent infections; some unusual for a young child. And I thought from what I heard in the sessions about Anika, that she was able to enjoy much of her life but these illnesses and infections did persist. I felt in the current situation with Anna, that the endangered ones were real and internal and that the only possibility for hope would come through continuing to track and challenge her belief that she would be less endangered by death than by life.

At long last Anna referred to mothers that were not only helpless in the face of "male violence" but also greedy and self-centered. She referred also to her friend's therapist who was a terribly inept and crazy person. She emphasized that her friend couldn't find any fault with her and exclaimed that she was so-o wonderful. I was able to make the link between her friend's blindness and her own. Anna had also spoken frequently about more experienced and more prestigious therapists who did well in their practices, a status she would never attain. These people were competitors not helping figures. Again I was able to link her feelings to me, adding that she hated me for having what she couldn't have. She began to cry, pleading that she didn't want to hate me or envy me. "But I love you," she opined. "You have helped me with so much that was twisted and stuck." I identified these thoughts and feelings as those of the traumatized infant, who dare not express her agonies for fear of losing her slim hold on her mother's care and concern. Anna became frightened in the session, feeling if she located and expressed her rage and hatred that it would destroy any possible bond. She would have to destroy our analytic work, just as she had felt with her own patients after the birth of their children – to be born is to be tormented by images of falling into an eternal abjection or black hole.

Another woman, "Polly," in analysis four times a week for five years came in contact with aspects of her emotional biography that had remained secretively buried. In many sessions she complained and worried about children that were at the mercy of inadequate parents. Her outrage over the neglect or misguided care of infants and children stimulated in her a "rescue worker" who would inform the parents of the miserable situation although to no avail. Often Polly felt herself to be the one in the wrong. She reported that her family members reacted as if she were peculiar or odd or yet again as someone who stirred up trouble. I intuited that the transformative effects of the negative, critical responses found their power in infantile projective identifications in which baby Polly turned herself into mother or mother's likeable and agreeable child. The conflict that raged in her about these two approaches and interpretations of child care, protection and loving concern was horrendous. In her analysis hypochondria emerged mainly in symptoms that were linked with hormones and allergies. Polly's panic and anxiety communicated the felt meaning of these symptoms if not the direct connection with infantile psyche soma events.[2] I hypothesize that the analysis made it possible for Polly's disorganized, chaotic and suffering infant to emerge.

The sessions presented the opportunity to complain to me. I felt that I was the inadequate parent who couldn't be awakened to her desperate infantile anxieties but alternatively someone who might be capable of responding appropriately. Her nephews and nieces often were the subject of her reports. This led back neatly to her criticism of her mother who as a dead mother was inert and unresponsive. The complaints about this version of her mother were filled with great disappointment, rage and hopelessness. A related outcome of her eternal and stillborn feelings about her mother was a grave inhibition in realizing many of her own capabilities. Actually she was the only offspring of a family of five that had successfully completed college and graduate school. Polly had gone on to find satisfaction in a chosen profession and had achieved fulfillment in many respects. However she often found herself hesitating or cutting off openings for her further development, outwardly and internally.

In another session some months later Polly associated to the inertia of her mother. She rarely moved from her chair these days leaving her father to attend to all their needs. Polly continued to speak from the point of view of incredulity, outrage and moral superiority. The tragic and profound feelings of hopelessness, helplessness and fear of fragmentation and abandonment, common to motherless babes, remain imprisoned in the capsule of disavowal. Polly's profound anxieties about her physical well-being seems to be the single channel for expression of her disturbed, traumatized infant self. The verbal protests recounting stupid and cruel treatment of infants and children charge the caretaker who is felt to be responsible for the suffering of the endangered victim but keeps the emotional life of the terrified little one in a distant place while the crusader carries on her mission. The emotional depth is kept as a somatic event.

2 I would like to refer the reader to the ideas appearing in the primitive mental states literature. The routes laid down in the psyche soma, prenatal and early postnatal life involving trauma neglect, overstimulation are stored in split-off capsules and left to work their influence in body aches, Crohn's disease, asthma, eczema and migraines for example. Bion's (1962a) beta element prime is significant here. These are not innocent sensory data but ones that have been expelled from the mind that would ordinarily accept them. In extreme circumstance bits of the mind itself are powerfully believed to be expelled as well. Anzieu's brilliant work in the skin ego as well as Frances Tustin's splendid discussions of normal and abnormal auto sensuality set the stage for viewing the depth of symptoms that were known as "psychosomatic." Also the work on attachment by Fonagy et al. (2004) and neurobiology by Schore provide dimensional maps for us to "see" the loss of functions which are meant to hold the sense of being and humanity together or not.

Another dimension has been introduced into the tirades of parental insufficiency. Polly remarked that her mother had a very hard emotional life; she had lost her own mother at the age of 3. This association marked the first time that Polly expressed more than critical outrage about her mother's lack of compassion and empathy. She made a thoughtful link between her absolute, unchanging image of her *mother* and circumstances that were beyond mother's control. Usually Polly expressed miserable frustration that her *mother and the other members of her family* have absolutely no common sense. She also wavers between interpretations of deliberate cruelty and stupid neglect. One young mother is cited often for stupid neglect. "The baby is not dressed for the weather" (which is extreme). She is deprived of her mother much of the time. She has been in day care from 3 weeks of age. Other children are neglected and put into danger as in the case of herself and her siblings undertaking vigorous sports and activities without supervision. Her nephew is prescribed and given the wrong and unnecessary procedure. A neighbor's boy appears to be suffering from a breakdown and indicates suicidal gestures. No one else sees the situation and if Polly signals alarm, she is met with incredulity or clear hostility. The rejection of her thoughtful diagnosis of the situation had in the past, sent her into shockwaves of doubt and guilt.

As I challenged the doubt by holding and interpreting the profound confusion about the legitimacy of the infant's plight, Polly began to gain more confidence in her compassionate and thoughtful observations. Signs of her pain, worry about further injury continued in her worries about her child. Indeed her anxiety about "Sally" seemed highly colored by her internal reality. Actually, Sally excelled in both academic and various sports and was capable of both loving and hateful feelings. Polly was able to give Sally a very intimate and loving environment, as was her father "Kyle." Of course I became anxious about how I was still felt to be letting her down and was also believed to be stupid or cruel in feeling her agonies.

Since she couldn't believe in the powers of maternal love and remained the "mother" herself, identified with a limited capacity to mother, and remained distant from her infantile feelings I was concerned that we were in an impasse. Polly's determination to find her emotional depth helped us to find chinks in the capsule of self-sufficiency but dangers lurked there as well in a layer of good-natured cooperation that flashed so instantaneously that any thoughts that were on the horizon of consciousness might be blown away.

"Laurie," another woman in analysis at the same time, helped to illuminate aspects of the dead mother relationship as it colored many of her serious relationships and self to self-emotional scenarios. The main consideration here is the powerful influence of the dead mother. Laurie is compromised by feelings of massive fragility. Her mind is dominated by an intense fear of detachment and a dread of being swept away by the needed person's demands and desires. The psychoanalytic process presents us with powerful vignettes of helplessness; these are received by me as a current of feelings sweeping me along. In thinking about this experience I have begun to realize that I saw an infant lying in a basket set afloat by a mother who couldn't keep her daughter with her or could only do serious harm to her infant. I wonder, is the appearance of the little female Moses in her basket a sign of disrupted bonding and is it the last effort to save an infant destined for extinction?

I think the distinction between these two patients is worthwhile. Though they are put together differently (we might think undefended and over defended) they both have the tragic legacy of a mother whose mother died. I suggest that the hopelessness that the neonatal or barely postnatal aspects of the self have remained in a deathlike state as a way of being with the mothering one. Polly took on the task of mothering all the children, including herself. The deepest infantile feelings remain with the mother who is indifferent to such feelings. We know that Polly's mother lost her own mother at 3 but we also have evidence in the transference that I am often believed to be a lethargic, uncompassionate and ineffectual parent (most commonly, mother). In Laurie's internal reality both male and female figures are experienced as potentially exploitative, greedy and in the case of boyfriends, dangerously hypnotic and seductive. I feel the eerie powerful male figures are partially constructed out of Laurie's infantile terrors with mother, her disavowed desires to be heard, noticed and confirmed, split off into a horrid nowhere space occupying the place where the container might be. I interpreted from this vertex. Laurie seemed involved and interested.

Growth of the daughter's subjectivity

Laurie came in after a few days' break due to work obligations; she seemed more relaxed and said that she felt happy. She began the session with a description of those feelings and commented that she didn't feel so entangled with people who would manipulate her and damage her sense of well-being. She felt better about her family and more compassionate about the conditions of their lives when she was a baby and child. She was particularly struck by the normality of the man she was dating. She especially liked that he did what he said he would do and found it very refreshing and the first time that she ever had that kind of relationship. I thought this must be our relationship or a new part of it. She shortly raised the idea of wanting a child of her own. She had previously tried to become pregnant in a past relationship but thought that she didn't have a reliable partner at that time. Laurie fell silent for several minutes. I inquired into her state of mind. She replied that if she wanted to talk about something that wasn't a problem or an issue she didn't know how to talk about what she had on her mind. I felt for her to have good things to talk about stirred up mother's envy and her own of a fertile mother. I also ventured that she seemed more familiar with a mother who was over-whelmed and angry not someone she could consult with and share experi-ences. Laurie readily confirmed my idea:

> I took care of others but didn't think about myself. I am still that way. I can fix up my sister's house or buy her things but can't do good things for myself. My house is still not finished but I decorated my sister's whole house. I don't feel too creative much of the time. Do you know why that is?

I found myself thinking of my grandson, then 10 months old, who could most usually find interest and support for his experiences. Drawing on that imagery I told Laurie that she felt that something was missing that she had referred to earlier, a not knowing how to talk about good things developing inside of her. I added that consulting with the breast and sharing feelings required two willing partners. As I spoke I thought about the lost infant inside who was bonded to a sadistic and teasing other. She brought up the idea of her mother's life in her generation. "She was meant to be a housewife but I don't think she counted on working outside the home as well. The contract as she knew it and expected it was broken." I thought about mother's childhood trauma, the death of her mother. I hypothesized that mother was not only overtaxed, partnered to an underwhelming husband partner but her con-sulting breast-mother died when she was 3.

Laurie spoke of her fear and hatred of being caught in that role or dilemma: "I would never let that happen to me." She brought up women in films such as *Far from Heaven* (2002). We began to talk about the film and other portrayals of women in the 1950s. I felt we were sharing our experience at several levels and that I was cast as the accessible consulting containing mother sharing her capacity for reverie.

I want to call attention to the idea that we were not bypassing the undigested emotional facts but that we were creating a new container–contained situation operating on several levels of mind (dreaming the dream and creating). I felt concerned that we might be avoiding something through a manic detour. I also had evidence that I was cautiously approached as a helpful presence. Laurie complained of feeling weak and achy as if she were coming down with an illness. She also cancelled most make-up sessions, which her work schedule required. I knew quite well from previous sessions that Laurie had her own black hole experiences and that she joined with the teasing figure as a way of holding her together and keeping her out of the nothing, nowhere experience. Her infant self had been lost in that dilemma, falling into nothingness or giving the baby over to a cruel, taunting presence.

In this particular session I felt different emotional qualities arising in the field between us. At this moment in the session she seemed to have more confidence in herself, I think due to her sense of a containing and dreaming mother-me. As part of her discovery of a more commensal partner Laurie ventured into an exploration of her shaky in and out faith in her creativity. She gave several examples of incidents of her pulling away from projects.

The most malignant aspect of the motherless child manifested in a profound chasm between the morally superior her and her painful feelings of deprivation, anguished envy and murderous competitive urges. Another danger lurked in her disavowed conviction that she was a martyr, sacrificing herself for the good of others or to the worship of an all-powerful cruel and tantalizing libidinal source. These two positions in her inner world grew from the agonized infant's burial in an overwhelming identification with her orphan maternal grandmother inside her mother. Laurie's free association narratives are constructed around an overwhelmed mother who she feels sad about and her intermittent rage at being so lost and an enigma to herself. In several sessions I have felt an enormous irresistible feeling of wanting to side with Laurie's sense of injustice verging on feared soul murder. I felt myself wanting to protect her and furthermore wanting to support her growing sense that she is both murderous and seriously wounded, though at the same time I feel seduced. The power of the seduction overwhelms me; Laurie continues to abnegate her responsibility for these feelings. I also feel the plight of the infant inside who wants so desperately to be found and to be seen (mirrored) as a respected infant. I hypothesize that these inventions and strategies are a step up from the exclusive dominance of the dead mother.

Another subject, "Karla," consulted with me, complaining of a terrible feeling of not being real. Karla is a 55-year-old, well-educated articulate woman. She had been married once for a short time and divorced after the birth of her son. The early sessions soon took on the coloring of melancholy, self-loathing or blaming and remorse of great intensity and despair. She also let me know that she had a serious illness five years before and ever since had "lost" part of her mental capacities; or they were badly diminished. Karla attributed this to the effects of the treatment for her illness. Her main themes centered around the loss of her intelligence and her deep remorse that she hadn't taken good care of her son, who she felt was withdrawn from birth, didn't make good eye contact and had a very hard time latching on. At this time in the analysis Karla also felt overcome by sinister, demonic presences that would threaten her with horrible reprisals, murder and torture. She also suffered from terrible and continuous anxiety. She believed that she couldn't get through the day or stay with basic responsibilities. She attributed some of her deficiencies to physical conditions but also to the demons that had all the authority and left her a weak and self-deprecating facsimile of herself. "Left her" is somewhat misleading because Karla believed this condition to be permanent and congenital. Analysis of the demons made some inroads into the origins and fantastic nature of their power. But as they were laid bare another situation emerged in the form of several states of mind that descended into chaos, violence, terror and severe disassociation.

I became aware of her absences not only through silences but also through changes in her speech. Her voice became without weight and had a dreamy quality. She spoke haltingly almost with a stammer. My response was bewildering to me. I became very irritated and noted that I felt taken for a fool, as if she were posing as a person in a relationship with me when she was barely there at all. Upon exploration Karla expressed a conviction that she was dead, without hope of coming back to life. I felt terrible pain in place of irritation; this relieved me suggesting a revival of her capacity to tolerate her emotions and signified the deepening of our relationship.

The narrative of her early days now emerged. Karla was placed in an incubator at birth due to low birth weight though she was not premature. According to the account, she did not see her mother again after birth for over a week. The patient's sessions have repeatedly presented themes of rejection leading to the idea that her mother did not recognize her and the baby Karla did not have the advantages of meeting the mother externally immediately after birth. Karla's unfolding projective identifications into me as the incarnation of the rejecting mother have included an infant trapped in an impervious tomb (the incubator?) a hated baby and a hating disgusted mother. In regard to these scenarios of rejection Karla fell into deep masochistic melancholy or disappeared psychically, her voice trailing off suggesting a ghost imploring me to pay attention but terrified of reprisals.

In the sessions or weeks that followed, the appearance of the ghost baby I found myself witness to many scenes of a traumatic nature. In one version Karla was losing her mind. She was a baby who was left alone and no one could hear her cries. Furthermore she felt lost in eternity, adrift outside time and space. However, at times she organized herself by bringing forward the rejecting, hating mother and bringing it into our emotional field. Suddenly I felt acute anxiety and a foreboding of terrible danger. Karla had become the fiendish rejecting *Mother* and I the infant about to be killed off. The emotional field deteriorated. Karla disappeared but this version soon placed me in the aspect of her experience of the ghost-baby. I no longer felt irritated, I now felt disembodied. I would like to suggest that I felt myself to be without the ordinary reassurances of existence, temperature, and weight or nearby signs of a companion. I am now inside the horror of the unbounded her with the phantasies that figure for Karen her derailment.

She elaborated on these experiences a few sessions later. Karen remarked that she had had a horrible experience that morning. She was leaving a meeting to come to her session and she suddenly saw images of a person who had been stabbed many times. There was blood everywhere. She had also been thinking about her son again. Her voice began to slip away and she began to weep in a pathetic helpless tone. "I never could help him enough to take hold and now he is going to live the same limited, mutilated life that I have been living." Karla continued that she had been realizing that she had been very destructive to herself that she had cut out parts of her in order to survive. But that it hadn't worked well. I connected the two cuttings and the mutilation. Karla readily agreed. I thought that the ghost-like voice and lack of presence were the reappearance of the cut-off parts.

Here is trauma laid bare. I think we can also hypothesize that the suffering of mother and mother's mother is passed on as a curse on the daughter's subjectivity. Karla's internal family history contained another hidden situation. Her family fled from Europe at the end of the nineteenth century, escaping from fierce anti-Semitism, pogroms and extreme economic hardship. My hypothesis is that though we can make links about the failure of bonding and attachment difficulties to Karla's depression and fragmented sense of herself, they may be intergenerational as well as idiosyncratic to Karla. I believe that once again we can see the parent's unconscious was burdened with the turbulent, dark dreads of being the prey or a sacrifice to an internal and external group of malignant "others" (see Chapter 3), thus Karla suffers from psychological impingements and deprivation and also from the projective identifications of mother into her infant (and child) of her own nameless dreads linked to unconscious knowledge of abjection and the fear of extinction. Karla carried the suffering infant with no hope of relief or ending but at the same time hated and excoriated. Her mental states are dominated by these themes. Much of the time she feels herself to be a scared rabbit caught in the headlights and a disgusting failure held in place by a sadistic superego.

Karla recently had a dream of an infant lying in her stroller accompanied by her mother and an older child. Presently the older child began to tear strips of skin off of the infant's face. The infant was terrified but the mother did nothing. Karla usually depends on her internal sister in her dreams and free associations. She speaks of her as sticking up for her and providing empathy in place of her mother. We examined the possibility of the appearance of another version of her sister. As yet this idea has not met with recognition in Karla's responses. We have however found another realization. She feels the realm of otherness as being stripped of any sense of safety and competence leading additionally to a terrible sense of shame. Karla's further associations led to the conviction that her mother, the protective mother, was inaccessible even prenatally. Recall mother smoked all through her pregnancy with Karla. She was incubated without contact with mother. On her arrival at home mother was not able to breast-feed her. In the analysis a good enough mother, me, is wanted but disappears easily with misunderstandings in the sessions and between the sessions. This pattern has much in common with the relation to the dead mother imago except that in the case of Karla, sadism and teasing play a larger role.

The inaccessible, sarcastic mother, similar to Rebecca's holocaust survivor mother (see Chapter 3), deadens the daughter's subjectivity by withholding but if the truth be known deadens the internal infant. In both cases, the dead mother and the dead infant, the daughter's subjectivity is encumbered with murder and death.

Identifications or mergers with the "dead mother" have largely remained in a burial ground of lost hopes and dreams for continuing mental liveliness creativity and compassion toward the self and the next generation. One might say that death of a family member is an unavoidable risk in human life. Though the legacy of the dead mother may be intergenerational and important when entering the analysis, the inner world of the daughter is revealed to be dominated by images of mother's body and mind that are mutilated, dying or dead. From this vertex we are able to inquire into the nature of the woman's thoughts, feelings and identification with her and her mother's female body, its reproductive capacities and *her* responsibilities for the survival of her family and group. Since we are still recovering from the fear of mother's body in the unconscious dream narrative of mental birth, women and female infants and children carry the sign of inferiority and men are signified as external actors who have already achieved mental birth.

Chapter 6

The daughter's body, Part II

Female heroines, circa 1990–2003

Contemporary culture re-presents the daughter's body in films and television. Before the burst of new Amazonian images transitional films, *Thelma and Louise* (1991), *Fried Green Tomatoes* (1991), and *Angie* (1994) are focused on women who are trapped in the mythology of marriage as it is woven around middle-class and working culture. *Fried Green Tomatoes* brings us into a special world, both contemporary and historical. Most critically the film brings us into the post-Civil War society, heavily laden with the basic assumptions of the antebellum south. Much like the film, *Far from Heaven* (2002), racism and passion are both juxtaposed and intertwined. Both films generously open up the ways in which the signifiers of the culture have placed and interpreted "the concepts" of gender and race. *Far from Heaven*, set in the 1950s in New England, brilliantly places us inside the psychic and social domains of the illness of the signifier (see Chapter 1) and provides us with another level or vertex that presents the critical unmasking of these signifiers and the real suffering involved in living out the distortions and lies that underlie the signifying structures. In the latter film emotions are presented as badly mutilated and perhaps beyond hope. Juxtaposition of the two films reveals the horror of the possibility of the perpetuation of prejudice at the level of dream and myth. However, *Fried Green Tomatoes* also offers us the possibility of psychic growth and transformation through the recovery of lost aspects of human experience in the individual and in the culture (Bion, 1967a). Idgie is the designated heroine or revolutionary who sets herself against the basic assumption group without compromise. There are other women in the film who are dedicated to the destruction of the status quo and those who are moved and inspired by Idgie's convictions.

In *Thelma and Louise* rebellion against marriage and the values that define women's lives serve as the central spine of the film narrative. Through the perceptions of the two heroines men are depicted as cruel self-centered bullies that are dangerous to women let alone not helpmates. The limits of Thelma and Louise's thinking are foreshadowed in their basic assumptions about men and relationships between men and women. These limitations lead to their suicidal act since they remain overcome by male power and values. We might argue that they have become rebellious and angry but lack visions of hope and transformation. If we compare Thelma and Louise with Idgie we are privileged to realize the signifying process from the vertex of the illness of the signifier in contrast to the transformation of the emotions underlying the mythic structures.

Fried Green Tomatoes brilliantly works through several layers of culture by providing us with a map of the transformations taking place in the inner realms of the characters. The film *Fried Green Tomatoes*, directed by Jon Avnet, is one of a series of films, including *The Piano* (1993) and *Angie*, that break with the tradition of women's compromised social and subjective situations within the usual film discourse. The film's narrative focuses on the changing relationship between women in a Southern rural setting (Alabama) over the course of the century. This setting allows many connections to be made between the races as well as the sexes as an integral part of the film. An older woman, Ninny Threadgoode, played by Jessica Tandy, not only is the narrator, but also serves as the conduit for many of the film's themes and characters. Evelyn Couch, played by Kathy Bates, is a woman in her mid-forties who learns about women's history and potential subjectivity through Mrs. Threadgoode's tales of her own generation's experience. Ninny's sister-in-law Idgie (Mary Stuart Masterson), and a close friend of the Threadgoodes, Ruth Jamison (Mary-Louise Parker), are two women born at the turn of the century who break radically from traditional culture. Their radical departure leads to the murder of an oppressive male. On a deeper level, it leads to the murder of old values.

The film is set in a refreshing psychic space that bursts out of what we have come to accept as the dominant film discourse of male subjectivity (Kaplan, 1990; Mulvey, 1988; Penley, 1988; Rose, 1988). In this film the filmmakers artfully place women as central subjects while at the same time capturing the residues of a social discourse in which women are placed as the other to male subjectivity, or as foils, scapegoats, sexual icons or victims utmostly a shadow figure imagined by men.

Another radical departure from dominantly male discourse – in which men speak to other men about their businesses, politics and interests; talk at or about women; and gaze at the female form – are the speaking women who speak through their own stream of consciousness or to other women about themselves. Though men as dominating characters figure in their thoughts, the conversation between women is the significant discourse. Additionally, women characters largely drive the narrative with the designated narrator of the tale a woman, Mrs. Ninny Threadgoode.

Her story told to Evelyn serves several functions. Mrs. Threadgoode is 82 when we first find her in her present recounting her personal and historical narrative to Evelyn, her new friend. Outwardly, the two are brought together happenstance. Compelled by duty to visit his mother, Evelyn's husband brings her with him to the Rose Terrace Nursing Home, where Mrs. Threadgoode has also been placed by the cruel destiny of old age and the deficiency of relatives still living or available. However, another level is working in the film narrative that transcends time, space and diachronic laws; on their way to visit his mother, Evelyn and her husband Ed take a wrong turn and Ed stops to get directions near the now retired Whistle Stop Cafe. Evelyn remains waiting in the car near the obsolete train tracks. She hears the approach of a train, and we know that she is connected to a dimension that her husband cannot hear. "What train?" he asks. Her empathic connection and fantasy spans several generations of women and illuminates the changing inner world of women from the early twentieth century to 1937 and finally to 1986. Soon after arriving at the old people's home, Evelyn meets Ninny, whose narrative tale is deeply embedded in the significance of the Whistle Stop Cafe. The train sound is paralleled by the lettering on the window of the cafe, "FRIED GREEN TOMATOES," more tangible than the sound of the train but also indicating significance from another time to Evelyn for whom it will take on new meaning and provide new signifiers for women's bounty, significance and strength. Mrs. Threadgoode's name (read as *good thread*) reiterates the tie between the generations of women.

Ninny Threadgoode takes much pleasure in recounting her mythic historical account of Idgie and Ruth. Their history remains very meaningful to her, and the viewer is privy to the depth of the identifications she has made with two of her close peers. Additionally, they stand for all women in her era and particularly for those whose specific histories and subjectivities can be known, recognized and told to others in an oral form.

Furthermore, Mrs. Threadgoode senses the need for narrative structure in Evelyn's mind. Clearly, the older woman finds Evelyn depressed, scattered and lost in the project of trying to fulfill her destiny as conventional wife and *other* to her husband. When we first see Evelyn, whatever hopes and ambitions she has are invisible. She seems to put all her efforts into trying to arouse her husband's interest. Evelyn is a latter-day version of the domestic ideal portrayed in nineteenth-century women's novels. Victorian ideological values, no longer exclusive or unchallenged as the correct guidelines for worthy womanhood, had narrowed down the mid-1950s myth of the woman at home, to constricted parameters of the attractive, sexy but family bound woman with no subjectivity of her own. The moral and religious purposes that cloaked female heroines' characters throughout the nineteenth century faded though they remained in tension with the newer concepts of women emerging at the end of the century.

The angel in the house undergoes many transformations from her inception in the late eighteenth century through the mid-twentieth century when Evelyn and Sylvia Plath came of age. In her earlier guise, the angel of the house might be seen as represented by Eva in Harriet Beecher Stowe's *Uncle Tom's Cabin* (1852) and Beth in Louisa Alcott's *Little Women* (1868). Virginia Woolf invented this term in juxtaposition to the need of a room of her own. The twentieth-century angel is depicted in the poetry of Sylvia Plath in which she presents herself as an angel of destruction.

In *Fried Green Tomatoes*, Evelyn represents a robotic Stepford wife, a scared rabbit caught in the headlights attempting to make an escape or widen her range of autonomy. Evelyn is pulled backward to the idea that her body is not hers. She is terrified to discover her vagina in the mirror at a woman's group meeting. Her attempts to take on such strategies as greeting her husband draped in Saran wrap reveals her deep emptiness and lost-ness.

Race and sex in cinematic discourse

From its inception, American film as a new public cultural discourse has reflected many of the ideologies of sexual difference. D.W. Griffith's racism, moralism, sexism and Southern mentality set the stage for the "new" discourse of cinema, which in fact claimed many values and rituals from older conservative American belief systems.

In *Fried Green Tomatoes*, anxieties about sexual difference and race are presented both at the surface and depth of their significance. Simultaneously women's subjectivity escapes repressive silence, develops along new lines and reveals new alternatives. Women's desires surface powerfully though in the context of crushing forces of ancient basic assumptions or belief systems.

The film's fresh significance grows from breakthrough in contrast to breakdown of significance. The current chain of signifiers is allowed to carry along integrating meanings associated with women as complete persons or subjects. The female characters in the film are of different generations, race and class and share a friendly, loyal and generous attitude towards one another. Furthermore, their lives are connected through their placement in the symbolic order, and as they descend from their grandmothers and mothers into their own generation, their relationship to the stereotypes, ideologies and myths of culture function like a drag backwards into the older unconscious signifiers of womanhood. A good example of this trend is seen in Ruth's compliant marriage to Frank Bennett. The film suggests here that a good woman becomes a wife. Simultaneously new messages flow from one unconscious to the other (Bion, 1962a). Evelyn stands out as a woman whose subjectivity is clouded by a muddled collection of ideas about who she is and how to find herself. She suffers from a terrible sense of worthlessness and emptiness. Ninny's response to her and the tale of Idgie and Ruth offer a center of meaning that evolves from female subjectivity.

We see Evelyn attempting to find her voice, her will, and sense of agency through several channels, some pathetic, bringing shame and ignominy; in others she achieves feminine competence, authority and self-respect. Within the narrative structure of the film, Ninny Threadgoode's character is remarkably free from cinematic rules of narrative and discourse in the syntax of castration that has disavowed much of the opportunity for the characters and the viewer to think through the existence of women's subjectivity and the assumption of their own lives and inner voice. We may see the narrative of Idgie and Ruth as new chains of signifiers that have broken free, as well as the ancient ones that insist on male superiority and the failed subjectivity of women.

The symbolic order, as defined by Lacan and Lévi-Strauss, is made up of the rituals, beliefs and customs of the society and culture. Bion explains that if new messiah thoughts are allowed to be realized in emotional experience, new meanings, significance and values enter the chains of signifiers and break up the status quo (Bion, 1962b). New patterns signifying women's lives differently allow new qualities and abilities to emerge, the core of Idgie and Ruth's text of desire. In *Fried Green Tomatoes*, male desire is insignificant in shaping the growth and maturation of their subjectivity; men are portrayed as friends or enemies (Big George and Frank, respectively) who form an aspect of the context of their lives but who are challenged as the arbiters of the formation of the symbolic order.

From earliest days Idgie refuses the demands of female gender defined in her childhood as lady-like, restrained and supportive of male subjects. In that context her sister's wedding day is an occasion for a wild attack on the symbolic institution of the wedding, particularly feminine attire. Only her admired and much loved brother Buddy understands her complex subjectivity and hatred of gender restrictions. The symbolism of Buddy's death in a freak train accident functions as a sign of threatened castration for that aspect of her. Ruth also suffers great grief at Buddy's death, mourning with Idgie, and the two are drawn together around their common loss. Idgie acts as midwife to Ruth's unborn female self, delivering her from the obligations of womanhood and the restraints of marriage shown in Ruth's joyless and bleak marriage to Frank Bennett. Ruth loves and accepts Idgie as her lover and friend, and the two women pioneer together beyond the constraints of the symbolic order's belief in the necessity and moral superiority of heterosexual marriage. Their homosexual attraction signals the film's radical point that women must embrace their femininity as their own as self-defined and expressed.

Within that framework Sipsey, the black woman, in her fierce devotion to Ruth, Idgie and the infant Buddy, murders Frank Bennett. The myth of women's proper moral victimization and sacrifice is undermined in this meta-narrative of a new holy family and provides a remarkable new chain of signifiers for Evelyn and Ninny. Ninny presents Evelyn with the gift of an alternative view to sacrifice and silence. A crucial aspect of subjectivity is the freedom to think and to speak. As I have discussed elsewhere, women for all time have struggled with inner and outer repression against their desires, put into thoughts and spoken or written (see Chapters 2 and 3).

Idgie has already found her voice and point of view in childhood and develops them more fully as she matures. Whatever Ruth's potential, Idgie nourishes and encourages a revolutionary. Spirit and discourse in her. While they reject and excoriate the male symbolic order, they create a rich independent alternative semiotic, substituting a strong subjectivity against victimization and eliminating the dominance of the master slave-belief system.

The significance of the Whistle Stop Cafe seems to convey the idea of good food in plentiful supply, fragrant, stimulating on the lips and tongue, and available in democratic fashion standing against capitalism and the Protestant work ethic of self-madness and survival of the fittest, encouraging instead community strength and interdependent care. Little Buddy's rescue from the jaws of Bennett's cruelty displays a devoted group that importantly integrates race and sexual difference out of love and care of the mother and child.

The image of a jar of honey placed at Ruth's grave, accompanied by a note from Idgie expressing eternal love and connection, conveys the significance of sweet feminine supply or the yield from women's bodies. In the scene at the beehive, Idgie proves her ability to manage the binary opposition between male and female, hard and soft, prickly and enveloping, strong and gentle (Cixous and Clément, 1975; Irigary, 1974, 1991; Kristeva, 1980a; Tustin, 1981b; Van Buren, 1989, 1991).[1] Think of the change from *Sleeping Beauty* in which the young princess is pricked by the decree of the wicked witch and is restored by others, particularly the prince. In the tale of Idgie, a young female manages to settle the balance between danger, bounty and sexual difference through her own efforts. The metaphor of the beehive and its contents signifies a breakdown of the binary opposition between male and female subjectivity and the emergence of pathways for integration. In the film *Fried Green Tomatoes*, we are privileged to participate in the birth of more unencumbered images of women and women's expressiveness and power.

---

1 The term "binary opposition" is used from Western logic to mean a dichotomous comparison between two sets of qualities. Feminist writers drawing on the philosophy of Derrida propose that sexual difference is organized in terms of a binary opposition in which women are compared to men as less than. The male qualities are present, strong, known, and capable, whereas women's might be mysterious, unseen, unknown, and dangerous. In this binary opposition, women are deprived of valued qualities that are attributed singularly to men.

The Hours

The Hours (2002), a contemporary film, is a filmic transformation of Michael Cunningham's novel *The Hours*, published in 1998. The film and the novel focus on the lives of three women, of different generations, whose lives come together through the emotional links and the mythic structures of women's inner worlds that they share. Each of the three women, Virginia Woolf, the brilliant early-twentieth-century writer, Laura Brown, a mid-twentieth-century housewife, and Clarissa Vaughan, a Manhattan editor who we find at the cusp of the twenty-first century, are wracked by depression, nostalgia and regret. Virginia Woolf, we are informed, suffers from a malignant form of depression; we are also pointed to the awareness that somehow she missed contact with the sophisticated analysts who practiced in England in that era. We have only to recall the treatment received by Sylvia Plath and Anne Sexton.

The other two women suffer from melancholia as well. Laura Brown's intense sensitivity and permeability may be linked to 1950s culture that placed some women in a coffin of home and family. The film, *The Stepford Wives* (1975) figures the nightmare version of that situation. The film suggests the terror that possesses women if they continue to surrender themselves to the cultural malaise after the horrors of World War II. In fact the film portrays men as having lost themselves as well. Their relationships are drained of any liveliness and emotional expression, bringing to mind the autistic spectrum with the appearance of mechanical-like behavior and lack of emotionality (Alvarez and Reid, 1999). In *The Hours*, Laura is presented as someone who cannot bear her daily life and stream of thoughts; we suspect that she is the epitome of the false self-disorder, or schizoid personality disorder but at the point that she can no longer continue to hold together the profound discrepancies between her outer façade and her inner withdrawal and pain (Fairbairn, 1946; Winnicott, 1985; see also Chapter 2). Her husband, Dan Brown, explains to his son and the viewer that Laura has always been withdrawn, out of the mainstream. He has no insight into Laura's suffering and is content to find gratification through "rescuing" Laura, pulling her into his wish for a post-war dream of home and family. Dan's vision of Laura is reminiscent of the fatally wounded bird that centers Virginia's disappointing visits with her sister Vanessa and her niece and nephews.

Clarissa Vaughan's depression is linked to a thirty-five-year-old folie à deux with Richard Brown, the revered poet who is also identified as the offspring (outcome) of Laura's depression and false-self maneuverings. This link signifies the sterility and malignancy of the legacy of hopelessness in regard to emotional pregnancy and birth. The two members of the couple are fixed in a moment of beauty and youth while mistaking appearance for inner reality. Or to put it another way they are caught in an idealization of the moment and themselves. The moment in which Richard catches a glimpse of Clarissa emerging from sleep and finding him outside at the beach is an apotheosis of realization. Later Clarissa, also known as Mrs. Dalloway, recounts to her daughter the exquisite moment of happiness that she felt with Richard. She adds, "Oh I thought that was the beginning of happiness, but it was happiness." The book and the film *The Hours* follows their manic flight into delirium. We find that Richard is the child of Laura Brown, who fled from her family and from her agony with emotional contact, bequeathing to her son raw emotional sensitivity and woundedness, redeemed only by his grave talent for poetry.[2] An interesting and tragic outcome of their deep and tragic idealization is the continuance of infantile disavowal. In the novel and the film, Richard becomes a melancholic,[3] without the solace of mourning the feelings of loss of Laura, his mother: Clarissa, bearing the names of Virginia Woolf's heroine and alter ego, Clarissa "her given name" and "Mrs. Dalloway," Richard's renaming of the present-day Clarissa, introduces us to the signifier, "Virginia Woolf." Cunningham's use of the presentation of Virginia Woolf taken down from her glorious days in London society, by her what? Her mental illness that could not be treated satisfactorily? Are we to understand this as more than biographical truth, as a signifier that brings together many facets of women's internal reality?

Certainly we find evidence in the story of T.S Eliot's wife Vivien who was placed in a mental hospital for nine years without re-evaluation. The film *Tom and Viv* (1994) provides us with another portrait of a women submerged in a capsule but identified as a disturbed woman who upsets the more proper people in her social set, elites who are clothed in a façade of exquisite manners and character. Viv is not a depressed or disassociated woman (Virginia Woolf, or Laura Brown) but a women who is prone to

---

2 We might understand Clarissa and Richard's supreme idealization of their adolescent epiphany through Klein's notion of the claims of the depressive position. The explosion of the capacity for consequences, depth and significance is enhanced not only by maturation and preparation for adult life but in particular by the final development of the corpus callosum. With this brain development comes the capacity for stereoscopic vision or as Bion conceptualized the new vision, binocular vision. Klein advised us that the capacity to integrate infantile splits brought along realizations of the pain of loss, lack of control, intense guilt and death anxiety (Klein 1928, 1940, 1952). Klein gathered together Freud's and Abraham's notions of melancholia and concluded that mania and the manic defenses surged at the release of the ego from the dominance of the damaged and guilty identification with the lost object. Recall Freud's explanation: "The shadow of the ego falls upon the ego" (Freud, 1914).

3 Given access to Richard's childhood experience with his mother the reader and the viewer would be hard pressed to imagine a journey into mourning and meaning; the novelist, Michael Cunningham and the filmmakers, Stephen Daldry, Scott Rudin and Robert Fox, interpret the absence of maternal reverie and internment within the myths of sanctimonious domesticity.

acting out her inner states that appear to be violent resentment, hostility and one would suspect envy. Viv seemingly has not given up on her own presence by misbehaving badly, according to the social decorum of the day. One scene shows Viv wielding a gun at a detested prominent woman. The gun in reality is a toy gun but her weird mockery has already unleashed powerful forces that aim to teach her a lesson and punish her for her eccentricity. Her husband T.S. Eliot feels overwhelmed by her as well and her brother-in-law helps to persuade Eliot to have Viv put away under the lunacy law, a device for "depriving crazy women" of their civil rights with little hope of getting them back. Indeed, there is an aspect of Mrs. Eliot that is determined to cause trouble but often for herself. Ultimately she refuses to accept help from a young army psychiatrist who wishes to reopen her case because it would mean acknowledging that her husband was not a perfect man. Another dimension that brings us inside her internal relationship to her famous husband is her absolute need to maintain the idealized image of his perfection and realize her talents and ambition through identification with him. Of course she then resents, envies and despises the Eliot who receives all the accolades and has walked away with her gifts (so she believes unconsciously). The massive split in Viv's internal world is never undone; she dies in the mental hospital of a heart attack after nine years' internment. The women in *The Hours* are also caught in a capsule of interior and exterior limitation.

What is the meaning of the signifier Virginia Woolf? How does it carry meanings across the generations on the diachronic plane? And what does it contain in the folds of the synchronic? To trace the meanings of Virginia Woolf, Clarissa and Mrs. Dalloway, over time, forms a line of connection that points to the failures of the resolution of the mother–infant couple to bless the daughter in her odyssey towards psychic birth. Each generation of women in *The Hours* suffer from severe emotional limitation. From another vertex they are very different from previous generations of women. Woolf enjoys the cutting edge circle of intellects and artists in the Bloomsbury group. She has access to new ideas and finds respect and encouragement there. Virginia Stephen (her maiden name) had already gained a remarkable exposure to the more significant writers of her culture through her father, Leslie Stephen, one of the intellectual aristocracy of his era. Linda Gordon (2001), in her biography of the writer, shows the remarkable influence that her father had on Virginia. Fortunately, Stephen possessed a gift for seeing through saturated belief systems and sniffing out and nurturing the unexpected and unknown in other writers; he was also able to find and cherish new paths in parts of his life. But such openness did not apply to his attitudes and relationships with women. Virginia's mother lived and died as the angel in the house and other people's houses as well. She was driven intensely by the calling of the sacrificial Victorian woman. Julia Stephen seemed to have worked out her depression, really melancholia, through giving her life to others. The more demanding this calling becomes, the more it produces melancholia. Her life was shadowed by unexpected and tragic loss, her first husband died suddenly and that event seemed to have set the course for her melancholic tendencies.

The same became true of Virginia, who lost her mother suddenly of an illness contracted while nursing the sick. Virginia was 15; then her older half-sister Stella suddenly died not long after Julia. In the next few years her brother died and then Leslie himself. At the death of her mother Virginia began to fight off the wish to die too. However, she became more than severely depressed, she suffered her first breakdown serious enough to the extent that she was placed in a sanatorium, shades of Vivien Eliot. Gordon (2001) makes clear to us that Virginia's repeated breakdowns took a great toll on her efforts to find her own subjectivity and her development as a writer. She was waylaid by her terrible states of mind, which included not only lifelessness, but also weird voices. In much of the writing that followed Virginia experimented with the quest of her women characters to find their thinking and speaking selves. Some fell ill and died during the journey as Rachael, in *The Voyage Out* (1915). But by the time of *Mrs Dalloway* (1925) Virginia Woolf was again ravaged by her mental illness. She tells us that she can barely hold on to any sense of hope for her continuing sanity. We see her with her sister Vanessa, as desperate for intimacy of a primitive sort. She plants a seemingly inappropriate kiss on her sister's lips. Laura echoes this intense desire with a kiss to her dear friend. Can we say that Woolf is parched from a meager supply of maternal reverie; in her case someone who will provide her mind with sturdiness, regulation and meaning? The character Virginia Woolf, or her meaning in the fictional narratives, is very soon to relinquish her grip on her mind and life itself. Her resistance to the pull into insanity is her commencing her book *Mrs Dalloway*. Virginia says to her husband Leonard, "I think I have a first sentence." However, she also says to him in her suicide note that her voices are coming again and she cannot endure another round of insanity.

I found myself asking why are we presented with this view of Virginia Woolf; and for that matter all the women in these recent films that seem to be clearly attempting to understand the social-psychological conditions of women's internal reality and their cultural social holding environment, nevertheless present these female subjects as badly handicapped? Woolf's enormous talent and significance as an agent for change is given meager attention.

In *Far from Heaven* "the angel in the house" is Cathy Whitaker. The filmmakers' added perspective in *Fall from Heaven* is their wisdom gained from reviewing that culture. They are very much inside "the nuclear" family daily life to the extent that the viewer is made painfully aware of the felt necessity for lies and deception imposed and embraced by the members of the family. Our heroine is framed as an understanding wife who has forsaken her desires (if she ever had experienced them). Dressed in outfits that recall Victorian stereotypes of severe control of women's bodies (see below the discussion in *The Piano* of the layers of clothes that confine Ada so inappropriately in the setting of the New Zealand mud), Cathy's outfits are parodies of the nipped waists and long full skirts of the 1950s. In this style the female body is draped so that there is no sign of the legs or for that matter the lower half of the body. Notice the coats that are flowing and resemble cloaks of the nineteenth century. They are also color coordinated. Cathy is dressed in this style in a peach silky dress with a green coat, generously shaped to accommodate the fullness of her dress. In this scene, she is carrying supper for her husband Frank, who she believes is overworking. She enters his office portrayed as the woman of mercy and compassion and is met with the brutal unmasking of the truth of her relationship. This scene also begins the unfolding of the complexity of emotional relations breaking out of social and personal repressive mythologies. The discovery used by Todd Haynes, the screenwriter and director, interprets the 1950s from the perspective of the turn of the millennium (the twenty-first century). The labyrinth of race and sex in the nuclear family and the connections to corporate life are satirically exposed in an idealization of the couple as Mr. and Mrs. Megacorp.

The introduction of Raymond Deagan, an insightful and sensitive black man, follows the tradition of one aspect of the mythology of black Americans; that in truth under the dread paranoid images of black men as rapists and black women as victims of these violent men (not the white males who had many interfaces with their domestic female slaves) lives a concept of black people as not caught up in the values of the white culture. The weavers and sponsors of the racism and sexual tension between the sexes have been largely what Donald Meyer has called the "moral middle" clinging to chards of Protestantism and success myths as their belief systems eroded before their eyes or from under their feet (Meyer, 1989).

The Piano

I was struck while viewing the film *The Piano* at the similarity between the heroine of the film and a current patient in analysis with me. Both women had profound disturbances in their ability to speak. The woman in the film, Ada, does not speak at all when we meet her and we learn that she stopped speaking at 6 years of age. While we learn from the later novel that while the precipitating event was her father's sharp rebuke at the dinner table, we are also made aware that her mother had died when she was born (Campion and Pullinger, 1994). Recall that the morals and manners of England in the nineteenth century defined women in very restrictive ways. Women were cut off from public life; they were not allowed to pursue higher education or training and they were not to serve in political offices of any kind including the church. Critically for this exploration, they were not to speak in public.

> My analytic patient "Molly" was not mute. However, her social and personal speech was severely constrained and was cut off from her emotional life. In the sessions my patient spoke, but her use of language was badly compromised. Her words seemed to float without any connection to her inner world or to either of us. She often lapsed into deadly silences. The presence of a vital and forceful subject would disappear behind a shell that prevented contact and the inner subject was left feeling hopeless and lost. As I thought through the etiology of the mutilated speech of these two women, the fictional Ada and my analysand Molly, I was confronted with the interrelationship between prevailing gender concepts and restricted subjectivity, as well as their personal pain and schizoid withdrawal (see Chapter 3).

As we know, Freud had made a case for women's inferior intellect and character. Freud tied women's lesser abilities to the absence of a penis or an already existing castration. The zeitgeist of his society and culture still based many of its beliefs and mores on the superiority of the male gender. Perhaps it is more accurate to add that the unconscious dread of mother's life-giving powers continued to haunt culture and language and was not yet brought under the analytic lens. The challenge to the dominant belief in women's inferiority arrived more clearly with the unmasking of the old order (see Chapters 1 and 2).

The Piano is constructed around the odyssey of a woman who is sent from Scotland to New Zealand for a marriage arranged by her father. The film opens with the arrival of Ada McGrath, a mute pianist, her daughter Flora, and their piano on the beach. The arranged marriage is to Alisdair Stewart, who appears to be a cool and rigid man. She soon falls in love with George Baines who, by contrast, is sensitive and kind. The plot and characterization spiral toward a climactic moment when Alisdair, jealous and enraged, amputates one of Ada's fingers. She eventually leaves the marriage and moves away to start a new life with George and Flora. It is here that she begins to find her voice and her own subjectivity.

From the first moments of the film, it is made clear to us that we are being contacted by an inner aspect of Ada's self that expresses a deep cleavage in the ongoing being of this woman. Jane Campion, the writer and director, looking back from the twentieth century at the shape of women's experience in the nineteenth century, conveys well the splitting between surface and depth, the inner and outer, the lost and the known aspects of woman's subjectivity. Ada speaks to us with her inner voice and we are informed that she has not spoken aloud since she was 6. The outer posture that Ada assumes betrays an angry, resentful, guarded presence that walls off and silences her inner speaking self (Anzieu, 1989; Tustin, 1990).

It seems clear that Ada is outwardly helpless to shape her destiny, represented in the sea voyage to a new world and in an arranged marriage to a stranger. Embodying aspects of the notion of women as commodities of exchange, she was passed from the house of one man to that of another's, representing a common dilemma for nineteenth-century women who were deprived of a respected place outside of marriage and forbidden to join their male peers in gaining an education.

From that context we are able to see one of the very significant layers of meaning of Ada's piano for her. Her piano is an extension of her subjectivity, which is otherwise baffled and strangled. This is poetically imaged in the clipping of her wings – the amputation of her finger – and the violent, sudden ensnaring of the piano's rope. Thus, in addition to the cultural, social web imposed on women in our era and Ada's, I propose that deeply private inner contours of emotional forces including desire, need and intense fear of intimacy, spin out further webs which pull the subject, Ada, toward death and away from life. Think of Ada's struggle with the rope used to hold the piano firmly in place. In this context the rope may be interpreted as a manifest signifier of a deadly aspect of Ada's psychic reality, something like a demonic presence, powerfully ensnaring her will and blocking her mental birth. The demon usually appears because of a profoundly defective surround in which the parents' states of mind are taken over by deeply unresolved emotional defects and deficiencies leading to chaotic, unregulated fields of emotional interaction shorn of empathy or the capacity for containment or detoxification (Bion, 1959, 1962a, 1962b, 1965; Grotstein, 1984; Joseph, 1982; Klein, 1928; Rosenfeld, 1987; Steiner, 1993b).

The demonic rope that pulls Ada toward a place where no voice is ever heard is an image of the forces of anti-life that owe their virulent strength to the raw wounds of the experience of premature separation or lack of the papoose or kangaroo opportunity to build up a feeling of postnatal at-one-ment. The experience of precipitous awareness of separate skin boundaries leads to the premature closure against the "not me" (Anzieu, 1989; Tustin, 1981b, 1990; Winnicott, 1945).

When we meet Ada she communicates the presence of a woman who is both ensnared in her family's and culture's language or symbolic ordering of sexual difference and an angry rebellious subject who refuses to speak a language that oppresses and interrupts her ongoing being or misrepresents her to others and to herself. In this context the piano is a substitute for Ada's voice and if used in this way provides us a map for refinding her voice – much as one sees in the metonymic and metaphoric substitutions in the analysis of a dream. In this mode of communicating the internal world, disguise, deception and faint murmurs from lost parts of the self mingle and form labyrinthine chains of signifiers. Campion pursues not only the sexual repression of the era of the film's unfolding but the painful problematic of sexuality as a continuum of the nature and growth of the self's interface with other than self, particularly the "skin-ego" mommy whose task it is to provide skin-to-skin netting for the protection for the newly hatching infant enduring postnatal psychosomatic experience (Anzieu, 1989; Tustin, 1981b, 1990; Winnicott, 1945). Anzieu links the development of the skin ego with the existence of the subject. The skin ego or immunity boundary frontier develops out of sensory exchanges that include all the senses (Grotstein, 1984). In the first few days and months of life the active reciprocal sensory communications and their reception form envelopes that provide the feeling of being wrapped and held together snugly in place of prenatal security (Anzieu, 1989). The envelopes also perpetuate the feeling of connection, in great part through the experience of a shared skin until the infant feels buffered enough to be inside his or her own skin without damage to her/his newly developing sense of postnatal existence. In this sense being and subjectivity are entwined. Without a whole, flexible skin ego or permeable membrane, the basic structure that provides the safety of being is extremely precarious. The horrific anxieties that arise under these conditions are felt to be life threatening to the extent that death seems a blessing. The anxieties are those of unembodiment, disappearance, skinless vulnerability, interrupted being and deep wounds and holes in the sense of being, metamorphosed as an unreliable skin that torments the subject with images and feelings of abandonment (skin that is torn or loose), strangulation (skin that is too small) or murdering, poisoning skin (Anzieu, 1989). Thus, a tough shell develops set against the possibilities of experience; the shell may often be personified as a devil, a demon or a tyrannical group that is set against the possibilities of life (Grotstein, 1979; Meltzer, 1975; Rosenfeld, 1987; Steiner, 1993b). Hence the subject is caught within a life and death struggle, terrified that his or her being will ebb away (leak away as liquid or evaporate like steam) or feels identified with and dominated by tyrannical and evil presences.

Faith in the solidity of one's self derives from experiences of sensory and mental intimacy. In the absence of the conviction of solidity a second skin maneuver develops that is often manifested as a persona committed to the death of the subject but also paradoxically felt to be the only protection from profound annihilation anxieties. Ada reminds us of a woman with a tough second skin, covering old wounds, scars and holes with a crusty impenetrable skin-shell, who rarely lets down her guard (Bick, 1968). Though we see her softening with her daughter, languishing in intimate sensuality and sharing in secret hilarious little jokes, her softness is deceptive since it is used as a barricade against the fulfillment of the wedding vows and against intimacy with others.

I would like to suggest in this regard that Campion has brilliantly intuited and illuminated the labyrinthine threads of the experiences of communicating and not communicating, of making contact and the failure to do so, and of a well-founded going-on-being contrasted with a core self or going-on-being that is fragmented, deprived of sustaining rhythms or burdened with endeadened enclaves (Anzieu, 1989; Tustin, 1981b, 1990).

When we see Ada and Flora at their embarkation, they present an expected portraiture of Victorian womanhood. Typically, they are outfitted in the confining silks of the woman of genteel background. Layers of fabric and devices or contraptions, the hoop petticoats and skirts, the corsets, which alienate them from their body-selves and choke off their sensory life, bind them up. But most dramatically their portraits are marked and defined by the stiff bonnets that frame their faces – much like the horse whose blinders limit severely its vision of the scenes moving past. However, the stylish frame's omnipotent reign is challenged by Ada's dark, stormy eyes, which reflect pain, tragedy and violent anger. We are relieved to see the life there although often expressed without joy or humor. Communication comes through the tempestuousness of her eyes and facial expressions.

Her daughter's voice serves as a conduit for Ada's inner feelings as well. "She says she doesn't want it," Flora screams as her mother's alter ego. Her face, though corseted in a way by a smaller version of the constricting bonnet, betrays passion and presence. We are both comforted and pained by the knowledge that Ada is speaking through her daughter just as she speaks through her piano. Flora's spiritedness is a legacy passed on by her mother, but the effects on Flora are profound as she is also mandated to enact aspects of Ada's Other at the expense of Flora's own inner discourse with her (M)Other (Grosz, 1990). Both mother and daughter are unable to communicate their experience in their own language. Ada's potential speech is burdened with the dread of the annihilation of her subjectivity and the recourse to silence. Flora brings to our attention a generational curse. Flora speaks, but must speak for her mother (Apprey and Stein, 1993b).

The film allows much latitude for us to conjure up the inner scenario of Ada's resistance and muteness. Campion demonstrates evocatively Ada's hatred of her fiancé and of male authority. Her hatred and restless contempt of the male demand offers a window into her point of resistance; she will not speak the language of the male symbolic order nor participate willingly in its customs, rituals and demands (Grosz, 1990; Lacan, 1949, 1977b).

Through Campion's satiric view, the ritual of wedding portraits is shown to be not only impoverished, but also desperate in its insistence to carry out the rituals that legitimize and anchor the individual's sense of placement and being. Campion's cinematic comments and the facial expressions of her remarkable heroine, Ada, unmask attitudes about the rituals of marriage as foolish and obsolete attempts at the ordering of society – including sexual difference. The juxtaposition of the Victorian costumes and rituals, suitable for an English interior with the rain-drenched tacky setting, conveys not only pathos but also the demise of the grip of these conventions.

Another scene that functions as a mirror for marital relations is the horror at the chopping block. The attack by Stewart on Ada's voice-finger explodes out of the deceitful, ironical charade of their marriage – arranged, peculiar in its odd matching, and founded on frozen solipsism. Though from another vertex we are witness to Ada's cruel and sadistic treatment of her husband: denigrating, humiliating and teasing. We know that Alisdair Stewart has been the recipient of all Ada's abandonment feelings while George Baines is the one who is privileged to receive her unconscious desires to be found inside her shell. Stewart is left to peer through a peephole into George's house as the lush sensual couple engage in passionate lovemaking. His painful illumination is proximate to the scene of another sensual couple romping robustly in bed. Ada gives her lavish favors to Flora, again placing Stewart as the cast out, tormented nursling and lover. The act of mutilation arises powerfully out of all these elements. Ada's terror that she will be dominated by the monster-man is transformed through her relationship with George, but Stewart remains the recipient of all Ada's projections of her internal monster-man fantasies in which he is the agent of the oppression of her being and expressive capacities. As she projects and splits away her dark animus, *he* ricochets back at her in the form of a hated or haunting presence. The deadly rope is one such phantom, the mutilation is a nightmare exploding into external reality, foreshadowed by the tale of Bluebeard and finally Stewart, who is made to play the ax man in Ada's internal dramas. Ada's battles with these demonic ghosts of emotional life will remain split off and in need of integration until Ada passes through ritual ordeals of mutilation and the defeat of her ancient seducer, the Devil who tempts with sacrifice and death. Earlier I noted that Ada had developed language though she was mute. I believe that Ada has chosen elective muteness because she can find no language of her own in Campion's well-drawn depiction of Victorian culture, but her muteness is also tied to deep pockets or enclaves of schizoid withdrawal in which communication hardly takes place or is directed only in the ways imagined by a solipsistic psyche or aspects that exist in a coma-like state. I believe Ada's internal world introduces us to all these possibilities. Semiosis begins at birth supported by the pas de deux of the mothering one and infant subject. The mothering mind assists the neonate and older infant with the powerful affective forces that are overwhelming and bewildering. Without the intersubjective system of sending, absorbing, containing and signifying, mental breakdown or serious disturbances, including schizophrenia, psychosis and psychogenic autism may develop (Grotstein, 1990a, 1990b; Tustin, 1981b). Preverbal semiosis arises out of skin-to-skin intimacy and the envelopes of the senses that wrap the infant in mother's gaze, the music of her sounds and the touch of her body. (M)Other's interest, buffering and mutual responses weave the patterning of a psychic skin that pouches the infant in a way that nurtures self-experience and provides the structures to gather together messages for parental reception (Anzieu, 1989; Feldman, 1987).

Parents can be "turned on" by their infant's appropriate evocations of emotional states by all the colors of affective life. But alternatively parents may dread the evocations of infantile experience, and distance themselves from the impact of signals and signs of raw need, helplessness, terror and ecstasy (Bion, 1962a, 1962b, 1965, 1970; Tustin, 1981b). Culture and language reflect and reinforce distancing in the ways in which we are already familiar within philosophical and psychological debates about the nature of reason in its relationship to the passions. Ada's relationships in adult life strongly suggest the obstruction of her semiotic capacities at their origins. Victorian childrearing theories, though they softened throughout the nineteenth century, vastly underestimated the infant's need for emotional bonding. Moral standards still dominated childrearing discourse and intrusive molding remained a dominant theme. The writings of Victorian women novelists present both the milieu of obedience and revolutionary discourse in the context of the impositions placed on their humanity and gender. Female children were to be seen and not heard under societal and cultural customs that were more oppressive than the rules that were applied to their brothers. The Brontës provide us with the background for Campion's reinvestigation of female subjectivity in the nineteenth century. Jane Eyre's voyage of self-discovery and Cathy's passion for Heathcliff foreshadow Ada's reclamation of her speaking self. However, we may also conjecture that deadly depression and states of de-realization haunted the authors from earliest awareness (Gilbert and Gubar, 1979; Gordon, 1995, 2001). For the purposes of the exploration of elective muteness and autistic-like states, my focus centers on the tragic obliteration of aspects of the self in such a manner that mental birth for these aspects is mutilated or prevented.

Clinical experience has put me in touch with mute and disassociated aspects of the self through nonverbal communication of experiences of haunting depression, states of numbness, terror, and anxiety. These are the communications that emerge within the new container and holding situation that has remained unheard by the (M)Other thereby forcing the messages into other channels and modes.[4] I imagine that for Ada to allow the shell to soften and to experience freely would be to feel ripped open, awakening to the pain and wounds that had been banished inside the mute

---

4 Mother is used by Lacan to designate two internal aspects of the mother–child relationship. The first aspect or signifier describes the internal relationship; the second includes Lacan's notion of the Other by which he means the discourse of the conscious mind with the unknown or unconscious contributions. The two discourses are often confused. For example, the analysand believes he/she is describing something called a mother when in fact the (M)Other is allowed to speak in the analytic exchange.

or lost selves. So Ada preserves her bristly shell; but her outcast feelings find a means of expression partially through her piano. Ada's piano, then, is the vehicle for her special language and a conduit for her split-off feelings as well.

In the film's narrative, Ada's shell is broken by the sensual-sexual attentions of George. He provides sensual, caring contact for a person whose most passionate communications are through her piano, foreclosing on speech and most social interaction with others. As I discussed earlier, Ada maintains a hostile attitude toward conventional society. I can imagine that her attitude is not exclusively antisocial but originates in a deep sense of damage that has to do with the failure to be met half way in the early encounters with love, acceptance and empathy with the breast-mommy as well as within the relationship with both parents.

Ada's relationship to George may easily be interpreted as a sexual awakening that gradually overcomes her withdrawn and hostile state toward adult intimacy (particularly understandable given the Victorian restrictions placed on woman's relationship to her body). Campion provides Ada with a lover and a physical relationship that not only releases her from the restraints of Victorian gender codes and customs, but more significantly, cracks the shell of her self-imposed fortress or "second skin" constructed perhaps against grave disappointment, rejection and frustration (Anzieu, 1989; Bick, 1968).

George gradually breaks through Ada's armor by entering first into her relationship with the piano. He offers to give back the piano in exchange for piano lessons. The surface plot indicates the wiles of a would-be suitor seducing an appealing and exciting woman. However, as we move through the series of scenes in George's cottage, the viewer is privileged to witness the awakening of Ada's senses and the restoring of her psychic skin to the extent that she is able to be touched psychosomatically. Though at first stiffening in distaste at George's touch, Ada gradually softens the barrier between inside and outside and not only feels moved by his desire for her and sexually aroused, but also feels safe enough to give up her armor and enter into a skin-to-skin relationship. George, not unlike an early mothering one, relates to Ada with great attention not as an object for his exploitation and fulfillment of preordained concepts of women, but as an object of desire that he deeply accepts and admires. The scene in which Alisdair Stewart peeps at them through a small opening in the door of George's home reveals the couple en face in various postures, the picture of skin intimacy as well as sexual excitement. Campion places Stewart on the outside perhaps as an editorial comment against stiff societal mores. As we know well, a crucial aspect of the development of subjectivity is speech. Speech develops out of containment and reverie in which the mothering one dreams and organizes the infant's primitive experience into elements of meaning. At the same time the psychosomatic skin registers experience from internal and external stimuli and in this way is the first recorder of experience – writing on the skin. In situations in which the early partner is not functioning to filter experiences or to provide dream alpha function (Bion, 1962a, 1962b), the infant subject becomes overwhelmed to the extent that fragmentation and or breakdown interferes with the development of preverbal semiosis and therefore its transformative marriage with language (Lacan, 1957; Muller, 1994). Since the infant is not able to filter and repress the mental and physical traumata, the possibility of speech, at least for parts of the personality, is overwhelmed. I believe that Ada's elective muteness is accompanied by deeper levels of failure in the formation of a boundaried self and the regulation of experience in ways that are catastrophic to the forming subject. We are interested here in Campion's exploration of the unborn psychic reality of female women and children. I imagine Ada to have been burdened with these dilemmas. The shadow of death is shown to fall heavily on her being as the piano slips into the sea. The piano, at this moment, reveals its complex significance in Ada's inner world. Ada's waning entanglement with the piano betrays its meaning as a refuser of life and the enemy of its possibilities as well as the preserver of her as yet silent speech. At her return from her journey into the deep, Ada surfaces and speaks with her inner words of this near death at the hands of her inner demons and of her divided self: "What a death! What a chance! What a surprise! My will has chosen life!? Still it has had me spooked and many others besides." Ada, Flora and the others seem to fall under the shadow of the ax, a theme foreshadowed by the shadow play in the theatrical presentation of the story of Bluebeard – a tale of the terrorizing murder of Bluebeard's many wives. In other words, Bluebeard is a tale of fabled male violent domination of women. Through this conceit Campion shares with us, the viewers, her perception of female nightmares of sexual difference.

As it happens in Campion's narrative, aspects of Bluebeard arise in Stewart. The ax falls not in the full act of decapitation, but a metonymic gesture of the part for the whole, quite horrible in itself and nevertheless damaging to the wholeness of this woman and her ways of communicating. Moreover, as discussed, Ada has behaved in cruel and tormenting ways that stimulate male cruelty toward women. Here we see a closed cycle of pain given and vengefully forced back into the sender. Stewart reminds us of a man *cut off* from the maternal body and the feminine in himself as well as the external substitute by which he attempts to seek re-entry and gain full possession (Klein, 1928; Kristeva, 1980b; Van Buren, 1992, 1993, 1994). The belief in masculine evil stems often from the interpretation that it is daddy or daddy-penis (in part object terms) that has forced the recognition of the experience of separation from mother. Molly, my analysand, has had many dreams of phallic-like objects attacking her security in the cave of the womb. The snake-like object is described as knocking her off her perch inside a womb-like enclosure or intruding upward into it in a way that Molly found to be life threatening. The early onset of these feelings (even prenatally) is often experienced like a curse on the subject's destiny (in either sex), but the manner in which the curse is interpreted very much depends on cultural mythologies of gender. I take Campion's view of the nightmare of the phallus to be represented by the scene at the chopping block in which the man Alisdair raises the ax against the woman Ada. The act also signifies powerful cultural mythologies in which women are cut off from their destiny by male practices and rites of physical and mental mutilation. I have in mind footbinding, clitoridectomies within the physical realm and prohibition on speech and communication within the psychological realm (Kristeva, 1974; Walker, 1982). All are mutilations of women's subjectivity. Elsewhere I have discussed in detail the compulsions to signify women as the embodiment of an unborn, undifferentiated, incomplete and overly dependent being (Van Buren, 1991, 1992, 1993, 1994, 1996). Here I reiterate one theme: women's placement in the symbolic order is limited by the association female with the realization of lack and the loss of "petite object a" (Lacan, 1957; see also Bloch, 1991; Feldman, 1987; Klein, 1928). In a labyrinthine twist of projective identification, the infant's loss becomes the mother's and for all infants who must suffer the pains of impotence and mortality as part of the legacy of mental birth, the female person is identified as the scapegoat or sacrificial figure (Girard, 1977; Tustin, 1981b).

I can imagine Ada and Flora to be caught in a generational mandate in which women are commanded from birth to suppress certain aspects of their beings (Apprey and Stein, 1993b). In addition to the nonsensory values associated with Victorian childrearing, female children were most often signified as the lesser of the two genders, to be dominated by wiser and more worldly "men." Recall that Victorian girls were not allowed to go to school, speak in public, or vote. These cultural commands and beliefs are the spoken or written words that inform through the ears and eyes. The nontangible or sensory feelings that are disguised and hidden in speech written or spoken are difficult to deconstruct. What are the messages passed on to each generation of women by their mothers, fathers, and La Langue that interfere with the validity of being and the growth of semiosis and speech? Flora presents to us a girl bound up with family mandates. Like her mother, she is in a powerful conflict between being and nonbeing. Mother encourages her rebelliousness through sharing her own profound revolutionary feelings, and in fact makes Flora her spokesperson for her belligerent and rebellious words, though simultaneously Ada passes on aspects of her own inner world associated with the limitations placed on women's subjectivity. Ada's attitudes toward life and sociability clearly impress Flora with the dangers of being a woman, but Flora's cartwheels in nonconstricting cotton underclothes, on the beach with George and the piano and mother, foreshadows a more nurturing creative Oedipal triad as well as the triumph of women's lively subjectivity, seen at the end of the film at the moment that Ada begins to speak aloud. Though Flora has been through a great deal of trauma, particularly her harsh exposure to realization of Oedipal scenes of violence, competition and the murder of parts of mother's body, Campion implies the damage to both mother and daughter are reversible. It seems to me that conversely, Stewart's vengeful attack on Ada's finger signifies damage to women's whole self and capacity through the ages. The scene at the chopping block depicts male physical power as a recourse to the loss of mother (part of growing up male is to *cut off* the attachment to mother and femininity internally and externally). Victorian modern Western myths of manhood were at the extreme at this time, and the growth of a mythic complementary relationship between the sexes was unimaginable for the most part (Van Buren, 1989, 1992, 1993). In Campion's cinematic tale of the recovery of female subjectivity, she elaborates on the theory of women caught as objects of the gaze of the cinematic eye (De Lauretis, 1984; Doane, 1987; Penley, 1989). As we move through Ada's odyssey we see her as moving from the object of familial and culture's projections to a subject in her own right. The writers on the gaze emphasize the oppression and mutilation of female subjectivity not by men but by concepts of sexual difference constructed in a cultural discourse fiercely committed to denuding and/or oppressing the full flowering of women's subjectivity and capacity to represent. In *The Piano*, Campion presents experiences of the woman subject imprisoned in a reactive silence and in autistic and/or schizoid enclaves, as discussed previously. It is possible to construct a hypothesis that films in the latter part of the twentieth century have continued to present women as hostage to a cinematic eye and a discourse that envisions women as persons who are sculpted out of male desire. Post-Lacanian critics have challenged the confusion in Lacan's notion that the Symbolic Order evolves out of the father function that creates and maintains space for differentiation and representation. The Law of the Father defines the symbolic function as necessarily male. The lack of a phallus is believed to be equivalent to the lack of the means to employ metonymy and metaphor – to move across the chains of signifiers searching for "petite object a" (Boothby, 1991).

It seems to me that this perverse interpretation of the origins of the signifying process stems from the confusion about the origins of psychic space. The infant's dilemma of giving up the myth of autochthony (Grotstein, 2000a) is painful to both male and female infants, but by way of manic denial, male gender is signified as having maintained omnipotence and control over the vicissitudes of life (De Lauretis, 1984; Doane, 1987; Furman, 1985; Goldstein, 1995; Irigaray, 1985; Kristeva, 1974; Van Buren, 1991). I think that the notion of the "King" as holding society together and providing a place for the power of the law to reside, is another of the misconceptions that spring from the fear of mother's powers to carry the fetus and give the infant life and nurture. An aspect of that fear is also an outgrowth of the potency of the parental couple, interpreted by the unbounded or unattached infant as having no need of them.

Campion seems to interpret the growth of Ada's subjectivity from the vertex of postmodern ideas, though I am not certain that her strategy is intentional. However, I propose that Ada's elective muteness is very much entangled with the premise that the Phallus as a boundary makes signification processes, including speech and symbolic structures, possible.

Lacan (1977b), though insisting that biology plays no role in the generation of his theory, understood woman as the funnel for male desire, placed in the position of the one who lacks the means to exercise desire through symbolic means. Lacan proposes that the Symbolic Order is born of male desire and though a woman can speak and write, *women* remain exiled from the Symbolic Order and signifying processes (Gilbert and Gubar, 1979; Lacan, 1977b). It seems to me that Campion links Ada's refusal to speak the language of her culture to the dichotomies imposed by Phallic culture, based on the Law of the Father and the terrors that infants evoke. I believe the use of this structure is found in many symbolic orders to mask or deny feelings of vulnerability (Butler, 1990; Gardiner, 1985; Grotstein, 1994; Jones, 1985; Van Buren, 1993).

Sullivan (1991) adds that women cast as antagonists and destroyers of the Symbolic Order are exiled from the culture and may not participate in its formation. The contrived structures of our manifest culture reflect the belief that women do not exist. Sullivan interprets the rationale that places women in the shadows of culture and society as the need for outer society to carry the belief that speaking adult males give birth to themselves and the cultural belief systems that dominate their era. The primordial mother is eliminated and replaced by the first signifier. When the child speaks he gains the privileged position of creator of the fabric of existence (Sullivan, 1991).

Lacan found a more sophisticated understanding of the matter of sexual difference. Between 1957 and 1973, it became clear to him that sexual difference was culturally contrived. The attraction to notions of women as nonexistent is found in the need for difference. Men can have the illusion that they do not suffer from lack and disorganization. They belong to a set, which is differentiated from the primordial mother who threatens the efforts to order and regulate society. Along these lines, Freud's theories of incest are not sufficient as cause but function to enable men to believe that they are free of mother (Sullivan, 1991). They are thus enabled to believe that they are whole and pass the hole or lack on to the signifier woman. Consistent with the postmodern perspective, Campion's heroine recovers aspects of her subjectivity – her voice, speech, and the lost selves that had been entombed with them. In this way we are able to break through the lens of the gaze, through the objectified image and to arrive at the place of the origins of troubled, if not endeadened, semiosis and the holes in the fabric of female being as a means to release the full dimensionality of female subjectivity.[5]

5 Mother is used by Lacan to designate two internal aspects of the mother–child relationship. The first aspect or signifier describes the internal relationship; the second includes Lacan's notion of the Other by which he means the discourse of the conscious mind with the unknown or unconscious contributions. The two discourses are often confused. For example, the analysand believes he/she is describing something called a mother when in fact the (M)Other is allowed to speak in the analytic exchange.

Conclusion

Mother's body as a major dream figure, mythological character and phantasied presence is created out of the attempts to realize "O" in its fullness and truthfulness. The original power of "O's" messages are unbearably full of emotional truth and since starting in the realm of infinity, they threaten to upset the status quo or emotional balance of the evolving mind. "O" is always on the horizon of our emotional awareness leading us or tempting us to transcend the already known, familiar and incomplete expressions of our feelings and emotions. "O's" fate is inextricably involved with the openness or closeness of the already functioning mind. Within the infant's fragile mind assistance to realize "O" is an exquisite necessity. With the lack of that partnership the development of the mind is vulnerable to detours of defense and distortion of the truth often organized as the best way to understand the truth and follow its moral imperatives. Psychoanalytic theory is no exception though its main purpose is to open the mind to its buried and troubling aspects. The Oedipus complex or myth is a central structure of the negotiations between different layers and functions of the mind. It combines elements of the infant's odyssey from prenatal awareness through gestation and birth into a readable template of evolution into personhood or subjecthood. It asks and answers what is my prehistory? What is my familial legacy? How do I attach and bond with the maternal and paternal figures to which my life is owed and protected? Can my family live by the truth of our emotional shared experience? How deeply can I find my personhood and live it out ethically? Or is it preordained that I will fail my children and myself?

The Oedipal narrative also includes within its themes the intergenerational tragedy or the failure of the previous generations to solve the riddle of the Sphinx. From our present context, we might think that the major force pressing from the deep and formless infinite is emotional truth. We can see in the drawings left in the French caves at Lascaux more than the outlines of the struggles of daily life, even though this task of recording in figures which can be read is such a radical innovation. The drawings sign the awareness of experiences placed on external palettes perhaps to read a deeper awareness of mortality and the impediments to the search for personhood, as the Oedipus myth makes clear. These drawings in the French caves may be an expression of the individual looking out at the world from inside the protective womb of the cave, signing both the tasks of survival and the longing to remain unborn.

The exploration of the dreams and mythologies of mother's body from the vertex of the daughter's emotional responses to conscious and unconscious messages and demands of her family, culture, society and her own dreams illuminates the disruptions of human feeling and thought from the matrilineal side of the narrative. The idea that every page of *Totem and Taboo* (Freud, 1913) are haunted by the internal mother, her subjectivity and wisdom obscured or erased brings forward the passions realized as in *The Voice of the Turtle*. In the earlier chapters, I have suggested the terrors of infantile helplessness must also be realized as an integral part of women's subjectivity. As a female infant she is often refused personhood, defined as a burden or mutilated in a ritual that is meant to decimate the power of pregnancy and childbirth, her very well-being is endangered and devalued. As I discussed, I found many of the women in analysis with me had fierce unconscious anxieties about their well-being as a female and as a mother who would have children of her own. They lacked the fruitful outcome of mother's loving reverie that would endorse their self-respect as persons. Often they were also deprived of father's loving endorsement of their womanhood. The absence of a solid and complex combination of the parental couple is also part of their difficulties in creating their own internal vibrant and resilient couple. The Oedipus myth and complex in the play by Sophocles, and Freud's interpretations of it, point to the parents' and the Symbolic Order's confusions about parental responsibilities and generational relationships.

We can appreciate the gradual revision of the myths and dreams of mother–daughter relating finding ready access to these revisions in the external sphere in the aspirations of young women today reflected in the increasing numbers of women pursuing advanced training and in increasing proportion to men in graduate schools and professional programs, law, medicine, mental health and the corporate world. Many of these women articulate their limited access to fully realize their potential. The glass ceiling is an important concept in the manifest descriptions of women patients who have achieved a large part of their climb into the external world. Limitations imposed by the "men" in their field seem to carry aspects of the illness of the signifier. It appears that the concepts of woman as peer, colleague and mother remain drenched with anxiety and the defenses against the dream of mother's body and early dependency and helplessness. Though at the same time the breach between male and female is slowly loosening its power. A critical sign of this is radical changes in the cultural and personal beliefs and expectations of the concepts of father and husband. Father's inclusion in the intimacy of parent–child relationships starting with conception and pregnancy and the states of mind that prepare for emotional involvement with one's offspring are more acceptable and encouraged. These changes are the outcome of many generations' reworkings of archaic conceptions of survival. Another book is needed to fill out this side of the mythologies of fatherhood, male personhood and coupling.

I think it is useful to think of a mixed picture of women's internal world. As discussed in Chapter 6 recent filmic presentation of women are structured around struggles to find contact with their body, sensuality, and crucially their own voice. In *The Piano*, Ada gives up her speech, the spoken word in particular. Campion lets us know that she can speak and think but only to herself. She is unpleasant and non-responsive when coerced or invited to relate. On one level she refuses to speak a language from which she is formally shut out thus she speaks only to herself. Her elective mutism is not completely devastating to her ability to formulate her feelings and thoughts but imposes extreme limits on her hopefulness that she might change, grow and find good nourishment in the "not me" world. Virginia Woolf, one of the central figures in *The Hours*, is portrayed from the vortex of her misery as a seriously and dangerously depressed woman. In actuality Woolf was a huge literary talent, one of the great geniuses of her time, who was often compared to James Joyce due to their common ability to break with the conventions of their era and to write brilliantly through their inhibitions, depression and enormous sensitivity to the unknown and uncertainty. Woolf does in fact commit suicide. I suppose as a viewer of the film and a reader of her biography one is left with great uncertainty. Her mental illness is a formidable reality. The film *The Hours* portrays her mostly as a troubled and eccentric woman, who is finally overcome by her Victorian female depression.

The film *Million Dollar Baby* (2004) is purportedly centered on a woman's reclamation of her lost sense of agency, social and personal. The heroine Maggie Fitzgerald, played by Academy Award winner Hilary Swank, is determined to break through into the man's world of boxing. She persuades a male trainer, Frankie Dunn, to take her on though at first he is extremely prejudiced against her pursuing a career as a prizefighter. He calls her girlie and adds that he doesn't train girls. She is not dissuaded, persists, and gradually wins over the skeptical trainer (played by Clint Eastwood). He is brought around and becomes deeply affected by her singular faith. But in the spirit of the movies of the 1930s and 1940s, the heroines, think Rosalind Russell, Claudette Colbert and even Katharine Hepburn, lose a part of their edge and over the course of the film somewhat tamed in order to fit society's definition as wife without a career. Though the heroine's destiny is badly compromised, one can say at least the films look at questions about women becoming active participants in the Symbolic Order. However, *Million Dollar Baby* starts out with a more extreme rebellion and ends with an old idea. The unconventional woman has to die as a victim. *Million Dollar Baby* ends with euthanasia. Maggie not only loses all that she accomplished but also has to die and no longer brings the disturbances of profound upheaval. It strikes me that this ending, despite all the hoopla of the Academy Awards noticeably for Hilary Swank, illuminates for us the mixture of attitudes towards women's bodies and minds.

Eating disorders display similar themes, in their most deadly form. Enslaved to some myths of superiority and sexual desirability teenage women, refuse the nourishment of their future as women and as persons. As discussed in Chapter 4, their bodies serve as the "embodiment" of the undreamt terrors of infantile mental life or acute vulnerability, projected into Mother's body and taken in by the subject and stored in their internal mother or surrendering aspects of their subjectivity to fit that maternal nightmare by turning those dark feelings toward themselves. Anorexia and bulimia are powerful suicidal enactments of these feelings in the tradition of female saints, religious martyrs, beliefs systems and individual development, centered around cruel and depriving attacks on the body and on the mind that can accept emotional life. As ascetics sexuality is shunned or made shallow. Though young women display their bodies, lately their belly buttons and parts of their behinds, their inner world remains distanced, confused and unprepared to couple in ways that promote growth and reach towards new meanings and emotions.

Working with the analysands discussed in the main chapters I saw and felt their profound ties to the internal mother as well as their placement in the early Oedipus structure developed by Melanie Klein, Wilfred Bion, D.W. Winnicott and the attachment theorists. In the attack on coupling, boys and girls may transform father into a powerful monster or a cowardly man who in either case is denigrated and hated.

Fathers and males are often designated most often as a rival but also more importantly is conflated with many manifestations of thirdness including developing the capacity to tolerate transitional space, the "not me" and concepts of the Other found in the dim awareness of thirdness, the concepts male/female remain profoundly burdened with terror and antagonism.

As clinicians we have the opportunity to resonate with woman's internal world that has been buried, disavowed and distorted. We would want to think about our own experiences within our emotional life. Many of us have not yet recovered from the dread fear of the early Oedipal figures that can dominate our subjectivity and prevent the voices from the deep to be heard and honored. Melanie Klein's concept of the bad mother is very significant as is Bion's concept of the container as illuminations of the failure of the mind to allow the evolution of "O," powerful emotions that threaten the status quo to the extent that the arrival of thoughts without a thinker or voices from the deep may be felt as a catastrophe. In analysis we experience in vivo, the pain and dread of old protective patterns as well as the deficits themselves arresting the evolution of emotional life and imprisoning the subject in limited and or deadly mental life. In my exploration of internal mother and daughter relationships I began to think and feel about their disavowed subjectivity (and mine) in more complexity and depth. I have more appreciation for the enormous responsibility that women subjects have to carry the fetus and give birth to their infant and nurture them well enough to survive and thrive within misconceptions, the failure of realizations to form so that the association of mother's body as the keeper of life and death emerges with out distortion, persecutory anxiety and disavowal. If mother's mother and her mother and father's mother and so on remain trapped by the unconscious messages that women's bodies are dangerous and are to be demeaned or murderously attacked the cycle is very difficult to break. Intense examples are provided in Western democratic societies by wife beatings and in Middle Eastern and African countries where extreme control and brutality continue. Infidelity is met with shaming and even death.

Psychoanalytic work with women today in an urban society has helped me to realize the mother–daughter relationship as imbedded in the early Oedipal dilemma. Crucial questions that relate to mothers and daughters in the inner world are: am I able to feel safe in mother's care? Am I able to feel protection from mother as well as father? Am I able to accept the concept of thirdness without an overwhelming sense of dispossession, envy and jealousy? Am I able to maintain a sense of judgment conviction about the ethical nature of my society, my family and myself? Am I able to develop and stand by respect for myself as a person and a woman?

At deeper levels the therapeutic questions, the symptoms, the poor functioning and the pain are profoundly tied to the mystery of the origins of meaning, nameless dread and the fears around survival. The dreams and signifiers of Mother's Body are messages from the deep that we must hear, resonate with and find the unknown thoughts without the thinker for our responses.

Bibliography

Alhanati, S. (ed.) (2002). *Primitive Mental States*, vol. 2: *Psychobiological and Psychoanalytic Perspectives on Early Trauma and Personality Development*. New York: Karnac.

Alvarez, A. (1992). *Live Company: Psychoanalytic Psychotherapy with Autistic, Borderline, Deprived and Abused Children*. London: Routledge and Kegan Paul.

Alvarez, A. and Reid, S. (1999). *Autism and Personality*. London: Routledge.

Anzieu, D. (1989). The notion of a skin ego. In *The Skin Ego: A Psychoanalytic Approach to the Self*. New Haven, CT: Yale University Press.

Apprey, M. and Stein, H. (1993a). A prefatory note on motives and projective identification. In *Intersubjectivity, Projective, Identification and Otherness* (pp. 102–128). Pittsburgh, PA: Duquesne University Press.

Apprey, M. and Stein, H. (1993b). Dreams of urgent/voluntary errands and trans-generational haunting in transsexualism. In *Intersubjectivity, Projective, Identification and Otherness* (pp. 131–136). Pittsburgh, PA: Duquesne University Press.

Ariès, P. and Duby, G. (eds.) (1988). *A History of Private Life Revelations of the Medieval World*, vol. 2. Cambridge, MA: Belknap Press of Harvard University.

Ariès, P. and Duby, G. (eds.) (1989). *A History of Private Life Passions of the Renaissance*, vol. 3. Cambridge, MA: Belknap Press of Harvard University.

Barthes, R. (1972). *Mythologies*. Trans. A. Lavers. New York: Hill and Wang.

Bick, E. (1968). The experience of the skin in early object-relations. *International Journal of Psycho-Analysis* 49: 484–486.

Bion, W.R. (1959). Attacks on linking. In *Second Thoughts* (1967). New York: Jason Aronson.

Bion, W.R. (1962a). Learning from experience. In *Seven Servants* (1977). New York: Jason Aronson.

Bion, W.R. (1962b). Theory of thinking. In *Second Thoughts* (1967). New York: Jason Aronson.

Bion, W.R. (1965). Transformations. In *Seven Servants* (1977). New York: Jason Aronson.

Bion, W.R. (1967a). Differentiation of the psychotic from the non-psychotic personalities. In *Second Thoughts* (1967). New York: Jason Aronson.

Bion, W.R. (ed.) (1967b). *Second Thoughts: Selected Papers on Psycho-Analysis*. New York: Jason Aronson.

Bion, W.R. (1970). Attention and interpretation. In *Seven Servants* (1977). New York: Jason Aronson.

Bion, W.R. (1977a). *Seven Servants: Four Works*. New York: Jason Aronson.

Bion, W.R. (1977b). *Two Papers: The Grid and the Caesura*. Edited by J. Salomao. Rio de Janeiro: Imago.

Bion, W.R. (1977c). Untitled. In *Taming Wild Thoughts* (1997). London: Karnac.

Bion, W.R. (1992). *Cogitations*. London: Karnac.

Bion, W.R. (1997). *Taming Wild Thoughts*. London: Karnac.

Blake, W. (1812). *Songs of Innocence*. London.

Bloch, H. (1991). *Medieval Misogyny and the Invention of Western Romantic Love*. Chicago, IL: University of Chicago Press.

Bollas, C. (1987). *The Shadow of the Object: Psychoanalysis of the Unthought Known*. New York: Columbia University Press.

Boothby, R. (1991). *Lacanian Reflections on Narcissism, Death and Desire: Psychoanalytic Theory in Lacan's Return to Freud*. New York: Routledge.

Butler, J. (1990). Prohibition, psychoanalysis and the production of the heterosexual matrix. In *Gender Trouble: Feminism and the Subversion of Identity*. London: Routledge.

Campbell, J. (1959). *The Masks of God: Primitive Mythology*. New York: Penguin.

Campbell, J. (1976). *The Masks of God: Occidental Mythology*. New York: Penguin.

Campion, J. and Pullinger, K. (1994). *The Piano: A Novel*. New York: Miramax Books Hyperion.

Chuster, A. (2005). Psychoanalytic interpretations and the ethical-aesthetic principles of observation. A paper presented at the Forty-fourth Congress of the International Psychoanalytic Association, July 2005, Rio de Janeiro.

Cixous, H. and Clément, C. (1975). *The Newly Born Woman*. Trans. B. Wing. Minneapolis, MN: University of Minnesota Press.

Cramer, B. (1986). Assessment of parent–infant relationship. In Brazelton, T.B. and Yogman, M.W. (eds.) *Affective Development in Infancy* (pp. 27–38). Norwood, NJ: Ablex.

Cramer, B. and Stern, D. (1988). Evaluation of changes in mother–infant brief psychotherapy: a single case study. *Infant Mental Health Journal* 9: 20–45.

Cunningham, M. (1998). *The Hours*. New York: Farrar, Straus and Giroux.

De Lauretis, T. (1984). Imaging. In *Alice Doesn't: Feminism, Semiotics, and Cinema*. Bloomington, IN: Indiana University Press.

Deutsch, H. (1955). The impostor: contribution to ego psychology of a type of psychopath. *Psychoanalytic Quarterly* 24: 483–505.

Doane, M. (1987). *The Desire to Desire*. Bloomington, IN: Indiana University Press.

Eco, U. (1979). *The Role of the Reader: Explorations in the Semiotics of Texts*. Bloomington, IN: Indiana University Press.

Fairbairn, W.R.D. (1944). Endopsychic structure considered in terms of object-relationships. *International Journal of Psycho-Analysis* 25: 70–93.

Fairbairn, W.R.D. (1946). Object-relationships and dynamic structure. In *Psychoanalytic Studies of the Personality* (1952, pp. 137–151). London: Routledge and Kegan Paul.

Feldman, S. (1987). Beyond Oedipus: the specimen story of psychoanalysis. In *Jacques Lacan and the Adventure of Insight: Psychoanalysis in Contemporary Culture*. Cambridge, MA: Harvard University Press.

Fonagy, P. (1999a). Child psychoanalysis. In Gelder, M., Lopez-Ibor, J. and Andreasen, N. (eds.) *The New Oxford Textbook of Psychiatry* (2001). Oxford: Oxford University Press.

Fonagy, P. (1999b). Psychoanalysis and other long-term dynamic psychotherapies. In Gelder, M., Lopez-Ibor, J. and Andreasen, N. (eds.) *The New Oxford Textbook of Psychiatry* (2001). Oxford: Oxford University Press.

Fonagy, P. (2001). *Attachment Theory and Psychoanalysis*. New York: Other Press.

Fonagy, P., Gergely, G., Jurist, E. and Target, M. (eds.) (2002). *Affect Regulation, Mentalization, and the Development of the Self*. New York: Other Press.

Fonagy, P., Gergely, G., Jurist, E. and Target, M. (eds.) (2004). *Affect Regulation, Mentalization, and the Development of the Self*. London: Karnac.

Freud, S. (1893–1895). *Studies in Hysteria*. In *Standard Edition of the Complete Psychological Works of Sigmund Freud*, vol. II. London: Hogarth Press and the Institute of Psychoanalysis.

Freud, S. (1900). *The Interpretation of Dreams*. In *Standard Edition of the Complete Psychological Works of Sigmund Freud*, vols. IV and V. London: Hogarth Press and the Institute of Psychoanalysis.

Freud, S. (1909). Some remarks on a case of obsessive-compulsive neurosis (The Rat Man). In *Standard Edition of the Complete Psychological Works of Sigmund Freud*, vol. X. London: Hogarth Press and the Institute of Psychoanalysis.

Freud, S. (1910). Leonardo Da Vinci and a memory of his childhood. In *Standard Edition of the Complete Psychological Works of Sigmund Freud*, vol. XI. London: Hogarth Press and the Institute of Psychoanalysis.

Freud, S. (1911). The case of Schreber. In *Standard Edition of the Complete Psychological Works of Sigmund Freud*, vol. XII. London: Hogarth Press and the Institute of Psychoanalysis.

Freud, S. (1913). *Totem and Taboo*. In *Standard Edition of the Complete Psychological Works of Sigmund Freud*, vol. XIII. London: Hogarth Press and the Institute of Psychoanalysis.

Freud, S. (1914). *Mourning and Melancholia*. In *Standard Edition of the Complete Psychological Works of Sigmund Freud*, vol. XIV. London: Hogarth Press and the Institute of Psychoanalysis.

Freud, S. (1920). *Beyond the Pleasure Principle*. In *Standard Edition of the Complete Psychological Works of Sigmund Freud*, vol. XVIII. London: Hogarth Press and the Institute of Psychoanalysis.

Freud, S. (1930). *Civilization and its Discontents*. In *Standard Edition of the Complete Psychological Works of Sigmund Freud*, vol. XXI. London: Hogarth Press and the Institute of Psychoanalysis.

Freud, S. (1939). *Moses and Monotheism*. London: Hogarth Press.

Freud, S. (1952). Project for scientific psychology. In *Standard Edition of the Complete Psychological Works of Sigmund Freud*, vol. I. London: Hogarth Press and the Institute of Psychoanalysis.

Furman, M. (1985). The politics of language: beyond the gender principle? In Greene, G. and Kahn, C. (eds.) *Making a Difference: Feminist Literary Criticism*. London: Methuen.

Gallop, J. (1982). *The Daughter's Seduction: Feminism and Psychoanalysis*. Ithaca, NY: Cornell University Press.

Gardiner, J. (1985). Mind mother: psychoanalysis and feminism. In Greene, G. and

Kahn, C. (eds.) *Making a Difference: Feminist Literary Criticism*. London: Methuen.

Gilbert, S. and Gubar, S. (1979). A dialogue of self and soul: Plain Jane's progress. In *The Madwoman in the Attic: The Woman Writer in the Nineteenth Century Literary Imagination*. New Haven, CT: Yale University Press.

Girard, R. (1977). Oedipus and the surrogate victim. In *Violence and the Sacred*. Baltimore, MD: Johns Hopkins University Press.

Goldstein, R. (1995). *And Then . . . Why Lacan?* Lima: Siklos.

Gooch, J. (2002). The primitive somatic psychic roots of gender formation and intimacy; sensuality, symbolism, and passion in the development of mind. In Alhanti, S. (ed.) *Primitive Mental States*, vol. 2: *Psychobiological and Psychoanalytic Perspectives on Early Trauma and Personality Development*. New York: Karnac.

Gordon, L. (1995). *Charlotte Brontë: A Passionate Life*. New York: W.W. Norton.

Gordon, L. (2001). *Virginia Woolf: A Writer's Life*. New York: W.W. Norton.

Green, A. (1980). The dead mother. In *On Private Madness*. London: Hogarth Press.

Green, A. (1986). *On Private Madness*. Madison, CT: International Universities Press.

Grosz, E. (1990). Sexuality and the symbolic order. In *Jacques Lacan: A Feminist Introduction*. New York: Routledge.

Grotstein, J. (1978). Innerspace: its dimensions and its coordinates. *International Journal of Psychoanalysis* 59: 55–61.

Grotstein, J. (1979). Demoniacal possession, splitting, and the torment of joy. *Contemporary Psychoanalysis* 15(3): 407–453.

Grotstein, J. (1980). A proposed revision of the psychoanalytic concept of primitive mental states. *Contemporary Psychoanalysis* 16: 479–546.

Grotstein, J. (1981). Wilfred R. Bion: the man, the psychoanalyst, the mystic. A perspective on his life and work. In Grotstein, J. (ed.) *Do I Dare Disturb the Universe? – A Memorial to Wilfred R. Bion*. Beverly Hills, CA: Caesura Press.

Grotstein, J. (1983). A proposed revision of the psychoanalytic concept of primitive mental states. *Contemporary Psychoanalysis* 19: 570–604.

Grotstein, J. (1984). A proposed revision of the psychoanalytic concept of primitive mental states II: the borderline syndrome, section 3. *Contemporary Psychoanalysis* 20: 266–343.

Grotstein, J. (1990a). The Black Hole as the basic psychotic experience: some newer psychoanalytic and neuroscience perspectives on psychosis. *Journal of the American Academy of Psychoanalysis* 18(1): 29–46.

Grotstein, J. (1990b). Nothingness, meaninglessness, chaos, and the "Black Hole" II: The Black Hole. *Contemporary Psychoanalysis* 26(3): 377–407.

Grotstein, J. (1993). Towards the concept of the transcendent position: reflections on some of "the unborns" in Bion's *Cogitations*. *Journal of Melanie Klein and Object Relations* 11(2): 55–73.

Grotstein, J. (1994). Projective identification reappraised: projective identification, introjective identification, the transference/countertransference neurosis/psychosis and their consummate expression in the crucifixion, the Pieta and Therapeutic exorcism, part I: Projective identification. *Contemporary Psychoanalysis* 30: 708–746.

Grotstein, J. (1997). The sins of the fathers . . . human sacrifice and the inter- and transgenerational neurosis/psychosis. *International Journal of Psycho-Analysis* 2: 11–25.

Grotstein, J. (1998). Numinous and imminent nature of the psychoanalytical subject. *Journal of Analytic Psychoanalysis* 43: 41–68.

Grotstein, J. (2000a). Autochthony (self creation) and alterity (cocreation): psychic reality in counterpoint. In *Who Is the Dreamer, Who Dreams the Dream?* Hillsdale, NJ: Analytic Press.

Grotstein, J. (2000b). Why Oedipus and not Christ? – Part I. In *Who Is the Dreamer, Who Dreams the Dream?* Hillsdale, NJ: Analytic Press.

Grotstein, J. (2000c). Why Oedipus and not Christ? – Part II. In *Who Is the Dreamer, Who Dreams the Dream?* Hillsdale, NJ: Analytic Press.

Grotstein, J. (2000d). *Who Is the Dreamer, Who Dreams the Dream? A Study of Psychic Preferences.* Hillsdale, NJ: Analytic Press.

Grotstein, J. (2007). *Into the Mind of a Mystic: Wilfred Bion's Legacy to Psychoanalysts.* London: Karnac.

Harrison, J. (1962). *Themis.* Cleveland, OH: World Publishing.

Hawkes, T. (1977). *Structuralism and Semiotics.* Berkeley, CA: University of California Press.

Hegel, G.W.F. (1977). *Phenomenology of Spirit.* Trans. A.V. Miller. Oxford: Oxford University Press.

Irigaray, L. (1974). *Speculum of the Other Woman.* Ithaca, NY: Cornell University Press.

Irigaray, L. (1985). *The Little Girl is (Only) a Little Boy.* Ithaca, NY: Cornell University Press.

Irigaray, L. (1991). *The Irigaray Reader.* Oxford: Basil Blackwell.

Jones, R. (1985). Inscribing femininity: French theories of the feminine. In Greene, G. and Kahn, C. (eds.) *Making a Difference: Feminist Literary Criticism.* London: Methuen.

Joseph, B. (1975). The patient who is difficult to reach. In *Melanie Klein Today: Development in Theory and Practice*, vol. 2: *Mainly Practice* (1988). London: Routledge.

Joseph, B. (1982). Addiction to near death. In Feldman, M. and Bott Spillius, E. (eds.) *Psychic Equilibrium and Psychic Change: Selected Papers of Betty Joseph* (pp. 127–138). London: Tavistock.

Kaplan, E.A. (1990). Motherhood and representation: from post-war Freudian figurations to post-modernism. In Kaplan, E.A. (ed.) *Psychoanalysis and Cinema* (pp. 128–142). New York: Routledge, Chapman and Hall.

Kennedy, R. (1997). Aspects of consciousness: one voice or many. *Psychoanalytic Dialogues* 6: 73–96.

Klein, M. (1928). Early stages of the Oedipus complex. In *Love, Guilt and Reparation and Other Works, 1921–45* (1975). New York: Delta.

Klein, M. (1931). A contribution to the theory of intellectual inhibition. In *Love, Guilt and Reparation and Other Works, 1921–45* (1975). New York: Delta.

Klein, M. (1940). Mourning and its relation to manic-depressive states. In *Love, Guilt and Reparation and Other Works, 1921–45* (1975). New York: Delta.

Klein, M. (1945). The Oedipus complex in the light of early anxieties. In

Contributions to Psychoanalysis, 1921–1945 (pp. 339–390). London: Hogarth Press.

Klein, M. (1946). Notes on some schizoid mechanisms. In Klein, M., Heimann, P., Isaacs, S. and Riviere, J. (eds.) *Developments of Psychoanalysis* (pp. 292–320). London: Hogarth Press.

Klein, M. (1950). Mourning and its relation to manic-depressive states. In *Contributions to Psychoanalysis, 1921–1945* (pp. 311–338). London: Hogarth Press.

Klein, M. (1952). Some theoretical conclusions regarding the emotional life of the infant. In *Envy and Gratitude and Other Works, 1946–1963* (1975). New York: Delacorte.

Klein, M. (1955). On identification. In Klein, M., Heimann, P., Isaacs, S. and Riviere, J. (eds.) *Developments of Psychoanalysis* (pp. 309–345). London: Hogarth Press.

Klein, M. (1957). Envy and gratitude. In *Envy and Gratitude and Other Works, 1946–1963* (1975). London: Hogarth Press.

Kristeva, J. (1974). About Chinese women. In Moi, T. (ed.) *The Kristeva Reader* (1986, pp. 128–159). New York: Columbia University Press.

Kristeva, J. (1977). Stabat mater. In Moi, T. (ed.) *The Kristeva Reader* (1986, pp. 160–186). New York: Columbia University Press.

Kristeva, J. (1980a). *Desire and Language: A Semiotic Approach to Literature and Art*. London: Basil Blackwell.

Kristeva, J. (1980b). Place names, desire and language. In Gore, T., Jardin, A. and Roudiez, L. (eds.) *A Semiotic Approach to Literature and Art* (pp. 271–294). Oxford: Basil Blackwell.

Kristeva, J. (1982). *Powers of Horror: An Essay on Abjection*. New York: Columbia University Press.

Kristeva, J. (1986). Freud and love: treatment and its discontents. In Moi, T. (ed.) *The Kristeva Reader*. New York: Columbia University Press.

Lacan, J. (1949). The mirror stage as formative of the function of the I as revealed in psychoanalytic experience. In *Ecrits: A Selection* (1977, pp. 1–7). London: Tavistock.

Lacan, J. (1953). The function and field of speech and language in psychoanalysis. In *Ecrits: A Selection* (1977, pp. 30–113). London: Tavistock.

Lacan, J. (1957). The agency of the letter in the unconscious. In *Ecrits: A Selection* (1977, pp. 146–178). London: Tavistock.

Lacan, J. (1977a). *Ecrits: A Selection*. London: Tavistock.

Lacan, J. (1977b). The significance of the phallus. In *Ecrits: A Selection* (pp. 281–291). Trans. A. Sheridan. New York: W.W. Norton.

Lévi-Strauss, C. (1963). The structural study of myth. In *Structural Anthropology* (pp. 202–212). New York: Basic Books.

Lichtenberg, J. (1989). *Psychoanalysis and Motivation*. Hillsdale, NJ: Analytic Press.

Maiello, S. (1995). The sound object: a hypothesis about pre-natal auditory experience and memory. *Journal of Child Psychotherapy* 21: 23–41.

Mancia, M. (1981). On the beginning of mental life in the foetus. *International Journal of Psycho-Analysis* 62: 351–357.

Mason, A.A. (1981). The suffocating super-ego: psychotic break and claustrophobia. In Grotstein, J. (ed.) *Do I Dare Disturb the Universe? A Memorial to Wilfred R. Bion*. Beverly Hills, CA: Caesura Press.

Matte Blanco, I. (1988). *Thinking, Feeling and Being*. New York: Routledge, Chapman and Hall.

Matte Blanco, I. (1998). *The Unconscious as Infinite Sets: An Essay in Bi-Logic*. London: Karnac.

Meltzer, D. (1975). The psychology of autistic states and of post-autistic mentality. In *Explorations in Autism: A Psycho-Analytic Study* (pp. 83–142). Strath Tay, UK: Clunie Press.

Meltzer, D. (1988). Aesthetic conflict: its place in development. In *The Apprehension of Beauty* (pp. 7–33). Strath Tay, UK: Clunie Press.

Meltzer, D. (1992). *The Claustrum: An Investigation of Claustrophobic Phenomena*. Strath Tay, UK: Clunie Press.

Meltzer, D. (2002). *Psychoanalytic Work with Children and Adults: Meltzer in Barcelona*. London: Karnac.

Meltzer, D. and Harris-Williams, M. (1988). *Apprehension of Beauty: The Role of Aesthetic Conflict in Development, Violence and Art*. Strath Tay: UK: Clunie Press.

Meyer, D. (1989). *Sex and Power: The Rise of Women in America, Russia, Sweden, and Italy*. Middletown, CT: Wesleyan University Press.

Muller, J. (1994). Clinical sexual psychopathology. In *The Analytic Dyad: Derrida, Heidegger, and Lacan* (pp. 83–142). New York: Routledge.

Mulvey, L. (1988). Visual pleasure and narrative cinema. In Penley, C. (ed.) *Feminism and Film Theory* (pp. 57–58). New York: Routledge.

Nobus, D. (1998). *Key Concepts of Lacanian Psychoanalysis*. London: Rebus Press.

Norman, J. (2001). The psychoanalyst and the baby. *International Journal of Psycho-Analysis* 82: 83–100.

Norman, J. (2004). Transformation of early infantile experience. In *International Journal of Psycho-Analysis* 85: 1103–1122.

Ogden, T. (1992). The dialectically constituted/decentered subject of psychoanalysis, II: The contributions of Klein and Winnicott. *International Journal of Psycho-Analysis* 73: 613–626.

Ogden, T. (1994). *Subjects of Analysis*. Northvale, NJ: Aronson.

Oliver, K. (1993). The prodigal child. In *Reading Kristeva*. Bloomington, IN: Indiana University Press.

Osterweil, E. (2002). Notes on the vicissitudes of intrauterine life. In Alhanati, S. (ed.) *Primitive Mental States*, vol. 2: *Psychobiological and Psychoanalytic Perspectives on Early Trauma and Personality Development*. New York: Karnac.

Paglia, C. (1990). *Sexual Persona, Art and Decadence from Nefertiti to Emily Dickinson*. New Haven, CT: Yale University Press.

Paul, M. (1997). *Before We Were Young: An Exploration of Primordial States of Mind*. New York: Esf Publisher.

Penley, C. (ed.) (1988). *Feminism and Film Theory*. New York: Routledge.

Penley, C. (1989). "A certain refusal of difference": feminism and film theory. In *The Future of an Illusion: Film, Feminism and Psychoanalysis* (pp. 41–54). Minneapolis, MN: University of Minnesota Press.

Piontelli, A. (1988). Prenatal life and birth as reflected in the analysis of a two year old psychotic girl. *International Review of Psycho-Analysis* 15: 73–18.

Piontelli, A. (1989). A study on twins before and after birth. *International Review of Psycho-Analysis* 16: 413–426.

Ragland-Sullivan, E. (1987). *Jacques Lacan and the Philosophy of Psychoanalysis.* Champaign, IL: University of Illinois Press.

Ragland-Sullivan, E. (1991). The sexual masquerade: a Lacanian theory of sexual difference. In Ragland-Sullivan, E. and Bracher, M. (eds.) *Lacan and the Subject of Language.* New York: Routledge.

Rose, J. (1988). Paranoia and the film system. In Penley, C. (ed.) *Feminism and Film Theory* (pp. 141–158). New York: Routledge.

Rosenfeld, H. (1987). Breakdown of communication between patient and analyst. In *Impasse and Interpretation* (pp. 45–73). London: Tavistock.

Rosenfeld, H. (1989). Destructive narcissism and the death instinct. In *Impasse and Interpretation* (pp. 105–132). London: Tavistock.

Roudinesco, E. (1990). *Jacques Lacan and Co: A History of Psychoanalysis in France, 1925–1985.* Chicago, IL: University of Chicago Press.

Sabbadini, A. (ed.) (2003). *The Couch and the Silver Screen: Psychoanalytic Reflections on European Cinema.* Hove, UK: Psychology Press.

Sandler, J. (1987). *From Safety to Superego.* New York: Guilford Press.

Schore, A.N. (1994). *Affect Regulation and the Origin of the Self: The Neurobiology of Neural Development.* Hillsdale, NJ: Lawrence Erlbaum.

Schore, A.N. (2002). Clinical implications of the psycho neurobiological model of projective identification. In Alhanati, S. (ed.) *Primitive Mental States,* vol. 2: *Psychobiological and Psychoanalytic Perspectives on Early Trauma and Personality Development.* London: Karnac.

Segal, H. (1957). Notes on symbol formation. In *The Work of Hanna Segal: A Kleinian Approach to Clinical Practice* (1981, pp. 49–68). New York: Aronson.

Sekoff, J. (1999). The undead. In Kohon, G. (ed.) *The Dead Mother: The Work of André Green.* London: Routledge.

Shlain, L. (1998). *The Goddess Versus the Alphabet.* New York: Viking.

Shlain, L. (2003). Periods/perils. In *Sex, Time and Power: How Women's Sexuality Shaped Human Evolution.* London: Viking.

Silver, A. (1981). A psychosemiotic model: an interdisciplinary search for a common structural basis for psychoanalysis, symbol-formation, and the semiotic of Charles W. Peirce. In *Do I Dare Disturb the Universe?* Beverly Hills, CA: Caesura Press.

Silverman, K. (1983). *The Subject of Semiotics.* New York: Oxford University Press.

Spitz, R.A. (1946). Hospitalism – a follow-up report on investigation described in Volume I, 1945. *Psychoanalytic Study of the Child* 2: 113–117.

Steiner, J. (1993a). *Psychic Retreats: Pathological Organizations in Psychotic, Neurotic, and Borderline Patients.* London: Routledge.

Steiner, J. (1993b). The retreat to a delusional world: psychotic organizations of the personality. In *Psychic Retreats: Pathological Organizations in Psychotic, Neurotic, and Borderline Patients* (pp. 64–73). London: Routledge.

Stern, D. (1985). *The Interpersonal World of the Infant.* New York: Basic Books.

Stern, D. (2004). *The Present Moment in Psychotherapy and Everyday Life.* New York: W.W. Norton.

Sullivan, R. (1991). Homo sapiens or Homo desiderans: the role of desire in human evolution. In *Lacan and the Subject of Language.* New York: Routledge.

Trevarthen, C. (1980). The foundations of intersubjectivity: development of interpersonal and cooperative understanding in infants. In Oldson, D. (ed.) *The Social Foundations of Language and Thought: Essays in Honor of J.S. Bruner* (pp. 316–342). New York: W.W. Norton.

Trevarthen, C. (1993). The self born in intersubjectivity: The psychology of an infant communicating. In Neisser, U. (ed.) *The Perceived Self* (pp. 121–173). New York: Cambridge University Press.

Tustin, F. (1981a). *Autistic States in Children*. London: Routledge and Kegan Paul.

Tustin, F. (1981b). Psychological birth and psychological catastrophe. In *Autistic States in Children* (pp. 78–94). London: Routledge and Kegan Paul.

Tustin, F. (1986). *Autistic Barriers in Neurotic Patients*. New Haven, CT: Yale University Press.

Tustin, F. (1990). To be or not to be. In *The Protective Shell in Children and Adults* (pp. 33–59). London: Karnac.

Van Buren, J. (1989). *The Modernist Madonna: Semiotics of the Maternal Metaphor*. Bloomington, IN: Indiana University Press.

Van Buren, J. (1991). A psychoanalytic semiosis of absence: or, the semiotic murder of the mother. *International Review of Psycho-Analysis* 18(2): 249–263.

Van Buren, J. (1992). The semiotics of gender. *Journal of the American Academy of Psychoanalysis* 20(2): 215–232.

Van Buren, J. (1993). Mother–infant semiotics: intuition and the development of human subjectivity. Klein, Lacan, phantasy of meaning. *Journal of the American Academy of Psychoanalysis* 21(4): 567–580.

Van Buren, J. (1994). The engendering of female subjectivity. In Van Buren, J. (ed.) Special issue: Female Subjectivity and Inner Illuminations. *American Journal of Psychoanalysis* 54(2): 109–125.

Van Buren, J. (1996). Feminine subjectivity, embodiment and reproduction. *Journal of the American Academy of Psychoanalysis* 24(3): 431–443.

Van Buren, J. (2004). Women's internal reality: birthplace or graveyard. *Journal of the American Academy of Psychoanalysis and Dynamic Psychiatry* 32(2): 303–320.

Van Buren, J. (2005). Discovery of the mother's body and the creation of the daughter's subjectivity. *The Psychoanalytic Review* 92(1): 117–136.

Walker, A. (1982). *The Color Purple*. New York: Washington Square Press.

Williams, P. (2004). Incorporation of an invasive object. *International Journal of Psycho-Analysis* 85: 1333–1348.

Winnicott, D.W. (1945). Primitive emotional development. In *Through Paediatrics to Psychoanalysis* (1975, pp. 145–156). New York: Basic Books.

Winnicott, D.W. (1951). Transitional objects and transitional phenomena. In *Through Paediatrics to Psychoanalysis* (1975, pp. 229–242). New York: Basic Books.

Winnicott, D.W. (1958). *Through Pediatrics to Psycho-Analysis*. New York: Basic Books.

Winnicott, D.W. (1960a). Ego distortion in terms of true and false self. In *The Maturational Processes and the Facilitating Environment: Studies in the Theory of Emotional Development* (1985, pp. 140–152). London: Hogarth Press.

Winnicott, D.W. (1960b). The theory of the parent–infant relationship. In *The Maturational Processes and the Facilitating Environment: Studies in the Theory of Emotional Development* (1985, pp. 37–55). London: Hogarth Press.

Winnicott, D.W. (1963). Communicating and not communicating leading to a study of certain opposites. In *The Maturational Processes and the Facilitating Environment: Studies in the Theory of Emotional Development* (1985, pp. 170–192). London: Hogarth Press.

Winnicott, D.W. (1985). *The Maturational Processes and the Facilitating Environment*. London: Hogarth Press.

Index

Page references to illustrations are denoted in *italic*

Printed in Great Britain
by Amazon